FREDERICK THE GREAT

Frederick the Great

A PROFILE

Edited by Peter Paret

WORLD PROFILES

General Editor: Aïda DiPace Donald

 HILL AND WANG   NEW YORK
A division of Farrar, Straus and Giroux

To GORDON A. CRAIG

Contents

Of the twelve selections in this volume, seven are appearing for the first time in English. Renate Morrison translated Hinrichs' essay; Elborg Forster translated the essay by Gundolf and the selection from Dilthey; the editor translated the pieces by Fromme and Mehring, and the selections from Barsewisch and Srbik. Lawrence Baack, Department of History, Stanford University, assisted the editor in preparing the manuscript for publication. The editor also gratefully acknowledges a grant in support of his work from the Center for Research in International Studies, Stanford University.

Introduction

TO THOSE CONTEMPORARIES who knew him best and were not overawed by him, Frederick appeared as a man of almost inexplicable contradictions. His character, the British ambassador reported in a dispatch in 1776, was strongly marked by a "motley composition of barbarity and humanity." On a visit to Potsdam three years earlier, Count Guibert, the military oracle of the waning *ancien régime,* took note of the constant shift from flattery to menace in the king's facial expressions: "He is never the same; one never knows where one stands with him." Guibert carried away the impression of a profoundly ambiguous personality, which he found confirmed even in such details as the king's costly snuffboxes, "which contrast strangely with his general simplicity."

An author-king, harsh and bizarre, was Voltaire's description soon after he had broken with his royal patron.[1] Still another French observer, Frederick's chamberlain, the Marquis d'Argens, liked to dwell on the inconsistencies in the king's behavior, adding, however, that he "knew no one whose contradictions were more logical." The significance of Frederick's personal ambiguities was enlarged by the young Herder, who discussed them in his treatise *Another Philosophy of History Concerning the Development of Mankind* as examples of the ironic disparity between intent and effect in human affairs. After praising the enlightened attitudes and policies of the great monarch, Herder continued that the "reverse side of the portrait" would show that despotism and suffering accompanied the king's "love of humanity, justice, and tolerance." The sense of mystery experienced by his closer associates at every stage of Frederick's life flowed into the general picture that Europe formed of the king, and fed the legends that attached themselves to his person in greater profusion than to that of any other statesman of the century. In these anecdotes and parables Frederick typically figured as the unexcelled warrior with a boundless tenderness for animals; the absolute ruler, who subjects himself to the state and its laws; the holder of supreme authority by divine right, who scoffs at ceremony and governs from a palace scarcely grander than a country house, without guards, protected only by his self-confidence. A political development provided intellectual weight to these legends concerning an astonishing human being: the equally surprising emergence of Prussia as a great power. Both man and state, in their activity and rapid evolution, seemed puzzling and contradictory.

That Frederick was not one of a hundred minor German princes, but a monarch who could affect the course of European affairs, rendered the complexities of his personality a matter of more than local interest. And up to a point, curiosity could be satisfied: the political and moral circumstances of Prussia served to put his figure into the sharpest possible focus. This had been the case even in Frederick's youth: the conflict with his father was waged openly for years and erupted into a European scandal. The conditions that

1. The attack occurs in the 1756 edition of Voltaire's epic *La Pucelle d'Orléans*. It was deleted in subsequent editions.

prevailed in Prussia after his accession did even less to obscure him from general view. At the same time they afforded quite exceptional scope to his unfolding personality. A young prince of talent succeeding to the throne of an ancient polity such as France or Austria would have encountered powerful resistance to his ambitions; court ceremonial and the constraining sophistication of society and culture would have enveloped him, as they enveloped Louis XIV, and turned him into their representative. In Prussia, Frederick William I and his son after him were innovators, not spokesmen. The state was young, poor, politically primitive, its social development stunted: Prussia provided a bare, unobstructed stage, on which the ruler acted alone.

The manner in which Frederick exploited his opportunities, beginning with the occupation of Silesia in 1740, altered the European state system and continued to determine events in Prussia long after his death. But this very extension of his political reach interfered with later assessments of Frederick as ruler and man. The knowledge that it was he, above all, who had made possible Prussia's eventual domination of Central Europe, and even more the consciousness of the tragedies and horrors of modern German history, almost inevitably affected interpretations of the man who died a few years before the French Revolution. The great historiographical debate over Frederick that began in the middle of the last century with Ranke and Droysen was shaped not only by the publication of the king's writings and by the opening of the diplomatic archives, but at least as much by the investigators' own political and social preferences. Scholars who welcomed the unification of Germany under the leadership of a militaristic, socially conservative Prussia thought very differently of the king than did those who hated or feared the new empire.

Such reactions are not unique to the study of Frederick. Dependence on the present, on the interests and passions of the day, is a constant of historical study, and for methodological reasons the impact of contemporary factors may be especially pronounced in historical biography. In his introduction to a collection of essays on Andrew Johnson, published in a companion series to the one in which this volume is appearing, Eric L. McKitrick suggests that "with few exceptions, the entire tone of what has been written about Andrew Johnson has been inspired and governed throughout by the authors' view of a single subject, Reconstruction. . . . Even their treatment of Johnson the man, their assessment of his early life, and their judgments of the personality traits that emerged from the influences of his Tennessee environment and carried over into his Presidency have been shaped by their approval or disapproval of the course he took with regard to Reconstruction." [2]

Andrew Johnson was narrow, ill-educated, opinionated; he had done tragically little to prepare himself for national leadership, which came to him through political expediency and the accident of Lincoln's assassination; and yet the study of his personality and of his rise from tailor's apprentice to the Presidency may afford unique insights into an individual who eventually played a significant role, as well as into American political life in general. But the insights are bound to be fuzzy if the historian keeps squinting at Johnson's policies between 1865 and 1869 and at the influence they exerted on later generations of Americans. Frederick, a far more gifted figure, whose period of political power extended not for a few years but for half a century, during which time his personality came into full accord with his position, requires even greater detachment on our part. If we wish to gain a fuller understanding of the man and the king, we must put out of mind what we know about Germany in the nineteenth and twentieth centuries and concentrate instead on the individual and on the whole range of his activities and interests as they appeared at the time. Most of the essays in this volume have been chosen with this in mind. Their authors discuss Frederick as administrator, soldier, statesman, political thinker, and writer. Two of the selections are accounts by men who observed Frederick on an inspection tour and in battle, contemporary reports that carry us beyond historical interpretation one step closer to Frederick himself. The historical essays inevitably refer on occasion to the impact that Frederick's reign had on subsequent events, but only the two concluding selections—by Franz Mehring and Heinrich von Srbik—address them-

2. Eric L. McKitrick, ed., *Andrew Johnson: A Profile* (New York, 1969), pp. vii–viii.

selves primarily to the question of Frederick's role in history. Both the Marxist critic, his vision of the past dominated by its social and economic inequalities, and the conservative Austrian scholar, with his ideal of a greater Germany fulfilling the international traditions of the Hapsburgs, regard Frederick as an intruder in a difficult historical process, whose ability and energy, far from working for the common good, led to detours and unnecessary tragedies. Other, very different interpretations are equally possible.

With the exception of these two pieces, the selections emphasize Frederick, not the long-term effects that might be imputed to him. But even if we stick as closely as possible to the man, we will not resolve all problems of interpretation. We will find it extremely difficult to blend the complexities of his character and behavior into an assessment that is balanced as well as comprehensive. For reasons that are suggested below, no historian has ever fully succeeded in this task, and it is in any case beyond the scope of a collection of writings of scholars with differing purposes and varied points of view. What can be done here is to indicate some key elements in Frederick's personality and to suggest both the variety of his concerns and the attempts he made to reconcile their frequently antagonistic character.

The contradictions of Frederick's personality that so impressed his contemporaries became apparent at an early age. The young prince was demonstratively out of step with his environment—an unmartial aesthete who appeared a coward in the midst of soldiers and finally provoked a complete rupture with his father. But even before he had reached the age of thirty the opposite side of his temperament had become dominant. Not only did he learn how to lead men in battle; he came to understand and exploit the interaction of violence and policy in war more clearly and ruthlessly than anyone of his generation. The conflict with his father had been profound, but in military matters as elsewhere Ranke's judgment holds true: Frederick William could not have wished for a better successor. That is not to say that Frederick's earlier passions were juvenilia, which the mature man discarded. Frederick took ideas as well as artistic and intellectual creation far more seriously than the convention of his age required. Throughout his life he tried to clarify and expand the structure of his thought in philosophy and literature, but especially in politics. His ruthlessness in diplomacy and war was accompanied by a concern for principles, for lessons to be drawn not only from the participation in great events, but also from their analysis, literary treatment, and distillation into theory. To an exceptional degree, Frederick combined the life of action and the life of contemplation. On campaign he played the flute, composed poetry, listened to readings of the great French tragedies and memorized passages that mirrored his feelings in the ideal sphere of pure syntax. His daily schedule in times of peace suggests even more clearly the intensity of the needs in both the realm of government and the realm of the intellect that demanded satisfaction. He rose between three and four o'clock in the morning and worked with his secretaries, officials, and soldiers until noon; after lunch he reviewed and signed the orders dictated earlier; the rest of the day was given over to literature, music, and conversation. This pattern, with seasonal variations to accommodate inspection tours and maneuvers, he carried on in an environment that he had painstakingly designed and controlled completely.

It is a weakness in the works of even the best biographers of Frederick that they fail to analyze adequately the relationship between action and abstraction in his life. Most historians have seemed content to point out Frederick's unusual combination of talents, praise the breadth of his interests, and then proceed to matters in which *they* were interested—usually political developments. Some scholars have even gone so far as to discount the intellectual sphere in his life as basically insignificant, its value consisting of either filling idle hours or providing a hypocritical mask for brutally aggressive policies. Since Friedrich Meinecke opened the door to our understanding of Frederick's political thought, such views are no longer tenable. Meinecke delineated the historical antecedents of Frederick's ideas, their growth and change under the impact of events, and the interaction of realism, energy, and conscience that characterized them. But Meinecke wrote as a historian of ideas and not as a biographer; therefore, his interpretation necessarily ignores many practical aspects of the king's life. The literature contains outstanding studies on most of these—on Frederick's administrative policies, his social attitudes, his diplomatic techniques, and so on; but valuable though these studies are, from a biographical point of view they remain partial explorations, presenting the whole man only by implication. Today, of course, many historians argue that reliable advances in understanding are less likely to result from conventional biographic treatment than from the study of larger phenomena in which the individual might have been involved, and to which such techniques as quantification and sociological analysis might be applied—Frederick and the expansion of the Prussian bureaucracy, for instance. Of those modern historians who have nevertheless attempted a comprehensive interpretation of Frederick, Gerhard Ritter has probably been the most successful. But his biography, which seeks to give a full value to every major element in Frederick's life, is too brief to serve as more than a guide to the yet-unwritten, detailed analysis that would equitably interweave political, administrative, military, intellectual, and psychological themes.

It may seem especially surprising that no biographer has yet systematically addressed himself to the significant psychological motives in Frederick's life: the conflict with his father; the male, sexually ascetic environment in which he moved from his late twenties on; or such seeming contradictions as his profound sense of realism coupled with impatience and an urge to gamble, which repeatedly betrayed him into errors of policy. The application of psychoanalytic concepts to the study of his life might advance our understanding of it considerably. Unfortunately the few attempts made so far to explore Frederick's psychological constitution and dynamics have been not only fragmentary but also ill informed. They have not made adequate use of either the remaining evidence or the scholarly literature that has grown up around it. Psychological interpretations of Frederick can hardly be enlightening unless the analyst knows the values, anxieties, behavior, and vocabulary of the eighteenth century. If we wish to probe the psyche of a man who lived two hundred years ago we are entirely dependent on the documentary residue of a culture that is radically different from our own. The overt contents of the documents must be interpreted for their genuine message, and the atmosphere that

they reflect and in which they were created must be recognized
before we can use the evidence to illuminate Frederick's psy-
chology and gain insights that might lead to wider historical as
well as biographical understanding. Without a mastery of the
scholarly literature, such understanding is impossible. A case in
point is the treatment of Frederick's sexual life by psycho-historians.
More than forty years ago the German historian Gustav Berthold
Volz analyzed every contemporary assertion that Frederick was
an active homosexual or that in his youth he had undergone an
operation that incapacitated him sexually.[3] Volz was able to demonstrate that none of the reports was supported by factual evidence;
that nearly all contained impossible contradictions of names, dates,
and places; and that all can be attributed to personal animosity
or to scandalmongering. Nevertheless even recent psychological
analyses of the king ignore Volz's research and continue to offer
interpretations of what have turned out to be inventions. Until a
scholar with the necessary psychological and historical competence
sets himself the task of tracing the interaction of emotional, intellectual, and political factors in Frederick's life, the assessment in a
recent review of yet another superficial biography will continue
to apply:

> Frederick had greater and more varied intellectual and personal
> gifts—and they were more constantly and variedly exercised—than
> any of those who have written about him, well-endowed though
> these writers have been. No one has solved the problem which he
> himself puts to us. How does one reconcile acts of treachery and
> egoism with other acts that bespeak integrity and justice, of high
> heroism with the pedestrian qualities needed for painstaking and
> exact administration, or care that the law should be codified and
> liberalized with a talent for creating and using military force and
> exploiting illegality?"[4]

It is difficult to imagine how such a complex individual would
have managed his life if he had not had considerable power to

3. Gustav Berthold Volz, "Friedrich der Grosse und seine sittlichen
Ankläger," *Forschungen zur Brandenburgischen und Preussischen Geschichte,* XXXXI (1928), 1–37.
4. Unsigned review of Nancy Mitford, *Frederick the Great,* in *The Times
Literary Supplement* (October 23, 1970), p. 1212.

make his wishes come true. This power he possessed to a greater degree than any ruler of an important state of his age, and he almost always had a strong urge to use it. With a considerable degree of success he molded state and society to his wishes, and, indeed, it was the Prussian state that served as the bond which held together—and stimulated—the disparate elements of his personality and his varied interests. The interaction between the political and military authority he wielded and his poems and philosophic speculations on these subjects is only one example of the link.

Once the relationship between the state and Frederick's inner life has been clearly recognized, we may after all risk the dangerous step of considering his personality, rule, and their subsequent influence as one. Frederick and his immediate ancestors had filled a politically underdeveloped society with new energy. It is a historical cliché that the collapse of the Prussian monarchy two decades after his death showed the artificiality and failure of the Frederician system. In fact, events proved the very opposite. For a state that was much inferior in size, population, and military and economic resources to be overwhelmed by the Napoleonic Empire was not surprising. That Prussia recovered within a few years, and largely through her own exertions, indicates better than anything else the energy and competence that Frederick had helped create. But this energy continued to be generated by a system that until the First World War operated in what may be termed the Frederician tradition of social conservatism. Frederick, more than his father, had sought to freeze the hierarchical structure of Prussian society into a system of mutually exclusive areas of responsibility, which responded to his desire for an efficient division of labor as well as to his faith in the landed nobility's innate competence for loyal service. All subsequent reforms and adjustments to changing conditions notwithstanding, Prussia and later the German Empire never entirely shed this heritage. Authority in administration, the army, and government remained largely the preserve of protected elites, while the vast majority of the population was prevented from developing political expertise and confidence.

In the face of rapid population growth, industrialization, the collapse of old spiritual values and their replacement by the ideals of nationalism, the political naïveté of the German bourgeoisie proved fatal. But we must take care in postulating cause and effects. If Frederick set Prussia on a certain course, it was a course whose later stages he could not possibly foresee. It should be added that later on in the nineteenth century men did not lack for opportunities to abolish the privileges of the old elites—the broadening of political responsibility took place in other states and was repeatedly attempted in Germany. There are many reasons why not enough came of these attempts—one being the model that Frederick had provided for the German people. But another factor antedated Frederick and was more important: the meagerness of Prussia's political and social resources—her backwardness compared to the rich political culture and the continuing vitality of classes, interest groups, and regions in the other states of West Europe— which until late in the nineteenth century could never provide Germans with an adequate political base from which to combat the excessive power of the executive and its supporters. The vacuum, which had made Frederick's political success possible and provided scope for the expansion of a powerful personality, also did more than anything else to determine the subsequent history of his state.

Stanford, California   PETER PARET
June 1971

Frederick II, 1712–1786

FREDERICK WAS BORN on January 24, 1712, in Berlin, son of the Prussian crown prince who thirteen months later ascended the throne as Frederick William I. The heir's early training was entrusted to a French governess and French tutors, sympathetic to the gifted boy; but they were gradually replaced by soldiers and by the king himself, who rejected serious education in the humanities and fine arts in favor of religious instruction, physical exercises, and military drill. By the time Frederick was twelve his relationship with his able, brutal father had become strained, and their antagonism—heightened by political intrigues in which the queen worked against her husband—grew more severe during the boy's adolescence. In 1730 Frederick attempted to escape conditions that he felt to be intolerable by running away to England. He was caught and court-martialed; a young officer who had helped him was executed. For a time Frederick's succession seemed in doubt; he was pardoned only after persuading the king of his repentance.

After serving an apprenticeship in the state bureaucracy for two years, Frederick was forced into an unwanted marriage with a princess from a minor German dynasty. Their relationship proved an unhappy one, and no children resulted from it. The crown prince and his bride were assigned a new residence at Rheinsberg, in the countryside near Berlin, where Frederick spent the years until his father's death in relative independence, studying history, politics, and literature, beginning his correspondence with Voltaire, and devoting himself to the writing of poetry and political essays, among which his tract against Machiavelli—arguing for the necessity of a statecraft guided by ethics—was the most significant.

Frederick succeeded to the throne in May 1740. The outbreak of hostilities between Great Britain and Spain in the previous year had already disturbed the international system, which was further agitated by the unexpected death of Emperor Charles VI in October 1740. The young king seized the opportunity to gain glory and to strengthen Prussia at Hapsburg expense by occupying Silesia and by supporting the imperial candidacy of the Bavarian elector. In two wars against Austria (1740–1742, 1744–1745), in which he proved himself an adroit diplomat and a commander of genius, he secured his possession of Silesia, which increased the population of the Prussian monarchy by nearly half. For the following ten years he engaged himself deeply in the administrative and economic work of the state. In general his policies did not depart significantly from the pattern set by his father, but they now served to finance and maintain an energetic foreign policy and a far stronger military establishment. By intensive planning and training, Frederick made the Prussian army into the most effective force in Europe. At the same time he sought to elevate the cultural level of his state and to enrich his own intellectual life. Steps were taken to reform the legal system, the severity of the penal code was reduced, the Academy of Science was reorganized, Vol-

taire, Maupertuis, Lamettrie, and other men of letters were invited to Berlin, and Frederick himself entered a phase of great
literary productivity. His writings on recent and contemporary history, and on the theory of military operations, far surpass the average standards of his day.

By the beginning of the 1750's the overseas rivalry between
Britain and France was detrimentally affecting Prussia's position
in Europe, while Austria was strengthening her alliances. To protect himself, Frederick, in January 1756, concluded a limited agreement with Britain, a miscalculation that helped drive France into
a coalition with Austria and Russia directed against Prussia. In
August, Frederick occupied Saxony to disrupt the military prep-
arations of his enemies. Seven years of war in Europe resulted.
British subsidies, the advantage of fighting on interior lines, the
quality of his troops, and his inspired generalship saw him through
severe fighting; but by 1760 Prussia's military capabilities had de-
teriorated, and only the death of the Czarina and Russia's withdrawal from the coalition saved him from defeat.

The remaining twenty-three years of his life Frederick devoted
to repairing the damage that the war had caused Prussia and to
furthering her economic development, without either modifying
the rigid caste structure of Prussian society or modernizing his
system of personal rule, which in the last years of his reign—his
vast energy notwithstanding—was beginning to falter under the
growing complexity of public business. In foreign relations he felt
compelled to ally himself closely to Russia while fearing her increasing interference in Europe. The first partition of Poland in
1772 was a response to both considerations. In German affairs he
now pursued defensive policies that supported the status quo and
strove to inhibit Austrian efforts at expansion. The short war of 1778
and the League of Princes, which he organized in 1785, demonstrated that Frederick did not mean to tolerate a reduction of Prussia's new authority in central Europe. He died on August 17, 1786,
in Sans Souci, the small palace that he had built in a Potsdam vine-
yard after the Second Silesian War as the ideal dwelling of a philosopher king.

PART ONE

Three Stages in Frederick's Life

CARL HINRICHS

The Conflict Between Frederick and His Father

IN THE GREAT autocratic monarchies, the hopes and wishes of an ever-present but powerless opposition have often made common cause with the natural impatience of the heir to the throne. Throughout the true monarchical period, the opposition and liberalism of crown princes were nuclei and gathering points for political parties; it did not matter whether these parties spoke for older power structures against the country's bold innovators, or for a newer world against the inflexible protectors of the old.

"Der Konflict zwischen Friedrich Wilhelm I und Kronprinz Friedrich," from Carl Hinrichs, *Preussen als historisches Problem*. Copyright © 1964 by Walter de Gruyter & Co., Berlin. Translation copyright © 1972 by Peter Paret.

Even the decision about the young future ruler's education (To what philosophy would he be exposed? Who would educate him?) was a matter of state, overtly or secretly influenced by factions. It was as important a question as is the question of public education generally in modern mass societies. Fénelon, for example, leader of those opposed in principle to the system and philosophy of Louis XIV's government, wrote *Télémaque,* a political and educational roman-à-clef, for his pupil, the heir apparent. In this book he contrasted a humanitarian, pacific, ideal state, serving the civic welfare of the masses, with the heroic, bellicose tendencies of the Great King aiming at the glory and enlargement of France. In most cases, however, opposition leaders and the partisans attached to the crown prince experienced bitter disappointment on the "Day of the Duped," when the new ruler, on reaching power, quickly grasped the iron necessity of his country's interests and policies that in the idle contemplation of his days as crown prince he had thought he might easily change.

Of the three most notable royal father-son conflicts in modern European history, two ended in the premature death of the heir. In the latter cases—the conflict between Don Carlos and his father, Philip II of Spain, and that of the Czarevitch Alexei with Peter the Great—the heir was not sufficiently great, strong, or flexible to maintain himself against the *raison d'état* embodied in the father and at the same time grow into the system by means of this very opposition. The third—and in human terms the greatest—of these conflicts developed differently. We refer to that of Crown Prince Frederick of Prussia with his father, Frederick William I. Crown Prince Frederick did not succumb; he withstood the test because he was driven by more than the confused, merely stubborn and pathological emotionalism of Don Carlos, or the uncontrolled enthusiasm of Alexei. Crown Prince Frederick's strong personality and his consciousness of his own rank kept his omnipotent father —to whom the court-martial entrusted his fate—from going to the last extreme. Furthermore, he was willing and able to learn from his experience.

This was not the first father-son conflict in the Hohenzollern dynasty, but it was the sharpest both in personal and philosophic

terms and the one fought through most dramatically and ruthlessly because it involved two well-matched opponents. The long
and laborious climb to power of Brandenburg-Prussia was marked
by the quarrel of Prince Frederick William—later the Great Elector
—with his father, George William, and with that father's favorite
and councilor, Schwartzenberg. Here we find the model of dynastic conflict, and the elements needed for such a controversy, in
Brandenburg-Prussia. First there are two foreign-policy orientations between which the rising state must choose: adherence to
the Imperial House of Hapsburg, or to its European opponents.
Secondly, the ministers and privy councilors out of power make
common cause with the "entire electoral womanfolk" to fight the
statesman in power and his foreign policy. And finally, the whole
opposition party joins the heir apparent, who is struggling for
independence. Through weakness, the father allowed this conflict
to smolder on fruitlessly until it was resolved with the ruler's
death. The next controversy, on the other hand, that between the
Great Elector and his son Frederick—the future first king of
Prussia—ended in reconciliation. Here, too, the struggle about
orienting foreign policies toward Hapsburg or Bourbon was combined with family quarrels, in this case with the argument about
providing for the sons of the Great Elector's second marriage.

In judging the conflict between Frederick the Great and his
father, it is extremely important to remember that Frederick
William I was the only one of the great absolute Hohenzollern
rulers who always obeyed his father totally, in spite of the fact
that he was also the one who probably embodied the deepest and
most unconquerable antithesis to his predecessor. Actually, Frederick William I would have had all the prerequisites for a particularly sharp conflict. No Prussian ruler left standing less of the
spirit and system of his predecessor, and none—while still crown
prince—had already developed his own program so deliberately,
inflexibly, and early. And yet he was the most loyal of sons. Even
as a boy he possessed deep religious feeling for legitimate authority,
for the necessity of mute subordination to the divinely ordained
superior power. While still crown prince, he was already very
conscious of the fact that he would be able to command the un-

bounded obedience his work required only if he himself did not rebel against the highest authority. *Nemo potest imperare nisi qui prius paruerit* had been one of the boy's mottoes. He was so imbued with an almost mythical respect for the king of Prussia as one inspired by a higher power that he refused to attempt to influence his father's decisions by personal advocacy. Only in the last year of Frederick I's reign, at a time of deep crisis and upheaval in the state, did he step forward, but always in outward agreement with his father, leaving the latter at least the appearance of taking the initiative.

As a result, Frederick William I found his own son's disobedience incomprehensible.

Their controversy contained all elements, both objective and subjective, of a political crisis in the absolute state. In the first place, there was the heir resisting the demands the ruler made for reasons of state. Secondly, there was an opposition party penetrating all levels of society, including those closest to the ruler and his family. This party opposed both the domestic and foreign policies of the regime, and thus brought about the third prerequisite: vacillation between the alternative foreign orientations, between adherence to the emperor or to the Western Powers.

The first of these forces was especially conspicuous because here was the case of an extremely gifted heir apparent—supplied with the weapon of critical, superior, and caustic speech—who learned to think for himself at an early age. Opposed to him a father, inarticulate both in words and expression, who represented principles which—in the extremely strained and dangerous position of the country—could afford but little play for personal idiosyncrasies. The founding of the Prussian state had been a desperately daring process, and its position in the European concert of powers rested on the fact that this country of, at most, middling size maintained an exceptionally competent army that would have been appropriate for a major power, thus forcing the dominant governments to treat her with consideration. Prussia lacked natural resources and was poor in both land and population, so that everything depended on ability, exertion, and strength of will. While other countries had gradually developed, Prussia had been created, and her continued existence depended on the iron resolution that held this creation together, and on the severity and perseverance of the military authority that directed not only the army but the civilian government and the economy. In Prussia, more than in any other state of that time, everything depended on maintaining this leadership. But Frederick William I lived in constant anxiety about his work, about the state that he had fashioned by the decisions and experiences of his days as crown prince and had built up with ruthless energy in ten years of terrible exertion. He had had a noble-minded mother, who tried to bring him in contact with Fénelon and Bayle, the fathers of a new Western European *Geisteswelt* based on the supremacy of common sense. He had been surrounded by French customs and culture, by wealth and beauty, music, art and great architecture, by everything for which his son was to eat his heart out. But he had pushed all that aside, had disdained it because this luxurious royal existence was possible only at the cost of an ignominious financial and political dependence on the maritime powers at whose side the minor vassal Prussia fought for the Spanish heritage in Europe and overseas. It was these powers who forced Prussia to deliver her eastern borders to the Russians and Swedes struggling for supremacy on the Baltic. His youth had been filled with vast political events—the blocking of France's drive for hegemony, the declining power of Sweden and Turkey, the rising power of Russia and Austria—which fed his conviction that the foundations of his state would have to undergo a complete revolution. And yet he did not deviate from his posture of tortured waiting and observing.

As crown prince, Frederick William I had lived through great events both in domestic and foreign affairs. His work was based on these experiences. By the time his son was growing up, his creation—the state—was firmly established. Thus it was not the function of this heir to develop anything, to create something based on his own experience. His youth had not been stamped by the distress of his country and people who demanded to be saved and restored. Since everything had already been done and provided by the father, and was functioning in the most marvelous and awe-inspiring way, the son needed only to adapt himself to

the finished work so that, in his own time, he might take over
the leadership of this creation, maintain it, and carry it on. There
was nothing left for Frederick to do on his own; he was to conform to his father's concept of the ideal heir, to be a part, a service-
able accessory to the whole, as was his father, the king, himself.
Frederick William's views of the type of heir Prussia needed were
contained in his Instructions to the Successor, written in 1722.

Frederick William I identified himself with his work to such an
extent that he believed this creation must necessarily collapse if the
heir did not share his own beliefs, his thoughts, his likes and dislikes—in short, if the heir was not his double. But the life and
work of Frederick William I rested firmly on the foundation of
the evangelical reformed faith he had accepted without the slightest
question or doubt in spite of his enlightened Guelph mother's
many attempts to win him over to her Western traditions. With
truly Calvinist conviction about predestination, he saw the extraordinary rise of the House of Brandenburg as the result of
Divine Grace descending upon the dynasty. He saw it as visible
proof that his family's rule was moral and according to God's
Will. The rise of the state, the flowering and power of Brandenburg-Prussia in this world, were tied to the preservation of high
moral standards in its rulers. If the heir to the throne abandoned
these standards, it could mean the loss of this Divine Grace and
therefore the cessation, regression, and destruction of the blessed
work of generations. To guarantee the continued existence of the
dynasty, the heir must be hard-working, ruthlessly frugal, a good
husbandman, punctual, simple—placing no trust in anything beautiful, brilliant, suave, or worldly or in "comedies, operas, ballets,
masquerades, and galas"—fearful of debts, unnecessary expendi-
tures, and extravagances—in a word, as much of a puritan king as
Frederick William himself.

The slightest hint of suspicious tendencies in the son had to
alarm the father; the smallest sign in that direction made the
ground tremble under his feet. Since Frederick William devoted
himself to his work with matchless passion, the storm clouds
gathered as suspicious signs multiplied.

It is clear that the king compared even his son's earliest development with his own childhood. Indeed, he issued instructions calling for the same, or almost the same, education. He must have noticed emerging differences with deep concern. He himself had been an unruly boy who was difficult to control and absolutely disinclined toward all instruction. The only things he had respected were his father as king of Prussia, and the avenging, punishing God of Calvin whom his tutor called on against his violent misdeeds, threatening the pupil with the doctrine of predestination. Frederick William did not overcome the effects of this doctrine until he was nineteen. From then on, he fought against it because he felt that, in excluding the possibility for changing human nature, and in its weakening effect on willpower, the doctrine of predestination endangered the state. The experiences of his own youth were reflected in the instructions he gave for his son's education. He banned the teaching of predestination as well as of Latin and ancient history. Though he had not wanted to learn Latin and history, he had nevertheless harbored the ambition of becoming a great soldier, of learning the trade of "commanding the armies of all Europe—do you know of anything greater?" His son, also, was to learn how to "act the great general" since "nothing in this world can give a prince glory and honor like the sword." What Frederick William demanded of his son in the name of the state was that he should be a good officer, a good Christian, and a good husbandman. But the "true love of soldiering" which had burned in him as a boy would not appear in the little Frederick. He was a "coward," a "milksop," afraid of gunfire; he fell off his horse; he wouldn't stand straight; he didn't keep his clothes and hair neat; he slept late, liked to be by himself and wander around aimlessly, or cower near his mother and sister where he early learned to read novels, play the lute, and engaged in other unmilitary and unnecessary tricks.

In his childhood, the king had voiced his likes and dislikes freely and openly; Fritz was secretive and reserved, acted superior, and tended to sarcasm. The king wanted to know "what is going on in this little head; I know he does not think as I do." When he tried to understand this strange and uncanny twelve-year-old, the king became terribly fearful about his life's work. He pleaded with him: "Fritz, mind what I tell you; always maintain a big army and a good one. You can't have a better friend, nor maintain yourself without one. Our neighbors would like nothing better than to bring us down. I know their intentions, and you, too, will get to know them. Believe me, don't think on vanity, but stick to what is real: always see to it that you have a good army and money, for the fame and security of princes are based on them."

In order to accustom the son to his own harsh way of living, and at the same time get to know him and keep an eye on him, the king wanted to keep Frederick with him as much as possible. The lad had to get up at the crack of dawn, wear an ordinary grenadier uniform, take part in the wear-and-tear of the king's own tempestuous schedule, including the reviews, inspections, and trips, down to the king's smoking sessions. He regulated his son's day by the clock from dressing, morning prayer, and breakfast until time to go to bed; everything was set down minute by minute. At fourteen, the crown prince was so exhausted "that with all his young years he looks and walks as old and stiff as if he had already taken part in many campaigns." The observer continues: "It is the intention of the king that he . . . should prefer the military to all other sciences, learn thrift and frugality early, and not fall in love with *Commodité* and *Plaisir*!" But it all turned out the other way; Frederick leaned toward good living, comfort, generosity, beauty, and luxury. The harshness and drill he endured made him detest his father's entire system: the unspeakable workload of the officials, the pitiless taxation, the severity with which the army was trained and disciplined. This entire world of barracks and efficiency was somberly ruled by renunciation, and it touched his dreaming young heart like an icy blast with the foreknowledge of his fate.

Young Frederick found the first means of expressing his individuality in religion and the radical interpretation of the Christian commandment of love and peace. This development was promoted by his religious instructor, the court preacher Andreä, who belonged to the religious opposition and who, against the king's orders, taught Frederick the doctrine of predestination. A royal "thunderclap" removed Andreä in 1725. Until his eighth year, the crown prince accepted religious instruction passively, but at that point he began to interpret what he had learned independently and to use it for his own purposes. August Herman Francke, the leader of the Halle Pietists, long remembered that at the age of seven the crown prince applied to himself with "a particular, God-given joy" the first Psalm: "Blessed is the man that walketh not in the counsel of the ungodly, nor standeth in the way of sinners, nor sitteth in the seat of the scornful." It was also at this age that Frederick on his own initiative composed an essay on "The Life-Style of a Prince of High Birth," which should be that of a pious Christian. Examining him in front of a large gathering, his father asked, "And when you grow older, won't you have to act like others of your station: overeat, get drunk, swear, scold, grow callous, and go whoring?" The king was pleased with the answer, "I'll hold to the Ten Commandments." But he also told a tipsy officer attending the king: "I would rather meet a hog than a drunk." When the officer excused himself, saying, "The king wants us to have a good time," the prince replied that, "One must obey God before men."

His statements of faith gradually became ambiguous and calculated as he made them into a weapon of his opposition—a telling weapon, since it was aimed at his father's conscience and religious scruples. From Luther's "Of Secular Authority" his father had learned to regard force and the sword as "a special service of the Lord." At the age of twelve or thirteen, Frederick found in this work a quotation that seemed to be directed to him personally, and it became the first vague expression of his own ideal concept of kingship as opposed to the bitter barracks-world of his father.

> Hence David of old dared not build the temple because he had shed much blood and had borne the sword; not that he had done wrong thereby, but because he could not be a type of Christ, who without the sword was to have a kingdom of peace. It had to be built by Solomon, whose name means "Frederick" or "peaceful," who had a peaceful kingdom, by which the truly peaceful kingdom of Christ, the real Frederick and Solomon could be represented. . . . All for this reason, that Christ, without constraint

and force, without law and the sword, was to have a people who serve him freely.[1]

Frederick referred to this quotation at table one day—though in the king's absence—when the conversation turned to war and battles. He ignored the fact that Luther justified force and the sword in spite of Christ's injunction to love. He read a completely personal and almost political meaning into this religious teaching. "Without constraint and force . . ."—but the state of Frederick William I was full of both: the groans of citizens burdened with billeting and taxes, the suppressed lordliness of Junkers forced into cadet academies, just as the obligatory early rising and the hard life of the crown prince. His developing personality, his pride and need for freedom were constrained by the dominating state. He dreamed of building Solomon's Temple, the imagined picture of a realm without constraint. It was his first awareness of the contrast between power and ethical absolutes. Out of the depth of its suffering, the child declared against power.

The doctrine of predestination, taught him against his father's orders, became yet another spiritual foundation upon which to base his opposition. He took the position that man whose nature was ordained by God could not change himself, and from there it was but a short distance to insist on the right of his own ego, his individuality. The young, developing personality already knew how to assert himself. He engaged his father on the latter's own ground of piety, with a self-confidence and tactical cleverness that are demonstrated in an event that occurred in June 1725 at the review of the Magdeburg regiments. Upon the king's complaining that the crown prince was frequently late, he replied that while the king had four persons to help him get dressed, he—the crown prince—had only one, and furthermore he needed time for prayers after he was dressed. The king was of the opinion that the crown prince could say his morning prayers while dressing, to which the crown prince objected: "Saving Your Majesty's pardon, one cannot very well pray if one is not by oneself; one would need some time

1. "Of Secular Authority," translated by J. J. Schindel, *Works of Martin Luther*, The Philadelphia Edition (Philadelphia: Muhlenberg Press, 1930), III.

exclusively for prayer"; and then came the well aimed: "On such a point one must obey God more than men."

But before long the crown prince left the religious world of his ancestors, his father, and his childhood, not even using it to provide him formulas for his resistance. Now, he entered the realm of philosophy, the world of the dawning Enlightenment. At the age of sixteen he wrote his first poem, first signed himself *Frédéric le philosophe,* and began to play the flute under Quantz's instruction. The original religio-metaphysical interest that had once fed on religious instruction developed into a youthfully enthusiastic desire to become acquainted with everything men had ever thought. He installed a library of some 3,000 volumes—secretly acquired with borrowed money—in a house near the palace. The books dealt with philosophy, history, theology, rhetoric, and poetry; but he cannot have done more than leaf through them. They represented the direction he was taking, the kingdom of his soul, the Temple of Solomon to which he fled from the harsh reality of Prussia, rather than real knowledge—which he was to acquire only later in Rheinsberg. He entered into the heritage of his grandmother, Queen Sophie Charlotte, who had been the first intellectual woman in the Grand Style in Germany and who had demanded from Leibniz to know the Why of the Why. Her major literary and philosophic lights had been Fénelon, the father of liberal principles of government and eighteenth-century sensibility, and Bayle, the enlightener, and the destroyer of dogmas. Now they also rose on the prince's horizon. Frederick William I said of his mother that she was a clever woman but a bad Christian, and while he always obeyed his father, he showed nothing but distaste and contempt for the alien world of his mother, with its French ideas and art. So in the conflict with his son there was an echo, at least, of the conflict with his mother, whose educational principles the king had never accepted. But there was also an element of himself in his son's tendency to retire into his own conceptual world. All the great Hohenzollerns were saturnine by nature and were periodically troubled by a sense of fatigue and uselessness in their labors. A yearning for peace and private happiness broke through in each of them according to his own personality: Frederick

William I wanted to live like a farmer, or a Dutch rentier, or even
an anchorite in a brown cowl; Frederick the Great, like a sage in
the midst of books and music.

The crown prince withdrew more and more. He considered only
very few people worth a serious word, and to the rest he presented
a "mocking face." On meeting persons whose world he rejected,
he could turn to ice, and that included almost everybody, since
aesthetes were not to be found around Frederick William I. The
crown prince drew that much closer to his beloved older sister.
Prince and princess—her lute and his flute—consoled each other.
In their inborn, stubborn, and childish melancholy, they invented
a secret language in which—at times quite recklessly—they made
fun of the king and his entourage. The king wanted to see Frederick fresh, alert, and cheerful; but the son was filled with thoughts
of death. Boyishly, he got hold of a picture of a skull and penned
his thoughts on death to go with it. On top of all this came
Frederick's first dissipations. These began during a visit to the
court of August the Strong, in Dresden, where he learned about
those "scandalous Plaisirs" and "sardanaphalic desires of the flesh"
that "have never been tolerated in our House," as Frederick William I wrote pleadingly in his Instructions to the Successor. The
secret debts grew.

The crown prince developed an unhealthy double life. He obeyed
his father and performed his duty—since 1728 he was lieutenant-
colonel in the king's own regiment—but only as far as he absolutely
had to; he did not hide the fact that he acted unwillingly and
under compulsion. Precisely this was the king's constant reproach:
that the only things Frederick did cheerfully, gave himself fully to,
were connected with his "effeminate" tastes and *petit-maître* habits.
Whenever possible, he got out of his father's sight, and lived his
own secret, hidden, and suspect life. Everything about the son's
public and private posture irritated the father every day and every
hour; he saw it as the handwriting on the wall—a warning that
the bankrupt French pomp of his predecessor would rise from the
grave he had sealed over with his treasury: that "the old histories
of my father will wake again."

Things came to a head, however, only as a result of the crown prince's alliance with the opposition.

Frederick William's hard regime encroached ruthlessly on all conditions of life, and on every level of society; the omnipotence of the newly secured state hung threateningly over the old society. The authority of the nobility had been broken; the great fortunes forced into the service of the state; and peasant and city dweller brought to a higher and more intensive level of labor. The army had been inexorably placed at the center of the entire government, and its growth was ruthlessly advanced by forced recruitment, which was practiced not only abroad but also at home until the system of selective conscription was introduced. Prussia, the military colony, lived precariously, and every screw was sharply tightened: "Every comfort must give way to the king's will; obedience suits the subject best."

This obedience was hardest on the court nobility dating from the lovely, shining days of the first king—Wartensleben, Kameke, Schulenburg, and Arnim. General Count Finckenstein and Colonel von Derschau, the crown prince's governors, belonged to this group. This feudal opposition was closely allied to a movement in the church that—in the name of the ideal, unconstrained realm of Christian welfare—opposed the tense, ever-present power state. What made the opposition dangerous was the fact that its members could find a focus in the queen.

Sophie Dorothea, wife of Frederick William I, was the last and least of the three Guelph Sophies, but she nevertheless breathed the same air and the same tradition as her grandmother, the Electress Sophie of Hanover, and her aunt, Queen Sophie Charlotte of Prussia. All three shared the pride and arrogance of the house of Hanover, which were even greater after Hanover's ascension to the English throne in 1714, and they looked down on the Prussian upstarts. Even on the Prussian throne, they showed the same loyalty to Hanoverian interests and preferences, the same predilection for the Great World, the same concern for architecture, literature, and music as appropriate to their station—a concern they passed on to Frederick the Great; and the same feminine thirst for power and intrigue. Sophie Dorothea was the least fortunate of the three in that she had the least scope in which to develop her character, living as she did with Frederick William I. She had been happy as crown princess in the days of the first king; she was pampered and influential, and ruled the court in Berlin. But when she tried to gain political influence at the time of her husband's accession, he —though he otherwise really loved her—had somewhat testily sent her off "to her needlework." That did not, however, stop her from playing politics in her own way. Since she was dominated by feminine and familial feelings, her politics had to be in favor of Hanover and England and the Western Powers generally, whose civilizing glow held her as much in thrall as they had her predecessor on the Prussian throne. In the name of her house, she also passed this heritage on to her son. She fitted poorly into the role of German housewife that was forced on her, and she was embittered because she could indulge in her predilections for the great world only secretly and penuriously. Daughter of the mightiest European ruler, she was constantly short of money. Unable to separate personal from external matters, she blamed Frederick William's entire system of government—whose originality and creativeness she did not in the least understand—for her drab and joyless existence as queen. As a result, she decisively grasped the leadership of the Fronde against the government, the most hated of whose principal supporters were Prince Leopold of Anhalt-Dessau and the minister of state General Frederick William von Grumbkow.

It was inevitable that the crown prince should associate himself with this opposition, for the queen, full of hate and suffering, had made confidants of her two older children, whom she used as spies against the king and his councilors. She encouraged the crown prince's aversion to his father's harsh regime and sought to prepare for the future by teaching him other principles of government. She was convinced that someday after her death the country would thank her for what she had done with her oldest son. It was here —among those who criticized his father's principles, who were the hundredfold echoes of his own unhappiness, before whom he could practice and show off his wit and scorn—that the crown prince grew into a politician. It is true that he was immature and rash; nevertheless, he did become a politician who pursued his objective through all vicissitudes, and worked toward one end.

The matter at issue concerned his own and his sister's English marriages, a family question as well as a question of policy. The family connection between Prussia and Hanover had become traditional, and with Frederick William's approval it was to be renewed in the younger generation: an English princess had been chosen for Frederick, the Prince of Wales for his sister Wilhelmina. Frederick William considered this double marriage a purely family matter that he could keep entirely separated from foreign policy, but the English were not inclined to "begin the story at the end"; that is, they demanded that political arrangements be concluded before the marriage could be allowed. But Prussia had just gone over to the camp of the German emperor. Since Sophie Dorothea wanted to bring about the marriages at any cost, she considered it her job to keep the king to his former French-English orientation.

Ever since the Peace of Westphalia, the larger German powers possessed the right to make war and peace, and had faced the fatal choice between independence and loyalty to the empire, between joining the house of Hapsburg or the alliance of its European opponents, alternatives that corresponded all too well with the double face of the Hapsburg dynasty as emperors of Germany and as rulers of an international Catholic realm.

Frederick William I's imperial patriotism was rooted in the experiences of his youth, in the German Empire's battle against Louis XIV's encroachments. It became unshakable when the emperor deferred to his legitimate claims to the Rhenish heritage of the Hohenzollerns, Julich and Berg, and then confirmed his support after the contract of Wusterhausen of autumn 1726. For the Pragmatic Sanction—the assurance of female succession in the Austrian dynasty, without which the Hapsburg empire would be dismembered in Europe—could not be carried through without the assistance of Prussia as the most powerful state in the empire. The king regarded the possible fall of the Hapsburg dynasty as a national misfortune: "An emperor we must have, so we stick to the house of Austria, and who doesn't contribute to that is not an honest German. If we accept a prince from the empire who doesn't have Austria's treasure and income, he will have to be supported by the electors, and that doesn't suit me or the others." But "no English-man or Frenchman is to rule over us Germans, and I will put pistols and swords in my children's cradles that they may help keep foreign nations out of Germany. They already want to command and give orders as if they were the masters. What would happen if one let the imperial authority fall into their hands?" Nevertheless, "We must ask the emperor to satisfy all complaints that one or another prince of the empire may have, and that the powerful states not be served so contemptuously by the imperial ministers as a prince of this corner or that. . . ." Unfortunately, although many in Vienna realized that the claims of Prussia, whose development could not very well be reversed, would have to be faithfully hon-ored in accordance with the obligations that had been undertaken, this view did not prevail. Instead, the Hapsburgs preferred to bind Prussia by dishonorable intrigues and double dealing. The agent of this policy was the imperial General von Seckendorff, who had been Austrian envoy to Berlin since 1726, where he had bribed and won over to his side the king's trusted adviser, Minister von Grumbkow, in whom he acquired a first-class tool. Prince Eugen assigned the two conspirators as one of their prime objectives the prevention of the English-Prussian marriages. Thus Seckendorff and Grumbkow stood against the queen and her entire faction: "Whigs" and "Tories" made up the "female" and the "imperial" parties.

Of course, the crown prince also worked ardently for the English marriage plans, and, since he knew as well as his mother that these plans could be realized only if Prussia was oriented toward western Europe, he also took up the fight against the pacesetters of the imperial alliance, that is, against Seckendorff and Grumbkow. The queen allowed herself to be advised by the French envoy, and probably even accepted money from France so that she might live a little more royally than her husband permitted. Rothenbourg received valuable information from her and the crown prince about the activities of the imperial party, but Grumbkow also had spread wide a network of spies that watched the queen and the crown prince. Not only in hour-long secret discussions, but also in anonymous letters, he hinted to the king what was going on around him and his family. He understood perfectly how to feed his observations to Frederick William, drop by drop, in a manner calculated to drive the king—who was irritable, living in "continual movement" and at times beset by delusions—into a complete rage.

The hatred between Grumbkow and the queen and her adherents had a long history. As early as 1713, at the time of Frederick William's accession, Sophie Dorothea wanted to get hold of a letter from England in which Grumbkow had called her husband a "brutal beast"; the talented gambler with the honest face still used such expressions on occasion. Through Prince Eugen, Seckendorff secured him a secret imperial safe conduct, for Grumbkow would be destroyed if anything happened to the king; his position, even his liberty, depended on the success of the imperial policy. Years earlier it had already come to a test of strength between Grumbkow and the female party when a Hungarian adventurer and member of the diplomatic demimonde, Klément, disclosed to the king the plans of a palace revolution against him, in which Dessau and Grumbkow were said to be the leaders. Unable to prove anything, Klément eventually ended on the gallows, but Grumbkow had known how to turn the affair against the queen: the accusations against him must have come from her and her party. The Klément affair left a thorn of fear and worry in the king's side; he knew that all Europe waited for his death and the breakdown of the concentration of German power in Prussia, which seemed to survive only through his constant exertions. He knew that plans for Prussia's partition existed in the European cabinets, and he also knew that his wife's regency or the premature accession of his rebellious and immature son would mean the end of Prussia. And now he received carefully measured information of secret dealings between the crown prince and foreign diplomats, heard tell of a party around the crown prince working toward the king's destruction. How easy it was to provide a deeper conspiratorial background for the fundamental resistance of the crown prince: his careless statements about his father's system of government, which were repeated to the latter; his ill-considered communications with for-

eign diplomats, of which the king learned! That in the highly
placed opposition there was some playing with dangerous conspiratorial ideas is shown in a report by the French envoy, which
also indicates how other countries viewed this game and promoted
it. "To disarm the father, one would have to provide the crown
prince with a party and bring a number of officers to his side . . .
I believe that would succeed. Anyway, one would have to educate
the young prince to a frame of mind friendly to France." The
documents of Frederick's interrogation after his arrest in 1730 show
that the king suspected his son of such leanings. The king thought
that by torture he could wring their last secrets from the crown
prince and Katte.[2]

But there is no evidence whatever that the crown prince really
harbored plans for an uprising against the king. It was surely a
case of speculations and hopes which the opposition and foreign
nations placed in the growing conflict between father and son.
Seckendorff and Grumbkow cleverly used such indiscretions. Wor-
ried, burdened by a basic difference in temperaments, the king was
already on bad terms with his son. Seckendorff and Grumbkow
drove him frantic. His mistrust became boundless, but he had to
control himself in order to observe, test, and finally convict. Spotty
information and suspicion rubbed against a thousand trifles until
the dangerously explosive character of the king searched the manner, appearance, and dress of the crown prince for some external
pretext upon which to vent, to break out, the pent-up raging anger.
The relationship between father and son became desperate and led
to physical abuse that aroused impotent hate and wild indignation
in the young crown prince, whose pride as officer and aristocrat was
severely hurt.

After the fall of 1728, which the royal family had spent together

2. Lieutenant von Katte, son of a Prussian general and nephew of a
general field marshal, agreed to help Frederick escape from Prussia. After
the attempt failed in August 1730, Katte was arrested and court-martialed.
He was found guilty of attempted desertion, secret communication with
foreign powers, and other crimes, but the majority of the court recommended lifelong imprisonment rather than the death sentence. Despite the
king's urgings the court refused to alter its judgment, whereupon the king
overrode the court and ordered Katte executed outside Frederick's cell.
[ed.]

in Wusterhausen, the situation seemed to leave the crown prince no normal way out of his difficulties with his father. The king demanded that he "conform" in every detail, but matters had now come to a point where, even if he were willing, he could give no more than the appearance of compliance. He had too much pride to snuff himself out by simple submission. The mere appearance of conformity, however, would not have satisfied the king. Frederick had come to the point where he had either to convince his father of the value of his own personality or else seek some other way out. He was not capable of realizing the first alternative because it was impossible to achieve self-knowledge and control while he lay under the pressure of a father who wanted to make him into a mirror image of himself. Frederick felt only that he could not fit into that mold no matter how grandiose it might be. He could explain neither to himself nor to other people what sort of a man he was, but clearly he was not the sort who could simply slip into a finished mold, a finished creation. His personality had to find its own way; it needed to be fed and developed; it required space for mistakes and detours. All this Frederick could not find in his youth because —in spite of all his secret attempts—it was impossible to escape his father's spell and that of the needs of the state that he represented. This is what made the childhood diseases of his genius so lengthy and severe. His father could see only these childish diseases, a vague meandering in spiritual and carnal fields. Frederick drifted into them for want of a direction of his own, a goal he could himself recognize. Terribly fearful for the state, the king tried to force his successor onto his own track. It was the age-old mistake of fathers who wanted to set their heirs on a firmly established track where they had only to roll forward, while the sons wanted to seek and find their own way. Frederick William I made this mistake in monumental style. If the personal road Frederick the Great found was after all a magnificent continuation of his father's, that was due mostly to the momentum of his father's work, which he could no longer evade after the crisis had finally come. Both father and son acted in full accord with their own natures and their own situations: Frederick was young, imprudent, and impetuous; the king was driven by the state he had created and by concern for its safety. The father wanted a rational successor who would place the needs of the state first; Frederick was as yet only a living, seeking young man athirst for freedom and growth. When hopes that his father would at last allow him to travel were finally wrecked, he was left only with the possibility of the English marriage, or with flight—or both. The fact that Frederick faced this last alternative without shrinking, and the manner in which he carried it out proved him to be a politician and a man of action.

CHESTER V. EASUM

Return from the
Seven Years' War

In 1762 Russia and Sweden withdrew from the coalition against
Prussia, France opened negotiations with Great Britain, and
Austria was too exhausted to carry on the struggle by herself.
Chester Easum discusses Frederick's conduct of the peace talks,
and the return of Frederick and Prince Henry, his brother, to
Berlin.—Editor.

From *Prince Henry of Prussia,* by Chester V. Easum. Madison: University
of Wisconsin Press, 1942, pp. 226–237. Reprinted with permission of the
author and Greenwood Press.

I am . . . a stranger here.—FREDERICK.

I am not in any way attached to anything in Berlin; the
memory of the past is very painful to me, and the life that
one leads there [now] seems quite insipid.

—HENRY TO FREDERICK.

FREDERICK'S PEACE TERMS were simple. He had only
to state them once, briefly, and adhere to them while Count
Kaunitz estimated the cost of another year or two of war, weighed
the danger of a Turkish invasion of Hungary, and brought his
colleagues and the empress-queen to the point of confessing their
failure. Frederick would cede no territory, not even Glatz; but
when Austria was ready to concede that point, peace was possible
at any time; and Austria had as good reason as Prussia to wish
that it be made quickly.

Unless Russia should intervene! Before formal negotiations had
begun, Frederick had received a letter from Catherine II that
ostensibly offered her friendly services as a mediator but looked
ominously like a threat. In it the empress reminded the king of
Prussia that she had been and still was in a position to ruin him,
and said she hoped he realized how difficult it had been for her
to avoid being drawn into the war.[1]

Catherine would evidently have liked to have a hand in drawing
up the peace treaty—a concession which Frederick had no thought
of making either to her or to any other outsider. Yet he dared not
offend her. He devoted three days of serious thought to his reply;
choosing not to risk an outright refusal of her offer of mediation,
he pretended merely to defer his acceptance of it.

Naturally, he wrote in self-justification. He knew, he said, that
the British, after having failed so shamefully to safeguard his interests in their own preliminary treaty with France, had revived at
St. Petersburg their old accusation that he did not really want to
make peace. "There are some kinds of peace, Madame," he replied
to that charge, "to which I am opposed, because they are contrary
to the dignity and the glory of any sovereign, no matter who he
may be. . . . Up to now," he said,

1. Arnold Schäfer, *Geschichte des siebenjährige Krieges,* 3 vols. (Berlin,
1867), II–2, 759–760.

the number of my enemies has put me into no position to make peace; and as long as these enemies announced openly that they proposed to exterminate the very name of Prussia, I could not have consented to a peace unless I were either frightfully irresponsible or completely imbecile.

As the Empress-Queen now finds herself almost isolated, it is to be hoped that she will entertain more moderate ideas. I have envisaged this war, Madame, as a great conflagration which one can finally extinguish only by getting rid of the combustible materials which serve to nourish it. . . . I have been the injured party in this unhappy war, and I have very ardently wished to see it ended in an honorable fashion, and above all that the structure of the peace should not be just plastered over but should be durable.

As the injured party, the king went on to say, he considered himself in a better position than any other belligerent to ask for damages; but out of the goodness of his heart, for the love of peace and for the sake of humanity, he would demand only the complete restoration of his territories. Who was the better friend of peace, he asked—the Austrian seeking conquests or the Prussian who sought only to hold what was his? The French were about to evacuate his Rhineland provinces and he had troops ready, he said, to retake possession of them; but he had heard that the Austrian government was planning to send troops from Flanders to try to anticipate him. As soon as that matter had come to a head, he averred, he had intended to ask the empress of Russia to mediate in the interest of peace—which he was, however, "obliged to defer today," not knowing yet just where he stood.

He concluded his letter with a long paragraph in praise of peace and of Catherine, its high priestess:

I have revealed to you, Madame, all that I have on my heart, fully persuaded that your Imperial Majesty will not abuse [my confidence], and that you will be convinced that an honest peace, far from being repugnant, will be very agreeable to me, but that I should prefer death to a shameful peace that dishonored me. There is nothing more praiseworthy than Your Imperial Majesty's readiness to work for peace; the benedictions of all Europe will be heaped upon you, among which I beg you to be so good as to give mine a prominent place. I do not doubt that there are ways to satisfy everyone and the Saxons, as Your Imperial Majesty very well says, provided that one has to deal with conciliatory and peace-minded spirits; [and] Your Imperial Majesty's good advice will contribute not a little to take the stiffness out of certain spirits [now] too unyielding. Finally, Madame, Your Imperial Majesty inspires in me a complete confidence; I rely entirely upon your precious friendship, which I beg you always to conserve for me, assuring you of the high consideration and distinguished sentiments with which I am, Madame my Sister, Your Imperial Majesty's good brother,

Federic.[2]

Provided that his pen could protect him from outside interference, the king knew he could deal directly with Austria and Saxony, confidently and without haste. On December 30 negotiations were begun at Hubertusburg between Freiherr von Fritsch representing Saxony, Collenbach representing Austria, and the Prussian Ewald Friedrich von Hertzberg. As Collenbach was little more than a mouthpiece for Kaunitz, and Hertzberg a messenger for Frederick, much time was sure to be consumed in correspondence between conferences; but Frederick was in no hurry. Hertzberg was instructed to demand only the restoration of the *status quo ante bellum,* to be as conciliatory as possible on all points except demands for the cession of any Prussian territory, and to be especially careful to say nothing that could offend the empress of Russia; but he was to make no gratuitous concessions. He was to demand no indemnities for Prussia, but to point out that it was only Frederick's moderation that restrained him from asserting such a claim. And he was to avoid hurrying the negotiation, so that the Prussian troops would not have to be withdrawn from Saxony before the end of February.[3]

Before the negotiations had begun, Frederick was able to predict

2. December 22 in Gustave B. Volz and others, eds., *Politische Correspondenz Friedrichs des Grossen,* 47 vols. (Berlin, 1879–1939), XXII, 409–410, cited hereafter as *P.C.*

3. Hertzberg's précis of his instructions is printed by Schäfer, II-2, 762. All the concessions he was authorized to make were to be kept *"au fond du sac"* as long as possible.

both their duration and their outcome. The really important points, he said on January 1, 1763, were "almost agreed upon"; only the details had yet to be settled, though the negotiation might be drawn out until the end of February and the evacuation of Saxony not be completed until March.[4]

Prince Henry had demonstrated throughout the war that as a military organizer and administrator he had not an equal in the whole Prussian army unless it was Frederick himself. Nothing, therefore, would have been more logical than that the command of the troops during the armistice, their withdrawal from alien territory, and their return to a peacetime footing upon the conclusion of peace should all have devolved upon him while the king concentrated first upon diplomacy and then upon the countless other problems of reconstruction. Neither of the brothers, however, could quite forget their bitter quarrels over the treatment of Saxony, or the prince's repeated offer to resign. Frederick, furthermore, was so tremendously relieved at the prospect of peace that he felt quite capable of handling the whole problem of demobilization and reconstruction singlehanded. Hence, having ceased to be indispensable, the prince found himself at once a supernumerary, and a little in the way. The army, which had needed two heads in wartime, could do better with only one in peace; and obviously that one must be the king.

Prince Henry was therefore free to go home, but it was a joyless homecoming for him. The princess was in Magdeburg with the court, and there she celebrated his birthday anniversary without him by inviting in a few guests—only a few, according to Lehndorff's account, because everyone there was in such an impoverished condition that an ostentatious affair would have been out of place. The prince himself was in Berlin, where he celebrated Frederick's birthday but not his own.

From Berlin he went on to Rheinsberg, where disappointment and further disillusionment awaited him. During his absence Baron Reisewitz, who had been in his service for many years, had been

4. Kurel W. von Schöning, *Militärische Correspondenz des Königs Friedrich des Grossen mit dem Prinzen Heinrich von Preussen,* 4 vols. (Berlin, 1859), III, 526; *P.C.,* XXII, 429, 430.

commissioned by him to complete the extensive improvements of
buildings and grounds which he had planned before the war but
had had to leave unfinished. Upon his return he was not only dissatisfied with the way in which the work had been done but found
that Reisewitz had gone heavily into debt, abused both the prince's
confidence and his credit, misappropriated considerable sums of
money, and forged his signature. Soon after the prince's return to
Berlin Reisewitz died suddenly at Rheinsberg. The official notice
stated that he had had a fever. Court gossip called it suicide.[5]

In the middle of February the court returned to Berlin; and
Prince Henry, whom Lehndorff was by then calling "the scourge
of our enemies," was there to receive the queen. It was a period of
great scarcity and high prices in the capital, but economic miracles
were expected whenever the king should be able to return; and in
the meantime Prince Henry, as the victor in the last great battle
and the first to return, was acclaimed wherever he went as the
savior of his country. The people of Berlin had to wait a long time
yet for their first opportunity to cheer their king.

It was, after all, quite in keeping with his character and with his
place in the life of his people that the First Servant of the State
should be the last to return from the war. Working—not tirelessly,
but unremittingly—in his headquarters in Leipzig, with his
thoughts running ever forward to meet and wrestle with the problems of reconstruction, never backward over the trials or the tri-
umphs of the immediate past, Frederick the battler was already
revealing himself as Frederick the builder. The hard-bitten old
Haudegen whose image was and is familiar to all the world was
giving way already to the *Vater des Volkes,* the patriarchal figure
of the hard-working patriot-king that was to become even more

5. Reichsgraf Ernst V. Lehndorff, *Dreissig Jahre am Hofe Friedrichs des
Grossen,* ed. Karl E. Schmidt-Lötzen (Gotha, 1907), pp. 452–453; Mitchell
Papers (British Museum, additional manuscripts 6802 to 6871 and 11260 to
11262), VI, 174, 183. Some of the Mitchell letters were edited and printed
by Andrew Bisset as *Memoirs and Papers of Sir Andrew Mitchell, K.B.,*
2 vols. (London, 1850). These will hereafter be cited as Bisset, and the
unpublished ones in the British collection as M.P.; Richard Krauel, "Prinz
Heinrich von Preussen in Rheinsberg," *Hohenzollern Jahrbücher,* VI (1902),
15.

familiar and dear to the minds of millions of Germans than that of the victor of Rossbach and Leuthen.

Prince Henry during that period had only an occasional glimpse of the peace conference at Hubertusburg or of life in Leipzig, as Frederick found time to describe them to him. At the same time the king was unconsciously describing himself in metamorphosis —cynically tolerant of the weaknesses of others, confessing many of his own but working ahead in spite of them, complaining of weariness but never stopping to rest. He had not shunned danger in war, and he would not shirk his duty in peace.

In response to Prince Henry's letter of congratulation on his fifty-first birthday anniversary he wrote: "I am getting old. . . . Soon I shall be useless to the world and a burden to myself. It is the fate of all creatures to wither with age; but for all that, one must not abuse the privilege [of age] and drivel about it." [6]

Although the treaty of peace had not yet been signed, Henry heard on February 2 that its essential points had been agreed upon and that the signing would be only a formality and would take place within a week. "You know too well my way of thinking," Frederick wrote, "to believe that I have signed a shameful peace or anything prejudicial to posterity. I believe that we have made the best peace possible in the present circumstances." [7]

A week later the prince received from Frederick a confidential report on the terms of the Treaty of Hubertusburg. All boundaries between Prussian, Austrian, and Saxon territories were to be re-

6. *Ibid.*, 482. The war had aged him noticeably, but he could not find time really to grow old.

7. *P.C.*, XXII, 497. Sir Andrew Mitchell's suspicions were unduly aroused when Prince Henry showed him what the king had written about the treaty. He could not imagine Frederick's writing the words just quoted unless he had actually made some cessions of territory and felt compelled to defend himself for having done so. M.P., VI, 185; Bisset, II, 339.

When he finally saw the treaty itself, on March 7, Sir Andrew wrote the king a letter of congratulation, filled with the most fulsome praise: "I have long recognized Your Majesty as the greatest of warriors, but today when you have known how to give tranquillity to Germany in so short a time and in so few words, I admire Your Majesty as the most skillful negotiator who has ever lived. Permit me, Sire, speaking for myself, to felicitate you upon an event so glorious and honorable for yourself and so advantageous for the human race." M.P., VI, 196; A. Schäfer, II-2, 762.

established as before the war. As a gesture of complaisance and to mollify the spirits of the Austrian royal family, Frederick, as elector of Brandenburg, had agreed to vote for the archduke Joseph II in the next imperial election. (Maria Theresa had thought she was making a very material concession when she offered to give up the title of Duchess of Upper and Lower Silesia. So long as he retained Silesia and Glatz, Frederick cared very little what titles she or anyone else kept or dropped.) Final ratifications of the treaty would not be exchanged before February 25, so the last of the troops would not get home before April. Then to set their house in order, as the king assumed Prince Henry had already begun to do at Rheinsberg! [8]

The magnitude of the task of reconstruction which lay ahead was already evident to Prince Henry, to whom Frederick's promise to show great results within a year sounded like a vain and ignorant boast. "The work that you will have to do," he said, "to remedy the evils that war has caused will be no small task. I am, nevertheless, assured that the pleasure of reestablishing order and abundance and bringing back the golden age will serve you as compensation for the pains you have suffered." [9]

The king was in fact concentrating so closely upon the first steps to be taken that he had not yet realized what a long way he had still to go, and he was somewhat oversanguine about it. With unutterable relief he had turned his back upon the war, and confidently he faced the future. Blind to any but his own conception of the paramount interest of the state, and refusing to look too long at the obstacles along any path he chose to take in its service, he suddenly announced his decision to reestablish the debased currency of his realm: "Our money will all be put on a better basis

---

8. *P.C.*, XXII, 514. Kalckreuth maintains, on his own credence only, that Frederick failed to notify the queen of the conclusion of the negotiations, and that she got her first word of it from Prince Henry, who sent Kalckreuth at once to carry this letter to her. He says further that she received both him and his message graciously, without revealing by the slightest sign that she saw anything unusual or that there was anything lacking in such a procedure. Friedrich Adolf Kalckreuth, *Paroles du Feldmaréchal Kalckreuth* (Paris, 1844), p. 318.

9. Schöning, III, 532.

in the month of June; I shall pay off all the state debts between now and then; after that, I can die when I please." [10]

On February 15, while getting off "couriers to all the courts," the king sent one also to his brother with a message eloquent in its brevity: "Peace is signed." In the words of the prince's reply, "Never was courier received with greater joy than he who arrived yesterday evening to bring me word of the peace. The letter which you have been so very kind as to write to me on this occasion," Henry went on, "has confirmed the good news, and has given me the joy of realizing quite vividly the magnitude of the triumph you have won in terminating so burdensome and so many-sided a war without losing any of your territory. It did not look as if things could end as they have, and I cannot help but repeat how fully I rejoice with you in this fortunate event. . . . I hope not only that you may some day see everything restored to its former splendor but that you may thereafter [live to] enjoy the fruits of your labor." [11]

Tacitly admitting the obvious fact which the gloomy prince had suggested—that he had been fortunate to lose none of his territorial possessions—the king openly refused to mourn over having acquired no new ones. "I do not personally regret that peace should be made on the terms already known to you," he wrote Henry. "If the state had acquired some new province or other, that would no doubt have been a good thing; but, as that did not depend upon me but upon fortune, that idea does not in any way disturb my tranquillity. *If I repair properly the ravages of the war, I shall have been good for something; and to that my ambition limits itself.*" [12]

The one categorical imperative which Frederick invariably rec-

---

10. *P.C.* XXII, 523. On June 1 new currency began to be issued which Mitchell said was considerably better than that of wartime but still below the prewar standard in value. The period of adjustment was one of great hardship for the poor, and for months the army seethed with discontent because it was still being paid at the prewar rate in wartime currency of greatly diminished purchasing power. M.P., VI, 223, 231.

11. Schöning, III, 536; Rudolf Schmitt, *Prinz Heinrich von Preussen als Feldherr im siebenjährigen Kriege,* 2 vols. (Greifswald, 1885, 1897), II, 293.

12. *P.C.,* XXII, 526. The italics are the author's.

ognized and never denied or sought to evade was his sense of duty.
"It is my duty in this situation . . . ," he wrote again, "to work.
If ever in my life I can do the state some service it is now, by
raising it again from destruction and, if it is still possible, by cor-
recting abuses and effecting reform where necessary. The task is
vast and manifold, but if Heaven accords me a few more days of
life, I shall complete it; if not, I shall mark out a course which
others may follow if they see fit." [13]

The details of the king's "vast and manifold" plans for reconstruction were of course not given in his letters to his brother; but
some of their general outlines were sketched there and the prince
was assured that every plan had been worked out in full detail
and orders issued for its execution. Yielding again to his old temptation to consider already accomplished anything he had once
planned and ordered, Frederick promised that changes would at
once become apparent. Unused army stores would be released to
relieve the food shortage and to depress the extortionate distress
prices then being charged for foodstuffs. All conceivable government aid would be immediately available for the rehabilitation of
agriculture and the rebuilding of the towns and villages. Within
two years not a trace of the war would be visible. [14]

Blandly ignoring the effects of the depreciation of the currency
(except as he announced his intention to put it back at once upon
a better footing), he was still as proud as ever of his refusal to levy
new taxes, and scornful of any monarch who would do so in time
of distress. "What a man!" he commented when reporting that one
of the first acts of the king of Poland and elector of Saxony, upon
regaining possession of the electorate, had been to levy new imposts.
Prince Henry denounced such taxation as ill-advised, oversevere,
wrong in principle, and altogether unreasonable; and Frederick
agreed that it was nothing less than inhuman for Saxon tax col-
lectors to follow right on the heels of the retiring Prussians; but

13. *Ibid.*, 534. Prince Henry, as regent, would have been one of the
"others" to whom the king here referred.

14. Although he tried hard enough, he could not quite hold to so rapid a
schedule; but he worked for years along the lines indicated. Only the social
and economic rehabilitation of the undistinguished thousands of discharged
officers and soldiers (many of them cripples) was seriously neglected.

they did not reopen the old question of the justification of their own exactions there.[15]

While he waited for exchange of ratifications of the treaty and planned for reconstruction, Frederick surveyed also the whole field of foreign relations and decided that his policy should thereafter be one of cautious reserve. As for Austria, he understood that (largely as a result of Prince Henry's last campaign, he said) both Kaunitz and Maria Theresa were thoroughly tired of war and disposed to reestablish and to maintain friendly relations with him. Yet it would always be wise for Prussia to remember the fable of the cat and the mice, "The cat is still a cat, no matter what it does."

His relations with Russia were, for the moment, reasonably satisfactory to him just as they were. He feared Catherine far too much to be willing to risk her enmity, but he would "make haste slowly" in courting her friendship.

France had already made peace with Great Britain and re-cemented her friendship with Austria. All the powers were more or less exhausted and weary of war. Hence Frederick hoped that the peace, which was about to become general, would last out his time. If it did not, France and Great Britain would, he thought, be the first to break it. In that case Prussia's wisest policy would be to make no alliance with either—and let them destroy each other if they would. One state's disaster might be another's boon.[16]

On March 1 he was able at last to report that he was to entertain that day, at Dahlen, the Austrian and Saxon negotiators who were to bring with them the signed and ratified copies of the Treaty of Hubertusburg. "Messieurs Fritsch and Collenbach are coming here after dinner today like Noah's doves with the olive branch in beak. You may believe that they will be well received, for the news that they are bringing makes it worth the trouble."

15. *P.C.,* XXII, 529, 534; Schöning, III, 537–539. Considerable numbers of Saxon *émigrés,* driven out by taxation and hard times, found homes in Prussia. Prussian soldiers were also permitted after the signing of the armistice to marry Saxon women, provided the brides were strong and healthy, brought with them substantial dowries, and were willing to accompany their husbands on their return to Prussia. Frederick reported to Prince Henry that deserters from both sides were guilty of some brigandage in Saxony as the armies withdrew. *P.C.,* XXII, 547.

16. *Ibid.,* 534, 538, 540.

He would himself be unable to return to Berlin for another month; but, cheered by the certainty of peace, he was able to jest about that. He would take care, he said, not to arrive on April 1 for fear his compatriots should take it as an "April fool's" joke and make fun of him.[17]

March 30 was the date eventually set for Frederick's homecoming from Silesia, where all the intervals in a series of triumphal entries and receptions had been filled in by the examination of reports, accounts, and estimates of the quantities of seed and building material and of the sums of money needed for the first steps toward reconstruction. He had written to the queen that he would have supper that evening with the family, but he had neither ordered nor forbidden a public reception. Because he had ordered none, he seems to have anticipated none; but for once the burghers of Berlin thought they should act on their own initiative and arrange a triumphal entry for the returning monarch.

All day the populace was out in the streets, buzzing with excitement. All afternoon soldiers and townspeople watched the route by which the king was expected to reenter the city, waiting for an opportunity to cheer him as he passed. As he still had not appeared when darkness approached, torches were handed out so that he might be lighted through the crowd and that the effect of the triumphal arches and other decorations would not be lost; but Lehndorff says that thousands of people returned to their homes "angry and embittered."

Those who stayed out faithfully to the last were doomed to an even greater disappointment. Toward nine o'clock the king finally appeared at the Frankfort gate, but in no mood or condition to play the part of the returning hero. He had traveled that day approximately seventy-five (English) miles over very bad roads. A halt at the battlefield of Kunersdorf had consumed some time and had not cheered his spirit much. All day long, wherever he stopped at a relay post to change horses, he had been surrounded by crowds of his subjects praying for miracles, and bedeviled by officials asking for favors either for themselves or for their districts.

17. *Ibid.*, 540. On the same day he wrote to d'Argens: "I do not wish to arrive there on the first of next month; the facetious might make fun of me and shout 'April fish' at me." *Ibid.*

And at the end of the ride he was expected to change from his traveling coach to a great gilded one, specially provided by his faithful Berliners, and parade the torchlighted streets of his war-impoverished capital like the Roman conqueror of a new province!

The next day he did it, to please them; but that night he could not. Phantom hosts of the dead from Kunersdorf and Torgau would have paraded between him and the cheering populace, and the torches would have lighted up once more in his memory the smoldering ruins of Küstrin and Dresden.[18]

So he only let them greet him at the gate; then as the cavalcade made its way into the city with the triumphal chariot in its midst, the king in his service-battered old traveling carriage dropped off the rear end of the parade and made his way as quickly as possible, by obscure cross streets and bypaths, to a side entrance of his palace, where he slipped inside unobserved.

He gained thus a little time to refresh and compose himself before going to meet the members of his family and the distinguished representatives of civil and military officialdom, of the nobility, and of the diplomatic corps who had been waiting all afternoon and evening in the anterooms of the palace to receive him. When he did at last appear he singled out Prince Henry for his first and most effusive greeting—which was presumably not difficult to do, as everyone, the prince included, was expecting him to do that. Then his other brother, Ferdinand; then came Ferdinand of Brunswick, and a public acknowledgment of gratitude for his splendid services. Then he asked Prince Henry who the other gentlemen were, and the prince presented them. To the Dutch minister, who had offered an asylum to Berliners when the Russians were in the city, he was especially cordial. To the Danish representatives he paid very little attention. Mitchell, his erstwhile companion on many a weary mile of road and on more than one actual battlefield, was greeted with civility, but that was all. As soon as

18. Two weeks before his return he had revisited Torgau, and in a letter to Prince Henry had referred to the battle there as one "which through the intervening years had given him some very bad quarter-hours." The letter is mentioned in a footnote in the *Politische Correspondenz*, but is not printed there—"*Mon neveu a vu aujourd'hui le champ de bataille, qui pendant plus de deux années, m'a fait passer de bien mauvais quarts d'heure.*" Schöning, III, 543; *Oeuvres*, XXVI, 271.

the introductions were over he retired to the family apartments.[19]

"Madame has grown fatter," was Frederick's first word of greeting to his queen after all those years of absence, according to Lehndorff. With Countess Camas, who had earned his enduring gratitude by understanding and sympathizing with him in his youth, he was much more demonstrative. At supper he sat with his sister Amelia on his right and the Princess Henry on his left, but he ate in silence and left it to Prince Henry, who sat on Amelia's right, to carry the burden of the conversation. It was nearly midnight when he arose from the table and, after standing apart for a little while with his sister and Princess Henry, dismissed the weary family gathering by withdrawing to his own rooms—alone.

Alone, in privacy and in silence, but not in peace! Closer than the hosts of the men of Kunersdorf and Torgau that had ridden the roads with him for years, closer than the princes, generals, and diplomats in his anteroom, more real to him than the surviving members of his family at that specter-haunted homecoming supper table, there had crowded around him unbidden, all evening, the faces and the spirits of those inseparable from the memory of his war-killed past. Old Schwerin, shot down as he defied the Austrians to stop him at Prague. Marshal Keith, who died as he dared them to drive him from his place at Hochkirch. General Goltz, of whom he had said: "I never had a more faithful friend." Prince William, who failed him, and for whose unhappy end he knew his other brothers still blamed him.[20] Margrave Charles, whose death had made providentially available the lands and revenues with which Prince Henry was rewarded for his victory at Freiberg. Wilhelmina, his best-loved sister, who had written from her deathbed that he must not spare Bayreuth to his own hurt or at Prussia's cost. His mother, who after every battle had rejoiced first over the survival of her sons and only then asked whether a victory had been won—and for whom he mourned afresh as Prince Henry

19. M.P., VI, 203, 216; Lehndorff, 456–460; Reinhold Koser, *Geschichte Friedrichs des Grossen,* 4 vols. in 3 (Stuttgart, 1912–1914), III, 170–174.

20. August William, second son of Frederick William I, and Frederick's presumptive heir, commanded an army in the summer campaign of 1757. He proved unequal to the task, and resigned in disgrace. The following year, at the age of thirty-six, he died of a stroke. [ed.]

had done on his first return after her death. All these and many
more were gone; but his memories of them so filled the atmosphere
around him that those who had replaced them seemed somehow
guilty of trespass. "But for the buildings," he wrote soon thereafter to his sister of Sweden, "I am as much a stranger here as
if I were in London." Never in his life had he known such loneliness as then—with all Europe agape at his achievements, all Prussia
waiting to acclaim him on his tours of inspection, and all
Berlin outside his palace windows to welcome him home from the
war.

Within the next few days there were public celebrations enough
to take some of the edge off the people's disappointment over
Frederick's homecoming; but the economic miracles they had expected of him were slow in coming to pass. The Jews, whom he
had used often for the thankless tasks of manipulating the currency and procuring supplies (and even for purchasing surplus
Russian army stores in Poland), were popularly suspected of
wholesale profiteering and were blamed and hated for all the
hardships incidental to the postwar deflation. "Jews and Chris-
tians," wrote Sir Andrew Mitchell, "are striving with equal Zeal
and Ardour who shall have Share in the Spoils of the People, but
it is hoped that the King of Prussia's Wisdom, Sagacity and Penetration will disappoint the flagitious Designs of the Money Brokers
of whatever Denomination." But the British minister in his critical
mood could see little virtue or ultimate utility in the king's generous grants of money to the devastated towns and provinces for
reconstruction purposes. "Mere Palliatives and Acts of Ostentation," he called them.[21]

The numbers of the discontented were swelled by many veterans
of the war, officers and soldiers alike, both those retained in the
military service and those dropped from it. Men discharged from
the army in the interest of economy felt that they had been dis-

21. M.P., VI, 206, 208, 234; Lehndorff, *Dreissig Jahre, Nachträge,* I, 369.
One of several firms to go bankrupt in Berlin that year was that of Gottkow-
ski, who had been particularly active in raising ransom money for the city
during the war. The king bought a porcelain factory from him in September,
to enable him to save something from the wreck of his fortune. F. to H., in
Oeuvres de Frédéric le Grand (Berlin, 1855), XXVI, 284.

inherited; those retained in it and paid in depreciated currency after the new money had begun to be issued thought they had been cheated. Discipline, which had inevitably been relaxed somewhat in the field, was at once tightened up again upon the return to garrison duty, and was found doubly irksome. Even the all-important wartime position of the armed forces was redefined by a general order which reminded the army that it existed for the defense of civilians and of their property, not for their exploitation or abuse, and threatened any officer or soldier guilty of imposing upon or abusing a civilian with punishment of the utmost severity. When Generals Finck, Schmettau, and Fouqué returned from imprisonment in Austria they were at once put under arrest to await the formation of the courts-martial that were to investigate the reasons for their failures.[22]

So Lehndorff wrote in his journal: "One sees people who are pleased and others who are not"; and Mitchell reported that while the profiteers erected triumphal arches and sang praises to the king, the people "who want Bread and have long felt the Calamities of War, are grown mutinous and almost outrageous." Things had indeed gone so far, Sir Andrew wrote secretly to the Earl of Halifax just three weeks after Frederick's return, that papers had been posted up on some of the most prominent street corners denouncing the king as a tyrant who deserved to meet the fate of Peter III of Russia, and calling for the redress of grievances under the "more humane" Prince Henry! [23]

Sir Andrew thought that the very existence of this movement of protest had been successfully concealed from the king, and that no steps had been taken to apprehend or punish the anonymous culprits responsible for it. Nor is there anything to indicate that Prince Henry knew anything about it. If either or both of the brothers had had any knowledge of such a movement their homecoming would have been even more tragically disappointing than it was, and their relations with one another would again have been embittered just when they should have been, and were in most respects, at their best.

22. M.P., VI, 205, 210, 215.
23. *Ibid.*

GEORGE PEABODY GOOCH

Old Age

THE NEGLECTED QUEEN had faded out of her husband's life. Though he always treated her with outward consideration and they met on ceremonial occasions, she bored him and he could bear anything better than ennui. She, on the other hand, kept a warm place for him in her heart, and her letters to her brother Prince Ferdinand of Brunswick, the distinguished soldier, are full of allusions to "our dear king." That of July 12, 1757, on the death of the queen mother, brings us very close to the lonely woman. "Only time can help. The loss is too great and I can never forget the friendship she showed me in recent years. She had real

From *Frederick the Great,* by G. P. Gooch. New York: Knopf, 1947, pp. 141–154. Copyright 1947 by Dr. G. P. Gooch. Reprinted by permission of Longman Group Ltd.

confidence in me and did justice to my attitude to her and the dear king. If anything could console me it is that I never failed in my duty to her and that she recognized it. She often gave me her blessing; if all her wishes are fulfilled I shall surely be happy. So I shall if God preserves him and arranges everything for the best, and if the king renders me a little more justice, this dear prince whom I love and adore as I shall to the end. What a satisfaction it used to be when I was with the dear departed and talked with her about this dear king and wished him every blessing! None of her children could regret her more than I." A single tender word from her husband, an occasional invitation to Potsdam, would have been balm to her heart, but it never came. His few letters are brief and impersonal, and she is never mentioned in his correspondence with friends and relatives. "Madame is fatter" was his chill greeting after the long separation of the Seven Years' War. Yet she never ceased to enjoy his respect. In his will drawn up in 1769, he begged his successor to allow her a suitable residence in the palace at Berlin, and to show her the deference due to the widow of his uncle and a princess "whose virtue never varied." But he wanted personality as well as virtue, and personality she did not possess. He found it in her younger sister Juliana, queen of Denmark, with whom he exchanged delightful letters in the closing years of his reign.

Frederick had long reconciled himself to a bachelor existence, but it was an unending grief to discover that his nephew and heir, afterward Frederick William II, possessed neither the public nor the private virtues needed for his lofty station.[1] "This animal is incorrigible," he complained to Prince Henry. The prince of Prussia, like his father before him, fulfilled the demand to supply the dynasty with princes, but he was useless for the serious tasks of government. There was little to be said for him except that he was good-natured and musical. The king was disgusted by his dissolute ways and by his dabbling in occultism under the guidance of his bosom friend Bischoffwerder. Prince Henry was too much of a *frondeur*, Prince Ferdinand too insignificant to be

1. Gilbert Stanhope: *A Mystic on the Prussian Throne*, is a popular biography.

much of a help. Old friends of his youth—Fouqué and Algarotti, companions of the happy Rheinsberg days, his *liebes Mütterchen* Countess Camas, Sir Andrew Mitchell, Schwerin, Winterfeldt and Seydlitz, heroes of the Seven Years' War, were gone. Yet he was too occupied as well as too much of a stoic to complain of loneliness. Though he was often irritable and sometimes lost his self-control, the hermit of Sans Souci, as he described himself, seldom gave way to low spirits. There is a pleasant family picture in a letter written during the summer following the return of peace in 1763. "I am expecting here a whole swarm of nephews and nieces in a few days. I am becoming the uncle of all Germany." Four years later he reports that he is surrounded by a whole brood of nephews and nieces. "They are good children and I am very fond of them. When I am with them I feel like a hen who has brought up some chickens and finally persuades herself that they are her own." His favorites were Henry and Wilhelmina, the younger children of August Wilhelm. "I resolved to please him," writes Wilhelmina in her unfinished *Memoirs,* "and that gave me a feeling of confidence the first time I saw him [after the return of peace] which I had never had with anyone before, as I am excessively timid. But from the first day of his arrival I answered his questions without embarrassment. That pleased him and he showed me a thousand kindnesses. From that moment I can truly say he was a second father to me, and his affection for me lasted till his death."

Frederick never lacked attached friends during the long evening of his reign. That he disliked the society of women is a legend: no woman ever influenced his policy, but if they were reasonably intelligent he was only too glad to cultivate their acquaintance. The lively correspondence with the Bavarian princess Marie Antonie, electress of Saxony and daughter of the Emperor Charles VII, extends from the close of the Seven Years' War till her death in 1780 and reveals both parties in a pleasant light. Though there are too many compliments for our modern taste, they are the expression of a genuine liking, for neither wanted anything from the other. The king saluted her as the most erudite and enlightened princess in Europe. She loved literature and music, and her two visits to Potsdam gave both parties unfeigned satisfaction. Prussia and Saxony had been foes, but Frederick had had his fill of glory and battle. "War is a scourge," he wrote in 1765. "It is a necessary evil because men are evil and corrupt, because it has always existed, and perhaps because the Creator desires revolutions to convince us that there is no stability under the sun. Sovereigns are sometimes compelled to oppose their open or secret enemies, as in my own case. If I have made people unhappy, I have been no less unhappy myself. But happily these wars are finished, and there is no sign of their speedy recurrence. While the coffers of the great powers remain empty we can cultivate the sciences at our ease. The recent bloodletting was so copious that I expect to finish my course in peace." Rulers, however, he explains in a later letter, were not wholly their own masters. "Men ought by nature to live in harmony: the earth is big enough to hold them, nourish them, occupy them. Two unhappy words, 'mine' and 'thine,' have spoiled everything; thence came interest, envy, injustice, violence, all the crimes. If I had had the good luck to be born in a private station, I would never have gone to law. I would have given even my shirt and made my living in some honest industry. With princes it is different. The opinion prevails that if they give way it is because they are weaklings and that if they are moderate they are dupes or cowards. Some easygoing and kindly rulers have been despised by their peoples. I admit that such false judges deserve disdain. Yet public opinion decides reputations, and however much one is inclined to brave the verdicts of this tribunal, one must sometimes pay it respect."

The Frenchmen who had enlivened the royal circle during the first half of the reign were gone. Voltaire was far away, Maupertuis and La Mettrie were dead, the eccentric d'Argens returned to his native land in 1768. Though rivers of blood had flowed during the Seven Years' War, Frederick still looked to France as the land of sweetness and light. He longed for another glittering star, but most of the celebrities were ruled out by their commitments, their character, or their ideology. Grimm's visits were welcome, but this Frenchified Teuton was too deeply pledged to Catherine the Great. Frederick disliked what he felt to be the arrogance of Diderot, though they had never met. He detested the dogmatic atheism of Holbach and Helvétius, though the latter spent a year as his guest while initiating the excise. Rousseau, the only man of genius except Voltaire, was personally and politically impossible. "We must succor this poor unfortunate," wrote the king to Lord Marshal Keith in 1762.

His only offense is to have strange opinions which he thinks are good ones. I will send 100 crowns, from which you will be kind enough to give him as much as he needs. I think he will accept help in kind rather than in cash. If we were not at war, and if we were not ruined, I would build him a hermitage with a garden, where he could live as he believes our first fathers did. I confess that my ideas differ from his as much as the finite and the infinite. He would never persuade me to feed on grass and walk on all fours. It is true that all this Asiatic luxury, this refinement of good cheer, indulgence, and effeminacy, is not essential to our survival and that we could live with more simplicity and frugality than we do; but why should we renounce the pleasures of life when we can enjoy them? True philosophy, I feel, is that which allows the use and condemns the abuse; one ought to know how to do without everything without renouncing anything. I must confess that many modern philosophers displease me by their paradoxes. I stick to Locke, to my friend Lucretius, to my good emperor Marcus Aurelius. They have told us all we can know and all that can make us moderate, good, and wise. After that it is a joke to say that we are all equal, and that therefore we must live like savages, without laws, society, or police, that the arts have corrupted our morals, and similar paradoxes. I think your Rousseau has missed his vocation; he was obviously born to become a famous anchorite, a desert Father, celebrated for his austerities and flagellations, a Stylites. He would have worked miracles and become a saint; but now he will be regarded merely as a singular philosopher who revives the sect of Diogenes after two thousand years. Maupertuis told me a characteristic story of him. On his first visit to France he lived in Paris by copying music. The duke of Orléans, learning that he was poor and unhappy, gave him music to copy, and sent him fifty louis. Rousseau kept only five, saying that his work was not worth more and that the duke could employ it better in giving it to people poorer and more lazy than himself. This great disinterestedness is surely the essential foundation of virtue; so I conclude that the morals of your savage are as pure as his mind is illogical.

One of the first books he read on the return of peace was *Émile,* and he was not impressed.

Why should he not try d'Alembert, mathematician and philosopher, author of the famous Introduction to the *Encyclopédie,* which embodied the ripe wisdom of the Age of Reason? He had been a member of the Prussian Academy since 1746, and had met Frederick at Wesel in 1755. "He seems a very nice fellow," reported the king to Wilhelmina, "gentle, clever, profoundly learned, unpretentious. He promised to come next year for three months and then perhaps we can arrange for a longer stay." The Seven Years' War intervened, but directly it was over he spent two months at Potsdam. The two men were strongly attracted to each other. Though no one could fill the place of Voltaire, the visitor was a first-rate conversationalist, and he combined high intellectual distinction with a nobility of character that the patriarch of Ferney lacked. The guest, however, had no wish to be tied, and in the same year he declined an invitation to be tutor to the Grand Duke Paul, heir to the Russian throne. There was no society to be found in Prussia, he complained, except with the king himself. Voltaire's experience could not be ignored, his health was poor, and Paris meant the salon of Mme Geoffrin and the loving heart of Mlle de Lespinasse. Though he greatly enjoyed the visit, he declined the flattering invitation to make Prussia his permanent home. "More penetrated than ever by admiration for your person and gratitude for your kindness," he wrote, "I should like to inform the whole of Europe what I have had the happiness of seeing in Your Majesty, a prince greater even than his fame, a hero at once *philosophe* and modest, a king worthy and capable of friendship—in fact, a true sage on the throne."

The host's reply was in equally vibrant tones. "I shall never forget the pleasure of having seen a true philosopher. He departs, but I shall keep open the post of president of the Academy, which he alone can fill.[2] A certain presentiment tells me that it will come, but that we must await the appointed hour. I am sometimes tempted to wish that the persecution of the elect may redouble in certain countries. I know this desire is in some measure criminal, since it involves the renewal of intolerance, of tyranny, of the brutalities of the human race. That is how I feel. You have had it in your power to put an end to these culpable desires which offend the delicacy of my sentiments. I do not and will not press you. I will await in silence the moment when ingratitude will compel you to settle in a country where you are already naturalized in the minds of those who think and are sufficiently cultivated to appreciate your merit." The king wrote from his heart, but his blandishments were in vain.

An affectionate correspondence, scarcely inferior in interest to that with Voltaire, continued till d'Alembert's death twenty years later, though they never met again. From beginning to end of this fascinating exchange there is not a jarring note. "Your works will live," wrote the king, "mine will not; I am only a dilettante." He apologized for his bad verses, but hoped they would send his friend to sleep. Though both men believed in the supremacy of reason, Frederick had far less expectation of its ultimate triumph: the average man, he felt, had no use for it. In some long and striking letters written in 1770 he explained his intellectual position in detail. "I think that a philosopher who set out to teach the people a simple religion would risk being stoned. Men desire objects that strike their senses and appeal to their imagination. Even if you could rescue them from so many errors, it is doubtful if they are worth the effort to enlighten them." Even skeptics were not beyond temptation, for the tendency to superstition was inborn in the human race. "If one founded a colony of unbelievers, in the course of years we should witness the birth of superstitions. Marvels seem to be made for the people. If one abolishes some ridiculous religion, something still more extravagant takes its place. I think it is good and most useful to enlighten man. To combat fanaticism is to disarm the most cruel and sanguinary of monsters.

2. A successor to Maupertuis was never appointed.

To protest against the abuses of monks, against vows so contrary to the designs of nature and the increase of population, is only to serve one's country. But it would be unwise and even dangerous to suppress those elements of superstition which are provided for children and which their fathers desire them to be taught."

The old king found the world as full of interest as ever, but he did not cling to life. When the queen of Sweden lost her husband in 1771, he reminded her that this was not the best of all possible worlds, as Leibniz had argued, but the worst. "When we enter our seventieth year," he wrote in 1781, "we should be ready to go directly the signal sounds. When one has lived a long time one ought to realize the nothingness of human things and, weary of the unceasing ebb and flow of good and evil fortune, should depart without regret. Unless we are morbid we should welcome the close of our follies and torments and rejoice that death delivers us from the passions that destroy us. After having maturely reflected on these grave matters, I expect to keep my good humor so long as my frail machine holds out, and I advise you to do the same. Far from complaining that my end is near, I ought rather to apologize to the public for having had the impertinence to live so long, for having bored it and wearied it for three quarters of a century, which is past a joke." D'Alembert, though the younger of the two, passed away in 1783, and Frederick's last letter restated the outlines of the blend of skepticism, epicureanism, and stoicism that formed his creed. "Man, it seems to me, is made rather for action than for thought; fundamental principles are beyond our reach. We pass half our life in shedding the errors of our ancestors, but at the same time we leave truth resting at the bottom of the well from which posterity will not extract it despite all our efforts. So let us enjoy wisely the little advantages that come our way, and let us remember that learning to know is often learning to doubt."

While the electress of Saxony, Queen Juliana of Denmark, and d'Alembert shed their radiance from afar, Frederick was not without pleasant companionship nearer home. The Jacobite brothers George and James Keith had left Scotland in their youth after the failure of the Old Pretender in 1715, and after many wander-ings had come to anchor in Prussia. James, the marshal, fell in the Seven Years' War. George "Milord Marischal," after filling the posts of Prussian minister at Paris and governor of Neuchâtel, was provided with a house in the grounds of Sans Souci. When the old man, who lived to the age of ninety-two, was no longer able to climb the hill, the king walked beside his invalid chair. Keith had seen much of the wider world which Frederick had always longed to visit, and he was a man of wide culture and lofty character; among the ornaments of the Round Table[3] none was more welcome. Since the death of Jordan and Wilhelmina no one came so close to the heart of the lonely ruler who, for all his stoicism and reserve, craved for a little human warmth. "I thought you knew you would always be well received," he wrote in 1764; "by night and day, in all seasons, weather, and hours, you will be received with open arms by your faithful friend."

Old men prefer the friends of their prime, but with the death of Keith and Pöllnitz, an entertaining old chatterbox, the last of Frederick's elder contemporaries were gone. The faithful Eichel left no successor of the same stature to perform the confidential work in the royal chancery, but Hertzberg was not only a valued counselor but a welcome guest at Sans Souci, often for weeks at a time. Only one new figure crosses the darkening stage. Lucchesini, a marchese of twenty-eight, then at the beginning of his distinguished career, attracted the king's attention while traveling through France and Germany in 1779, and accepted an invitation to settle down as chamberlain. From 1780 onward they met almost daily at the Round Table, where the talk sometimes lasted for hours. Students have reason to be grateful to this cultivated Italian whose diary, covering the period May 1780 to June 1782, is our best source for Frederick's later table talk.[4] That the host did most of the talking and repeated his anecdotes did not matter, for Lucchesini was a good listener and their scope is de-

3. Gooch's rather inappropriate translation of the German *Tafelrunde,* referring to the company that regularly assembled at Frederick's meals. [ed.]

4. *Das Tagebuch des Marchese Lucchesini,* edited by Oppeln-Bronikowski and Volz.

scribed as immense. The prince de Ligne, who knew everybody and was himself one of the wittiest of men, has given us a vivid report in his memoirs of the king's conversation when he accompanied the emperor Joseph to the meeting of the monarchs at Neustadt in 1770 and when he spent a week at Potsdam in 1780. "The king's encyclopedic range enchanted me. The arts, war, medicine, literature, religion, ethics, history, and legislation were discussed: the great epochs of Augustus and Louis XIV; good society among the Romans, the Greeks and the French; the chivalry of Francis I; the frankness and valor of Henri IV; the renaissance of letters since Leo X; anecdotes of clever men; the slips of Voltaire, the touchiness of Maupertuis, the charm of Algarotti, the wit of Jordan, the valetudinarianism of d'Argens, whom the king could send to bed for twenty-four hours by remarking that he looked ill. He talked of everything imaginable in a rather low voice."

An incisive analysis of this complicated veteran by Sir Andrew Mitchell's successor, Sir James Harris (afterward Lord Malmesbury), in a dispatch dated March 17, 1776, emphasized "that motley composition of barbarity and humanity which so strongly mark his character. I have seen him weep at tragedy, known him to pay as much care to a sick greyhound as a fond mother to a favorite child; yet the next day he has given orders for the devastation of a province or by a wanton increase of taxes made a whole district miserable. He is so far from being sanguinary that he scarce ever suffers a criminal to be punished capitally, unless for the most notorious offense; yet in the last war he gave secret orders to several of his army surgeons rather to run the risk of a wounded soldier dying than by the amputation of a limb increase the number and expense of his invalids. Thus, never losing sight of his object, he lays aside all feelings the moment that is concerned. And although as an individual he often appears and really is humane, benevolent, and friendly, yet the instant he acts in his royal capacity these attributes forsake him and he carries with him desolation, misery, and persecution wherever he goes. Though they feel the rod of iron with which they are governed, few repine and none venture to murmur." [5] The ambassador, like various other people, hints at unnatural vice, but there is no foundation for such scandalous talk.

While Frederick was writing the story of his campaigns and rereading his favorite French authors, the Augustan Age in Germany was dawning; Lessing and Klopstock, Herder and Wieland, Goethe and Schiller were beginning to fill the world with their fame. The romantic productions of the *Sturm und Drang* period, with *Götz* and *Die Räuber* at their head, could hardly be expected to appeal to the lover of classical tradition; the *Messias* was remote from his ideology, and Herder's cult of the *Volk* conveyed no meaning to an autocrat. Lessing and Wieland, on the other hand, children of the *Aufklärung,* spoke a language that he could well have understood. The former spent several years in Berlin and Breslau, and, though a Saxon, applauded Prussian victories. Through the mouth of Tellheim, in *Minna von Barnhelm,* he preached the gospel of military honor, and the noble plea for toleration in *Nathan der Weise* would have gone straight to the ruler's heart. Yet Frederick, who knew the name from his fleeting association with Voltaire, had no idea of his solid merits, and twice rejected the suggestion of his friends that he should be appointed Royal Librarian and Keeper of the Gem Collection.

"Since my youth I have not read a German book, and I speak it badly," confessed Frederick to Gottsched during their conversations at Leipzig in 1757; "now I am an old fellow and I have no time." Yet his neglect of the intellectual springtime of his country, however regrettable for himself, may be regarded on balance as a blessing. He had commenced his reign by allowing uncensored liberty to the Berlin press, but the privilege had been quickly revoked. "Do not talk to me of your liberty of thought and the press," wrote Lessing to Nicolai in 1769. "It reduces itself to the permission to let off as many squibs against religion as one likes. Let somebody raise his voice for the rights

5. Gooch's incomplete quotation deletes important qualifying statements. [ed.]

of subjects or against exploitation and despotism, and you will soon see which is the most slavish land in Europe." Wieland declared that, while he felt the greatest admiration for the king of Prussia, he thanked heaven that he did not live under his stick or scepter. He had always had a heavy hand, and it was far better for the mind of Germany to develop on its own lines than to be cramped by the patronage of the crown. That was also his own view, as he explained to Mirabeau at their second and last meeting on April 17, 1786. Why was the Cæsar of the Germans, asked the visitor, not Augustus as well? Why did he not think it worthwhile to share in the fame of the literary revolution of his time, to quicken its tempo, to support it with the fire of his genius and his power? "What could I have done to favor German writers," replied the king, "compared with the benefit I conferred by letting them go their own way?" On reflection Mirabeau agreed. "I regard it as a very minor misfortune," he wrote in his *Monarchie prussienne,* "that German literature lacked the support of the great. It is the same with writing as with trade: it detests compulsion, and compulsion is the inseparable companion of the great."

The interesting little treatise, *De la littérature allemande, des défauts qu'on peut lui reprocher, quelles sont les causes, et par quels moyens on peut les corriger,* published in 1780, is the only one of Frederick's writings that continues to be widely read. The root of the trouble, he argues, is in the language, *à demi barbare,* which it is impossible even for a genius to handle with effect. "I seek in vain for our Homers, our Virgils, our Anacreons, our Horaces, our Demostheneses, our Ciceros, our Thucydideses, our Livys. I find nothing. Let us be sincere and frankly confess that so far belles-lettres have not prospered on our soil." Germany had produced philosophers, but not poets or historians. German culture had been thrown back by the Thirty Years' War. "To show you how little taste there is in Germany you have only to go to the play. There you will see the abominable pieces of Shakespeare translated into our language, and the whole audience in transports as they listen to these ridiculous farces worthy of Canadian savages. I thus describe them because they

sin against all the rules of the theater. These rules are not arbitrary: you find them in the *Poetics* of Aristotle, where the unity
of place, time, and action are prescribed as the sole means of
making tragedies interesting. One can pardon his strange digressions, for the birth of the arts is never the time of their maturity.
But here is a *Götz von Berlichingen* on the stage, a detestable
imitation of these bad English pieces, and the audience demands
the repetition of these disgusting platitudes." That the critical
standards of the public might be superior to his own never entered his head. Goethe's name is not mentioned, and Lessing,
then in his last year, is ignored.

What could be done? The royal critic refused to despair, for
Germany had produced great men, among them Leibniz who
had filled Europe with his fame. The first task was to perfect the
German tongue. The classics of all languages, ancient and modern, should be translated, so that writers and readers might
learn from the best models. France had shown the world what
could be achieved. The "crude and graceless works" of Rabelais
and Montaigne had only bored and disgusted him, but in the
seventeenth century her authors set the standard for the whole
continent. Secondly, university methods must be reformed from
top to bottom. Philosophy should be taught in its historical
evolution from the Greeks to Locke, with comments on the
various schools. Professors of law should trace the growth of
their science. Professors of history should devote special attention to the fortunes of Germany, particularly since Charles V,
and should emphasize the significance of the Treaty of Westphalia, "because it became the basis of Germanic liberties and
restrains the ambitions of the Empire within just limits."

After all this fault-finding and the astonishing revelation of
ignorance it is a pleasant surprise to find the old man lifting up
his eyes to the hills. Various handicaps had prevented the Germans from advancing as speedily as their neighbors, but late-
comers sometimes pass their predecessors in the race. This might
happen in Germany quicker than they expected if the rulers had
a taste for literature and encouraged the best writers with praise
and rewards. "Let us have some Medicis, and we shall see some

geniuses. An Augustus will make a Virgil. We shall have our classical authors; everyone will wish to read them and profit by them; our neighbors will learn German; the Courts will speak it with pleasure, and our language, refined and perfected, will spread all over Europe thanks to our good writers. These bright days of our literature have not yet come but they are drawing nigh. I announce to you that they will appear, though I am too old to witness them. I am like Moses and I gaze from afar at the Promised Land." When these words were written the partnership of Goethe and Karl August was five years old, all Europe was reading the *Sorrows of Werther,* and the *Urfaust* was in manuscript; but at the time of Frederick's death only five of the eighteen academicians were Germans. The best of several rejoinders came from the sturdy old champion of Germanism, Justus Möser, author of the *Patriotische Phantasien* and the *History of Osnabrück.*

Frederick's mood in the last year of his life was one of tranquil resignation. "I have lived over seventy years in this world," he wrote to Charlotte, duchess of Brunswick, who had lost a son; "and during that time I have seen nothing but the strange freaks of fortune that mingles many painful happenings with a few that are favorable. We toss without ceasing between many anxieties and certain moments of satisfaction. That, my dear sister, is the common lot of man. Young folk ought to feel the loss of their relatives and friends more than the old; for the former have long to dwell on their sorrow, whereas people of our age will soon be gone. The dead have the advantage of being sheltered from the strokes of fortune, while we who remain are exposed to them day by day. These reflections, my good sister, are not exactly consoling. Fortunately your wisdom and your disposition have given you strength to bear a mother's grief. May heaven continue to help you and to preserve a sister who is the happiness of my life."

We are indebted to Zimmermann, the celebrated Swiss author and doctor, for our last glimpses of the old ruler a month before his death.[6] Having lost faith in his own medical advisers, he be-

6. *Über Friedrich den Grossen und meine Unterhaltungen mit ihm kurz vor seinem Tode* (Leipzig, 1788).

sought the court physician at Hanover to pay him a visit. "Eight months ago I was violently attacked by asthma. The doctors here gave me all kinds of drugs, which made me worse instead of better. Your reputation having spread throughout northern Europe, will you come for a fortnight? I am sure the duke of York will allow it." Zimmermann paid his first visit on June 24, and for over a fortnight he saw the patient twice a day. He found him at Sans Souci in an easy chair with an old hat on his head, his blue coat stained yellow and brown with snuff, a terribly swollen leg resting on a footstool. "All the fire and all the power of his best years shone in his eyes and often made visitors forget his wasted body." "You find me very ill," remarked the king, and it was obvious that the end was near. Yet he proved a most refractory patient, sometimes flatly refusing to take the prescribed medicines, sometimes devouring large quantities of indigestible and highly spiced foods in which he had always delighted. His mood varied with his health, sometimes gentle and winning, more rarely terrible and harsh. The two men took to each other from the first, and the doctor was deeply moved when the time came to part. Removing his hat and speaking with indescribable dignity and friendliness, Frederick said: "Adieu, my good, my dear Mr. Zimmermann. Do not forget the good old man you have seen here." We would gladly exchange some of the realistic medical details for more of the talk that enlivened their meetings on the better days.

When Goethe visited Berlin in 1778 he was disgusted by the abuse of the ruler to which he had to listen; yet there was a pervading sense that he was not as other men, and the rough military verses of old Gleim were current coin. The memoirs of General von der Marwitz contain a striking snapshot of Frederick in the year before his death as he appeared to an eager schoolboy. Returning from a review of his troops, he was received by Princess Amelia before her palace in the Wilhelmstrasse. The crowd, having accompanied him with acclamation as he rode on his white horse, stood bareheaded at the door through which he had passed. "Yet nothing had happened: no pomp, no salvos, no music, no recent event. Only a man of seventy-three, badly dressed and covered with dust, returns from his exhausting daily task. Yet everyone knew that this old man was working for him, that he had given his life to this task, that he had not missed a day for forty-five years. Everyone saw also the fruits of his labors, near and far and all around. When one looked at him, reverence, admiration, pride, confidence, in fact all the nobler sentiments were experienced." The old stoic neither expected nor craved for survival after death. He was content in the knowledge that he had spent himself to the uttermost in the service of his country and that he had won fame far beyond the visions of his flaming youth.

PART TWO

The Administrator, the Soldier, the Statesman

WALTER L. DORN

The Prussian Bureaucracy in the Eighteenth Century[1]

THE UNIQUENESS, the extraordinary strength, but also the weakness of modern Prussia lay in the fusion of the economic and military power of its nobility with the order, system, and efficiency of its bureaucracy. The combination of these two basic

Reprinted with permission from the *Political Science Quarterly*, XLVI (September 1931), 403–423.

1. The older Prussian literature is concerned more with the juristic than with the functional aspect of Prussian administration in the eighteenth century. This is notably true, in spite of its title, of J. Isaacsohn, *Geschichte des preussischen Beamtentums* (Berlin, 1884); also of C. Bornhak, *Geschichte des preussischen Verwaltungsrechts* (Berlin, 1885), II, and C. Bornhak, *Preussische Staats- und Rechtsgeschichte* (Berlin, 1903). These general works must be considered antiquated today. See G. Schmoller's criticism, *Jahr-*

elements of the Prussian state warded off the rising tide of the strongest currents of nineteenth-century liberal thought and ceased to be a decisive factor in Prussian politics only with the Revolution of 1918. Whatever judgment one may eventually pass on the Prussian army as an instrument of social organization and discipline, no one conversant with the evolution of modern Prussia can fail to see that the Prussian bureaucracy was for many decades the most creative force in Prussian history. Established in the first quarter of the eighteenth century by Frederick William I, under Stein and Hardenberg this bureaucracy not merely reformed itself but adapted the Prussian state to the conditions of modern life, and in the first half of the nineteenth century played a leading role in Prussian politics.

At no time, however, in the entire course of its history did it perform services of greater importance for the future of the Prussian monarchy than in the second half of the reign of Frederick the Great. Under the guidance and inspiration of this enlightened

---

bücher für Gesetzgebung und Verwaltung, X, 244. Entirely juristic in treatment are the brief studies by Hubrich, "Grundlagen des preussischen Staatsrechts," Verwaltungsarchiv, XVI, 389–496, and the brief summary by F. Giese, Preussische Rechtsgeschichte (Berlin, 1920). Useful for the structural aspects of the Prussian administration of this period, though not written with complete command of the best materials, are the introductory chapters of the two studies by Ernst v. Meier, Französische Einflüsse auf die Staats- und Rechtsentwicklung Preussens im 19. Jahrhundert (Munich, 1908), pp. 3–127, and Die Reform der Verwaltungsorganisation unter Stein und Hardenberg (Munich, 1912), pp. 1–110. A brief but unsatisfactory introduction is G. Schmoller, Preussische Verfassungs Verwaltungs und Finanzgeschichte (Berlin, 1921). Of fundamental importance for the years immediately before and after 1740 and based on complete command of the best archive materials is the volume by O. Hintze, Behördenorganisation und allgemeine Verwaltung in Preussen beim Regierungsantritt Friedrichs II, Acta Borussica (Berlin, 1901), VI, part 1. The writer of this article, which deals chiefly with the years from 1740 to 1786, is deeply indebted to Professor O. Hintze for his generous, patient, and thoughtful assistance in the study of these materials in Berlin. The principal source for the following study is the excellent documentary publication begun by B. Schmoller and continued by O. Hintze: Acta Borussica, Die Behördenorganisation und die allgemeine Staatsverwaltung Preussens im 18. Jahrhundert (Berlin, 1894–1926), I–XII [hereafter abbreviated A.B.]. The last volume ends with the year 1763. For the period from 1763 to 1786 the Geheimes Preussisches Staatsarchiv has been consulted wherever possible.

autocrat, the Prussian bureaucracy contrived to produce, on the economic resources of what was then the least prosperous section of Germany, a public revenue which was greater than that of Russia on the accession of Catherine II, with a per capita burden of taxation no greater than that of Austria and considerably less than that of France.[2] It managed to support the army of a first-rate power on the resources of a third-rate state and at the same time accumulated a large reserve in the public treasury; it opened up the mining industry in Silesia and in the Ruhr district; it carried through a project for extensive internal colonization in urban and rural districts which added upward of 300,000 inhabitants to the sparsely populated provinces of Prussia, thus making in 1786 every fifth inhabitant a colonist; it did much to introduce the improved British agricultural methods among the backward Prussian peasantry; it liberalized the craft guilds and adapted them to the needs of capitalistic industry while it endeavored to execute, and not altogether without success, a comprehensive plan to industrialize an almost wholly agricultural country. While in Great Britain, Hanover, and Saxony the civil service was still controlled by the system of official patronage, Prussia was remarkably free from it; nor was it possible here to purchase or inherit an office as in France. After 1770 and even before, no Prussian official was appointed to office without having undergone a special training and passed several examinations. Prussian civil servants were neither very numerous nor were they handsomely paid, for to *travailler pour le roi de Prusse* had become the byword of Europe.[3]

The intense pressure and severe discipline under which the Prussian bureaucracy labored is comprehensible only as a natural reaction against the intense pressure that arose from the insecure and precarious position of Prussia among the powers of Europe. Without his army the role of the Prussian monarch in the international politics of Europe would have been utterly negligible. To

2. G. Schmoller, "Historische Betrachtungen über Staatenbildung und Finanzentwicklung," *Jahrbücher für Gesetzgebung und Verwaltung,* XXXIII (1909), 1 *et seq.*

3. In 1925 one out of every 46 inhabitants of Germany was a civil servant while in eighteenth-century Prussia it was only one out of 450. I. D. Richter, *Finanzmaterialien* (Berlin, 1789), III, 32.

support the growing financial needs of this army was the pivotal function of the Prussian bureaucracy. All improvements in administrative methods and the wider scope and greater intensity of bureaucratic activity were made to serve the supreme end of producing a maximum public revenue. In the process this bureaucracy became a remarkably effective administrative instrument, if one which, with the progress of the century, it became steadily more difficult to manipulate from a common center. The Prussian bureaucracy of the eighteenth century was not without glaring defects, but whatever its shortcomings, it was superior, *mutatis mutandis,* to the German bureaucracy of our own day; indeed, it may be said that, whereas in postwar Germany the larger private business corporations possess a more highly rationalized and economical bureaucratic organization as compared with the German state, in eighteenth-century Prussia the situation was reversed.[4] The civil servant of Frederick II was still capable of instructing the Prussian merchant in more efficient methods of accounting, just as he was more active in searching for markets than the manufacturer himself.

In its architectonic structure the Prussian bureaucracy possessed certain peculiarities not found in the more familiar French system. In the French bureaucracy the modern monocratic official, the ministerial *chef de bureau* in Paris and the *intendant* in the provinces, predominated in all branches of the administration, while in Prussia all administrative activity was gathered in boards or "colleges," as they were called, which subjected the individual civil servant to group discipline and collective responsibility. Not only were there no Prussian equivalents for the French ministries in 1740, but the four members of the supreme Prussian administrative body, the General Directory, exercised identical functions in different provinces in such a manner that each was dependent upon the other three for decisions even in his own department. In provincial affairs the French *intendants* had their Prussian counterpart in the seventeen provincial chambers (*Kriegs- und Domänen-Kammern*), where the principle of group solidarity was observed with even

4. For an analysis of postwar German administration see O. Aust, *Die Reform der öffentlichen Verwaltung* (Berlin, 1928), pp. 123, 142.

greater consistency than in the General Directory. In this Prussian bureaucratic mechanism authority was more effectively centralized than even in France, just as there was a greater uniformity in the application of administrative maxims, partly because of the incessant personal intervention of the Prussian monarch in all branches of the administration, partly because the organization of the Prussian civil service into collective boards made supervision and control from above at once more difficult and more necessary. Not only did these provincial chambers exercise less discretionary authority than the French *intendants,* but they were bound by elaborate written instructions which embraced the entire range of their activities and provided an invariable rule for every administrative act.[5] Doubtless, the French bureaucracy offered freer play for personal capacity and initiative, as can be seen by recalling the careers of such reforming *intendants* as Le Pelletier de Beaupré, Aubert de Tourny, Turgot, and Trudaine. In Prussia, however, where feudal forces continued more vital and where consequently it was more necessary to combat the feudal conception of office, administration was systematically calculated to eliminate all personal influence whatever, first by fettering the individual civil servant to a collective board, then by subjecting both to bureaucratic regulations of imperative and canonical authority. The Prussian bureaucracy was dominated less by personalities than by the *règlement.* Of the two bureaucratic systems the French was technically sounder, although the Prussian bureaucracy was not less efficient and perhaps more active.[6]

5. The *commission* issued to the French *intendant* contained only a general description of his duties, not as in the case of the Prussian instructions, given to the provincial chambers, a detailed *règlement* which was to serve as a permanent guide of official conduct. The *intendant* Tourny, on going out to his *généralité* after his appointment, had first to correspond with his subdelegates to learn the exact nature of his duties. M. Lhéritier, *L'Intendant Tourny* (Paris, 1920), I, 243. The French Comptroller-General not infrequently encouraged his *intendants* to take the initiative in the reform of local administration. Thus Comptroller-General Orry felicitated Tourny on the initiative he had taken on several occasions. Lhéritier, I, 62.

6. If de Tocqueville pronounced laxity of execution the chief characteristic of French administration under the old régime, he was touching on a general evil of administration in the eighteenth century. A. de Tocqueville, *France Before the Revolution* (London, 1872), p. 84. It was less conspicuous

The greater uniformity of bureaucratic procedure and administrative maxims characteristic of the Prussian system was admirably suited to the undifferentiated feudal and agrarian society of the heart of Prussia, east of the Elbe River. It harmonized but poorly with the free industrial communities of the Rhenish provinces, where Prussian bureaucrats were perpetually at daggers' points with the native population.[7] It was in the region east of the Elbe that this bureaucratic hierarchy with its General Directory, provincial chambers, local commissaries (*Steuerräte*), and municipal magistrates became the veritable *ecclesia militans* of the Prussian monarchy, amalgamating heterogeneous provinces into a compact unit and disciplining the people to the needs of a Spartan military state. In a profounder sense than was true of the army, the Prussian bureaucracy served as the loadstone which attracted and absorbed into the service of the monarchy the most industrious and intelligent section of the population, thus binding their interests closely to those of the state. Like another Society of Jesus, here was an organization in which military discipline, absolute subordination, and centralization were complete. Prussian municipal magistrates could neither adopt a budget nor lodge a complaint without the consent of the local commissary, and he, not equipped with independent competence, reported all matters to the provincial chamber, which body, having made a preliminary decision, finally referred the matter to the General Directory. But this complicated meshwork of boards and individual officials had the supreme function of collecting data, correlating facts, drawing up balances of trade or contracts for leasing the royal domains, preparing budgets and drafting statistical reports, in other words of supplying the autocratic king, the highest civil servant and only real man of action in the realm, with the indispensable information on which to base his decisions.

Never did absolute monarchs take their autocracy more seriously

---

in Prussia, though certainly not unknown, because persistent financial pressure did not permit it and because in the course of the century Prussian bureaucratic control devices became more effective.

7. To be sent to the Rhenish provinces was for the Prussian official equivalent to being exiled to Siberia. *A.B.,* X, 456.

than the Hohenzollerns of the eighteenth century. Mirabeau could truthfully say that the Prussian government had become for the science of despotism what Egypt was to the ancients in search of knowledge.[8] Prussia was and remained the classic country of monarchical autocracy. Any study of the Prussian bureaucracy as an operating concern must begin with the central bureau or "cabinet," as it was curiously called, of the Prussian king.

Prussian administration in the eighteenth century was rooted in the fiction that the king knows everything, that he can do everything and does everything that is done. From Frederick William I onward, all matters which were decreed by the higher administrative bodies appeared in the form of royal orders issued by the king in person.[9] The artisan to whom the royal guild statute was a solemn guarantee of his economic security; the peasant who received a marriage license; the merchant entrepreneur who was exempted from the payment of duty on importing a specified article, all of them received their privileges from the king. When on Sunday the village pastor read a patent or an ordinance from the pulpit, it was the king who addressed the assembled congregation, even when the document in question had been issued only by a subaltern authority.[10] This fiction was not merely an administrative device which had taken possession of the popular imagination. Frequently it was no fiction at all. For the bitter quarrel with the obstructionist feudal estates of the numerous provinces of the kingdom had forced on the Prussian monarchs the settled conviction that Prussia could thrive only under an autocracy, that only a

8. Comte de Mirabeau-Mauvillon, *Die preussische Monarchie* (Leipzig, 1793), I, 87. I quote from the German edition because it has the advantage of the copious notes of Mauvillon, who collected most of the material for Mirabeau.

9. M. Hass, "Aktenwesen und Kanzleistil im alten Preussen," *Forschungen zur Brandenburgischen und Preussischen Geschichte,* XXII (1909), 52.

10. This created a curious confusion which the uninitiated reader of Prussian administrative documents will find perplexing, as in the following document: *"Wir Friedrich Wilhelm etc. finden Eure Anträge zweckmässig, indessen können wir darüber nicht beschliessen bis darüber an unser General Direktorium berichtet sein und dieses nach vorhergegangener Communication an unser Justiz-Departement die Befehle unserer Höchsten Person eingeholt haben wird."* This document was written by a provincial chamber using the name of the king.

king who in person attended to diplomacy, military affairs, finance, and current administration could effectually concentrate all the resources of his kingdom and apply them at the point where they were most urgently needed. Frederick the Great was convinced that the large independence of the French ministries was wholly unsuited to Prussia, for under a monarch like Louis XV it inevitably resulted in "lack of system, because each minister possessed a system of his own." [11] He was convinced that the Prussian king, to be able to construct and follow a rational system of politics, must be the actual head of all the departments of the government.[12] It was quite in keeping with this principle that in Prussia administrative tasks were allotted to the various departments in such a manner that the king was literally the only person in the kingdom whose purview embraced the entire field of administration, domestic, military, and foreign. The system was so conceived that the king alone came into daily and intimate contact with all the branches of administration. The full burden of coordination, therefore, could not possibly fall into any other hands save his own. Even in purely domestic affairs the General Directory, with entire provinces and departments withdrawn from its jurisdiction, could not serve as an adequate modern central coordinating body. No one but the king possessed complete information of the total public revenues of the kingdom.[13] But this was equally true of other branches of the administration. It is obvious that under these circumstances Prussian ministers could not become, as was the case in France, vehicles of opinions and programs, but must content themselves with the more modest functions of royal clerks who attended to such administrative bagatelles as the king chose to surrender to them. Autocracy could not have been carried to a greater extreme.

Unlike the French king, the Prussian monarch did not make his decisions in the council chamber in the presence of his assembled ministers. As a matter of fact the Prussian king rarely saw his

11. *Testament politique* (1768). G. B. Volz, *Die politischen Testamente Friedrichs des Grossen* (Berlin, 1920), p. 190.

12. *Testament politique* (1752). Volz, p. 77.

13. A. F. Riedel, *Der Brandenburg-preussische Staatshaushalt* (Berlin, 1856), pp. 76 *et seq.*

ministers. Apart from the annual "review of ministers," usually held in the middle of June, at which the king met his ministers to approve the budgets and to discuss with each one the affairs of his department, the king saw them perhaps once or twice a year.[14] He remained in Potsdam, immured in his royal chambers, while his ministers labored in Berlin, and no official, not even a minister, ventured to appear at the royal palace without a written leave of the monarch. All transactions were negotiated in writing. They sent him their reports, memorials, and requests, and the king replied by means of cabinet orders. It would have been difficult to improve on the order and regularity that prevailed in the royal cabinet.[15] Every evening when the courier from Berlin arrived, five secretaries arranged the letters according to the nature of the business and placed each group into a sealed portfolio to be laid before the king early in the morning. One of these secretaries, Mencken, has left us a description of Frederick the Great at work in his cabinet:

> He began his work early in the morning with foreign affairs; he had already read the deciphered dispatches of his ambassadors

14. On these "reviews of ministers" we have only a few scattered sources from ministers themselves. "Denkwürdigkeiten des Ministers v. Schulenburg." *Forschungen zur Brand. u. Preuss. Geschichte, XV* (1902), 411. There is one by Minister v. Hagen, K. H. S. Rödenbeck, *Beiträge zur Bereicherung und Erleuterung der Lebensbeschreibung Friedrich Wilhelms I und Friedrich des Grossen* (Berlin, 1836), p. 383. After having discharged the accounts of the previous fiscal year and arranged the various budgets for the ensuing year (there were many budgets as there was as yet no unified central treasury system), the king employed the occasion for explaining his administrative policies. Special conferences with individual ministers were held only on extraordinary occasions, although they became more frequent after the Seven Years' War as anyone can see who has examined the "Minüten" in the *Geheimes Preussisches Staatsarchiv.* Schulenburg reports that in 1781 he had several conferences with the king every week. *Forschungen zur Brand. u. Preuss. Geschichte, XV* (1902), 410.

15. For the organization of the royal cabinet in the days of Frederick II see Baron v. Diebitsch, *Specielle Zeit- und Geschäftseinteilung König Friedrichs II* (St. Petersburg, 1802); also Schöning, *Friedrich II, Über seine Person und sein Privatleben* (Berlin, 1808); C. W. v. Dohm, *Denkwürdigkeiten meiner Zeit* (Lemgo, 1814–1819), IV, 93, 670 *et seq.;* H. Hüffer, *Die Kabinetsregierung in Preussen und Johann Wilhelm Lombard* (Berlin, 1891), p. 44; O. Hintze, *A.B.,* VI, part 1, 59. On the origin of this royal cabinet, M. Lehmann, *Hist. Zeitschr.,* LXIII (1889), 266–271.

and now he dictated to his secretary an answer to every dispatch, whether important or not, from the first letter to the last, often several pages. Thereupon he dictated to another secretary answers to all letters on domestic affairs, to reports of the chambers on accounting and finance, and to the reports of the military inspectors on the army. Some of these he had already decreed by marginal notes. While this was being done, another secretary prepared a brief extract of all less important letters and petitions from private persons. This was then placed before the king who decreed each item in a few words.[16]

This done, the secretaries retired to write out the orders in full. Late in the afternoon these completed cabinet orders were once more brought to the king for examination and signature. They were always brief, pointed, stripped of superfluous verbiage, quite unlike the unctuous verbosity of the documents which officials sent to the king.

The chief merit of this system was its rapidity. All matters were dispatched forthwith, if circumstances did not require a special investigation. Since everything was done by letter and the king's mind worked with extraordinary speed, there was no reason for delay.[17] It should be remembered that the military order and precision of the king's life in Potsdam was conducive to hard work, that he had with him neither wife nor family, that there was neither court nor French court etiquette, that he never observed a religious holiday and never was distracted by undesired interruptions.[18] There was something like puritanical zeal in his unremitting application to work. His secretaries and ministers testify to the tyrannical discipline which he exercised over his mind and body.[19] With punctilious regularity he disposed of everything as soon as it came to him, sometimes issuing as many as thirty or forty cabinet orders

16. Mémoire of Mencken. Rep. 92 Friedrich Wilhelm II, B. VII, a4. *Geheimes Preussisches Staatsarchiv.*

17. See the comments in one of the most profound contemporary studies of the king by Christian Garve, *Fragmente zur Schilderung des Geistes, des Charakters und der Regierung Friedrichs des Zweiten* (Breslau, 1798), I, 156.

18. Garve, I, 158.

19. Mémoire of Mencken cited above and also the interesting diary of Minister von Heinitz printed in *Forschungen zur Brand. u. Preuss. Geschichte,* XV (1902), 440.

on a single day, and rarely did he postpone any matter from one day to another. Nowhere in the entire Prussian bureaucratic system was there such impeccable order as in the cabinet of the king. Just as each hour of the day, each week and month, so the entire year was arranged in such a manner that no business crowded on the heels of another. A calendar on his table indicated not only the duties of each day and week, but informed him when all outstanding reports, replies, and other matters fell due.[20] Even when in May, June, and August of every year the monarch regularly embarked on his inspection journeys through the provinces his secretaries and correspondence accompanied him.[21] Any official who addressed himself to the king could expect an immediate answer. He could even calculate, according to his distance from the royal residence and the time required by the post, the very day when he was to receive his answer. If he did not receive his answer then, none would be forthcoming at all.[22]

This extreme concentration of administrative leadership and control required not only a monarch of great capacity for work, but a man of large intellect and good judgment, for the slightest relaxation or error at the center was sufficient to drive legislation and initiative imperceptibly into the bureaucracy. To be sure, Frederick II was one of those rare persons who are always equal in capacity if not in temper. He was the essence of practicality and good sense. He knew his kingdom as an open page. Yet it was impossible for even so industrious a man as Frederick II to read all the lengthy reports and documents which accumulated in his cabinet. He was compelled to order his ministers to send reports of no more than two folio pages, stating briefly the reasons pro and con. At the beginning of every document sent to the royal cabinet there was a succinct summary of the matter dealt with to serve as a means of rapid orientation. The king was forever threatening officials with disgrace and dismissal if their reports were not

20. I. D. E. Preuss, *Friedrich der Grosse* (Berlin, 1832), I, 343. (Anonymous), *Observations sur la constitution militaire et politique des armées de sa Majesté Prussienne* (Amsterdam, 1778), p. 35.

21. E. Pfeiffer, *Die Revuereisen Friedrichs des Grossen* (Berlin, 1904); C. Dohm, IV, 626; A. F. Büsching, *Der Charakter Friedrichs der Zweiten* (Halle, 1788), p. 28.

22. I. D. E. Preuss, I, 345.

drawn up with the utmost brevity, an insistence which had the result that the official might daily spend hours of futile labor in the aggregate not on what action he must take—that was probably simple enough—but on what phraseology would pass the barrage of royal criticism. These reports which came to him from all administrative authorities were not always intelligible to him. He frequently found it necessary to order his civil servants never to employ a Latin or German bureaucratic jargon which he did not understand.[23] But these were minor difficulties easily simplified by ingenious devices in which every bureaucracy is fertile. The basic difficulty of the system was of another sort.

The main anxiety of the Prussian monarch must be to maintain his autocracy in the face of enormous difficulties which came from crowding affairs of such variety and complexity into his cabinet, affairs which often required a thorough investigation and an expert technical knowledge of detail. If under the modern democratic system a bureaucracy with its special training, expert knowledge, and continuous professional experience often exercises a decisive influence on legislation, even in matters of finance, in spite of parliaments and legislatures, its influence was no less subtle and strong even under an exceptionally intelligent and active king such as Frederick the Great, not to say a king who had a conscience in the matter of attending in person to the entire range of administrative problems. While the king resolutely insisted that all impulses must proceed from him alone, he incessantly dealt with officials whose specialized functions and mastery of every detail in their circumscribed field gave them much the same advantage over the king which the modern expert has over the dilettante legislator. The king's withdrawal from personal contact with his officials to the secrecy of his royal cabinet, where he was at leisure to make his decisions alone, was no real solution of the problem. The escape from the person of the expert made the monarch all the more dependent on the documents which the latter sent him.

23. This difficulty was increased by the fact that he was not completely master of the German tongue and by the circumstance that the "Cameralistic" jargon which was used by Prussian officials was heavily spiced with Latin phrases which were "pure Arabic" to him. *A.B.*, X, 385.

Instinct and reason might have convinced another man that the system required a degree of autocracy which was impossible, yet Frederick II was inflexible on the principle that neither his ministers, nor the General Directory, nor the provincial chambers could be allowed any initiative as independent administrative bodies. He wrote to the provincial chamber of Breslau in 1783, "You have no right of initiative whatever. All matters must be reported to me directly. The General Directory must do so likewise." [24] After the Seven Years' War the volume of public business swelled to such unprecedented proportions that no single person, however industrious, could inspire and control all measures which were necessary, but the king still firmly held to the principle of exclusive royal initiative and control.

Frederick II was shrewd enough to realize that his bureaucracy was not an impersonal machine which could be manipulated by a capricious master, but a body of men with opinions, passions, and habits hardened by routine, a body over which he could maintain his ascendency only by the severest military discipline. To retain that ascendency he assumed the studied pose of infallibility. As a matter of principle he never revoked an order and never openly admitted an error. Frederick managed his bureaucracy in the spirit of the general who places obedience above wisdom. If serious mistakes did occur, he was convinced that the continuity of uniform measures would soon remedy the harm caused by such intermittent errors. Without prompt and obedient response to royal orders the king's autocracy must become illusory. When Frederick suspected a minister of dissent, he brusquely declined all the latter's recommendations, even though he might later advance them as his own.[25] To criticize the king's measures openly was to court disas-

---

24. R. Stadelmann, "Preussens Könige in ihrer Tätigkeit für die Landeskultur, Friedrich der Grosse," *Publicationen aus den Preussischen Staatsarchiven* (Leipzig, 1882), XI, 236. This was an injunction which he repeated frequently but not frequently enough to indicate that it was generally violated. *A.B.*, X, 110.

25. Diary of Minister v. Heinitz, *Forschungen zur Brand. u. Preuss. Geschichte*, XV (1902), 444; W. Schultze, "Ein Angriff des Ministers von Heinitz gegen die französische Regie in Preussen," *Forschungen zur Brand. u. Preuss. Geschichte*, V (1892), 195.

ter. The unhappy Ursinus, one of the most brilliant officials in the General Directory, paid heavily for some mildly critical observations on the king's commercial policy by being condemned to push the wheelbarrow in the Spandau prison.[26] It was inevitable that a king so jealous of his authority should sometimes give instructions to his ministers on matters concerning which he should have listened to them. Wöllner, not always the most enlightened critic of Frederick II, is correct in stating that Frederick frequently gave orders on matters of detail on which it was impossible for him to be thoroughly informed.[27] On such occasions the king might suspect the incompleteness of his information, but he was convinced that the ignorance of others was greater.[28] This royal intervention in technical matters not infrequently disturbed the orderly process of administration, for which officials were nevertheless held responsible.[29]

Against such disturbing interference the only effective weapon was to resort to concealment or even to deception, of course always within the prudent limits of safety. Ministers practiced it and the General Directory also on occasion had recourse to it. Minister von Schulenburg, who in his memoirs avers that it was useless to attempt to conceal anything from the king because sooner or later he discovered almost everything,[30] was himself a past master in the

26. I. D. E. Preuss, *Urkundenbuch zur Lebensgeschichte Friedrichs des Grossen* (Berlin, 1834), III, 92–103. The case has been discussed by O. Hintze, *Die preussische Seidenindustrie im 18. Jahrhundert* (Berlin, 1892), III, 167–168. Frederick sent Ursinus to the Spandau prison on the charge of corruption although the charge was not substantiated. What angered him was the "impertinent relation" which the General Directory had sent to him, of which Ursinus was the author. He rightly suspected that the General Directory opposed his tariff policy, but he could not explain this opposition except on the basis of corruption or insubordination. Not wanting to send his ministers Hagen and Blumenthal to prison, he had to use Ursinus as a scapegoat. Minüten, Rep. 96, B 68. *Geheimes Preussisches Staatsarchiv*.

27. Wöllner's lectures to Frederick William II on important state affairs. April 28, 1786. Rep. 96, 208C, Acta. *Geheimes Preussisches Staatsarchiv*. H. Hüffer, *Die Kabinetsregierung in Preussen*, p. 60.

28. Garve, I, 158.

29. B. Rosenmüller, *Schulenberg—Kehnert unter Friedrich dem Grossen* (Berlin, 1914), p. 297.

30. Denkwürdigkeiten Schulenburgs, *Forschungen zur Brand. u. Preuss. Geschichte*, XV (1902), 402.

art of concealing matters which might provoke a confusing cabinet order if the king were informed of them.[31] When this same Schulenburg was appointed president of the provincial chamber of Magdeburg in 1770 he began to report faithfully the precise quantities of grain which were exported from this province each month. He promptly received from the General Directory the advice that henceforth he would do better to choose more adroitly the materials upon which he reported to the king, for the latter was inclined to be too hasty in prohibiting the exportation of grain entirely, much to the harm of the province.[32] But there were instances of systematic deception which could not be justified on the ground of uninformed royal intervention. Officials sometimes resorted to it when they encountered insuperable practical difficulties, to report which would only provoke a storm of royal criticism of their incompetence.

The most notorious offender in this glib and oily art, the man who deceived the king more than any other, was the Silesian minister Hoym, of whom Frederick II once said that he was really the only official who fully understood the Prussian monarch.[33] This nimble-witted minister understood not only how to omit from his reports items which he knew to be unpleasant to the king but did not scruple to falsify facts. He added 20,000 to a Silesian population report because he knew that Frederick liked high population figures.[34] In spite of the king's express orders to settle only foreign colonists in Silesia Hoym permitted his underlings to use native Prussian inhabitants for this purpose, insisting only that the colonists along the principal road over which the king ordinarily

---

31. Rosenmüller, pp. 118, 251, 261. In 1785 v. Schulenburg wrote to Sandoz Rollin, the Prussian envoy in Madrid, that he should not send to the king specific information on the Silesian linen trade with Spain because, *"il est impossible que le Roi entre dans le détail de leur gestion (la société maritime et administration de bois de construction), et que si Sa Majesté trouve dans les rapports qu'on Lui fait des réflexions isolées sur ces articles, il peut facilement être determinée à donner des ordres qui troublent la marché générale." Ibid.,* p. 394.

32. *Ibid.,* p. 21.

33. H. Fechner, *Wirtschaftsgeschichte der preussischen Provinz Schlesien* (Breslau, 1907), p. 21.

34. E. Pfeiffer, *Revuereisen Friedrichs des Grossen,* pp. 95–96.

traveled on his inspection journeys must be foreigners.[35] Under
Hoym's regime in Silesia an incident occurred which is without
parallel in the history of the Prussian bureaucracy in the eighteenth
century. It was one of the central features of Frederick's agrarian
policy to secure for Silesian peasants hereditary tenures of their
holdings. The energetic Schlabrendorff, Hoym's predecessor in
Silesia, had caused much bad blood among Silesian nobles in a vain
effort to carry out this measure. No sooner had Hoym assumed
control of Silesian affairs than all trouble suddenly ceased. He announced that now serfs held secure hereditary tenures and that the
matter was permanently settled. But in 1785 a special commission
sent to upper Silesia reported to the king that almost nowhere did
serfs possess hereditary titles to their holdings. To satisfy the angry
king Hoym was compelled to exhibit the strongest indignation,
for suddenly it became apparent that the reports of the rural commissioners (*Landräte*) had deceitfully misrepresented the facts for
years; that, while the orders of the king had been executed on
paper, things in reality remained as before.[36] And this was the
province where administration proceeded as smoothly, as Frederick
said, as a piece of music.[37] Indeed, Hoym understood the king only
too well.

This silent contest between the monarch and his bureaucracy
thus took on different aspects. Sometimes it was the result of official inertia and reluctance to deviate from the established bureaucratic routine; sometimes it was prompted by an effort to forestall
or render harmless confusing orders which issued from the cabinet
of the king; again it might be the result of an official propensity
to interpret royal orders generously enough to suit either the circumstances or bureaucratic convenience. Rarely was it the result of

35. J. Ziekursch, *Hundert Jahre schlesischer Agrargeschichte* (Breslau,
1915), pp. 171–173; E. Pfeiffer, p. 99. On one occasion the king forbade the
provincial chambers to collect perquisites from private citizens, allowing
them only the stipulated fees for the documents which they wrote for such
people. Hoym forbade his subordinates to use the word "perquisites" and
ordered them henceforth to employ only the word "fees." But everything remained as before. J. Ziekursch, *Preussische Jahrbücher*, CXXX, 300.

36. Dessmann, *Geschichte der schlesischen Agrarverfassung* (Strassburg,
1904), pp. 5 *et seq.*

37. *A.B.*, IX, 668.

actual corruption.[38] This contest never developed into open bureaucratic opposition, and on the single occasion when consistent opposition was secretly attempted, the king discovered and scotched it at once.[39] But the contest was none the less real and involved more or less the entire bureaucratic hierarchy. It was even rumored that in the persons of the king's private secretaries it entered into the royal cabinet itself. Contemporaries had an overwhelming sense of the influence and importance of these men.[40] Living constantly at the center of affairs, they were informed on everything that happened. They frequently had access to information which never reached the king himself. A shrewd secretary who worked with the king day after day for decades and knew all the latter's limitations and behavior patterns, could, on occasion, place the facts before his master in such a manner as to influence his decision; he could, to be sure at some risk, withhold a letter entirely or delay informing the king of it until he could take advantage of a propitious moment; he could in writing out a cabinet order which the king had turned over to him for expedition either moderate its language or give it a deadly edge.[41] We find these secretaries corresponding freely with ministers and other officials, offering them good counsel on drawing up documents and approaching the king

38. Among Frederick's ministers there was but a single instance of corruption during his entire reign. Görne was guilty of malversation of funds. H. Friedberg, "Friedrich der Grosse und der Prozess Görne," *Hist. Zeitschr.,* LXV (1890), 1 *et seq.*

39. This happened when Frederick in 1766 called into existence the French *Régie* to collect the excise tax throughout the kingdom, thus taking this branch of the service out of the hands of the old bureaucracy. At first this bureaucracy offered a consistent silent resistance to the new *Régie*. J. Ziekursch, *Preussische Jahrbücher,* CXXX, 283.

40. L'Abbé Denina, *Essai sur la vie et le règne de Frédéric II* (Berlin, 1788), pp. 419, 423 *et seq.;* Scheffner, *Mein Leben wie ich es selbst beschrieben* (Leipzig, 1823), p. 194; C. W. Dohm, *Denkwürdigkeiten meiner Zeit* (Lemgo, 1819), IV, 114; A. F. Büsching, *Der Charakter Friedrichs des Zweiten* (Halle, 1788), p. 214.

41. K. H. S. Rödenbeck, "Beitrag zur Beurteilung der Stellung der Geheimen Kabinetsräte unter Friedrich dem Grossen," *Beiträge zur Bereicherung und Erleuterung der Lebensbeschreibung Friederichs der Grossen* (Berlin, 1836), p. 337; H. Hüffer, *Kabinetsregierung in Preussen* (Berlin, 1891), p. 46; H. Hüffer, *Forschungen zur Brand. u. Preuss. Geschichte,* V (1892), 156.

with proper caution. Ministers in turn sought their favor with a cautious solicitude and often requested them to suggest to the king matters which they did not venture to propose themselves.[42] It is quite probable that now and then their intervention thwarted the intentions of the king. But to do so consistently without discovery was impossible. In his long reign Frederick the Great punished but a single secretary because of irregularities on the nature of which we are not accurately informed.[43]

42. Ministers were sometimes compelled to correspond with these private secretaries to have cabinet orders interpreted. Timid officials often asked secretaries to suggest measures to the king and not infrequently with success. When in 1772 Hertzberg desired the newly annexed portion of Poland to be called West Prussia, he submitted his request to Secretary Galster. See M. Bär, *West Preussen unter Friedrich dem Grossen* (Leipzig, 1911) I, 84. When Domhardt, the president of the provincial chamber in West Prussia, needed additional officials for his chamber, he communicated his wish to Galster. M. Bär, *West Preussen, Quellen* (Leipzig, 1911) II, Nos. 201, 652. Minister Massow of Silesia kept up a continuous correspondence with Secretary Eichel, asking for advice in dealing with the king. He invariably called upon Eichel before appearing before the king in Potsdam. *A.B.,* X, 134. See also the voluminous correspondence between Secretary Stetler and Magusch, the chief of the government tobacco monopoly, printed in K. H. S. Rödenbeck, *Beiträge zur Bereicherung* etc., pp. 343 *et seq.* There is no doubt that Secretary Eichel, although incorruptible, exercised greater influence than even a minister. Many officials, among them a minister, owed their appointment to him. R. Koser, *Preussische Staatsschriften aus der Regierungzeit Friedrichs II* (Berlin, 1877), I, XIX.

43. We do not know the reason why the king sent Secretary Galster to the Spandau prison. Denina tells the story that Galster and his wife sold grants of petitions sent to the king. L'Abbé Denina, *Essai sur Frédéric II* (Berlin, 1788), p. 424. Denina probably had the story from A. F. Büsching, *Charakter Friedrichs der Zwitten* (Halle, 1788). But it should be noted that Galster, who was released from Spandau after a year, brought suit for libel against Büsching and compelled the latter publicly to disavow the charge for want of evidence. See K. H. S. Rödenbeck, *Beiträge zur Bereicherung* etc., p. 339. Thiébault regards Galster as a martyr of autocracy. Thiébault, *Mes souvenirs de vingt ans de séjour à Berlin ou Frédéric le Grand* (Paris, 1805) IV, 130–136. But the testimony of Thiébault, who usually repeats every piece of irresponsible gossip, is worth very little. We know only that Minister von Zedlitz and others expressed their sympathy for Galster in writing. Thus we do not know whether Galster was innocent, or, if he was guilty, what was the nature of his offense. Some of these private secretaries became wealthy men on small salaries. But this was not necessarily the result of corruption. They received gifts from petitioners both before and after the king's decisions. Because their life was one of slavery the king also often

To imagine that Frederick was oblivious to these tendencies in his bureaucracy would be both to mistake his suspicious nature and to underrate his active intelligence. He cherished the inveterate belief that his officials were bent on deceiving him, deceiving him often, as he once admitted, with the best intentions.[44] He inherited this distrust from his Hohenzollern ancestors. The Great Elector had already written in his political testament, "The more civil servants, the more thieves." With Frederick II, however, this distrust became an integral part of the bureaucratic system. Unreserved confidence he reposed in none of his ministers. He kept them in a perpetual state of uncertainty as to what he thought of their honesty and capacity, and one could easily duplicate the instance of the minister who received a letter from the king in fear and trembling expecting his immediate dismissal but received instead the Order of the Black Eagle. It was especially subordinate officials whom he regarded with ineradicable distrust. He once wrote to the provincial chamber of West Prussia that among a hundred officials you could always hang ninety-nine with a good conscience, for if a single official was honest it was much.[45] He spent much time and thought on devising adequate guarantees for the accuracy of reports and reliability in the faithful execution of his orders. Some measure of guarantee he found in the annual journeys through his kingdom which he undertook with great regularity from May until August of each year. During these months he proceeded from province to province, examining officials and interviewing private citizens, personally inspecting public enter-

---

gave them costly gifts. Count Esterno, the French ambassador in Berlin, reported to Paris in 1786 that ministers paid pensions to these secretaries to fetch decisions in accordance with their desires. See Franzisco Agramonte, *Friedrich der Grosse, Die letzten Lebensjahre* (Berlin, 1928), p. 55. It is impossible to control the accuracy of this statement. It is quite possible that this may have been the case, especially during the last months of Frederick's lifetime when he was almost continuously ill. But as long as the king was in good health he was never easily duped. His suspicious nature would soon have discovered any dishonesty in a secretary with whom he associated every day in the year.

44. Taken from a conversation with his Minister v. Horst. G. B. Volz, *Gespräche Friedrichs des Grossen* (Berlin, 1919), p. 139.

45. M. Bär, *West Preussen, Quellen,* II, No. 275.

prises and inquiring into the condition of the peasants, and consulting with burgomasters, merchants, and manufacturers.[46] In this way he attempted to make himself in some sense independent of written reports and control in person the execution of his orders.[47] So imbued was he with the necessity of these journeys that he commended them to his successor as an indispensable means of controlling his officials.

Yet all this did not alter the fact that he was chiefly dependent on written reports and that attempts to control the bureaucracy must proceed from the royal cabinet itself. To prevent bureaucratic hoodwinking the king employed a number of safeguards. He frequently struck upon the expedient of committing the task of reporting on any particular piece of business to two or three different officials, none of whom was aware that others were engaged in the same mission.[48] When he did not wholly trust an official he charged

46. These journeys usually followed definite routes, although from time to time they were altered to surprise officials. In any case they always brought him to the provincial capitals, Magdeburg, Breslau, Cüstrin, Stargard, Graudenz, and Stettin. After the Seven Years' War he never visited Königsberg because of his dissatisfaction with the conduct of East Prussians during the war. We have detailed reports of these journeys from the rural commissioners and local commissaries, burgomasters, and other officials. These reports have been admirably exploited for Silesia by E. Pfeiffer, *Revuereisen Friedrichs des Grossen, besonders die schlesischen nach 1763 und der Zustand Schlesiens von 1763–1786* (Berlin, 1904), pp. 33–41.

47. A typical illustration of the manner in which the monarch controlled his officials on these journeys may be found in the following document which the king sent to the chamber in Graudenz, June 6, 1780: "*Sr. M. haben auf der jetzigen Herreise die hiesige Provinz gar nicht in dem Zustande gefunden wie Höchstdieselbe billig erwartet. In drei Jahren sind Sie nicht hier gewesen und in der Zeit hätte allerdings Vieles gebessert sein müssen. Allein die Kammer hat Nichts getan, um Nichts sich bekümmert, sondern alles so hingehen lassen und Jeden so wirtschaften lassen wie er gewollt, woraus denn nichts anderes als die grösste Unordnung entstehen konnte.*" Then follow specific instructions as to what he expected them to do and a declaration that he would hold them to the strictest accountability or dismiss each one of them. Graf Lippe-Weissenfels, *West Preussen unter Friedrich dem Grossen* (Thorn, 1866), p. 148.

48. When in 1766 merchants and manufacturers complained of lack of labor and of markets he ordered three separate investigations by three different officials. Minüten, September 26, 1766, Rep. 96, B. 39. *Geheimes Preussisches Staatsarchiv.*

an underling with secret supervision.[49] To control his ministers, he regularly corresponded with the presidents of the provincial chambers, and to assure himself of the veracity of the latter he often dealt with the individual members of the provincial chambers.[50] By this continuous correspondence with officials and their subordinates, by controlling ministers through their subalterns and subordinates through their equals, the king tapped extraordinary sources of information which, besides the ordinary channels of information . . . acquainted him with everything he seriously desired to know. Now and then shady facts might be cloaked by an impenetrable smokescreen of bureaucratic verbosity. Now and then the king might even become the unconscious dupe of his bureaucracy. But the fact remains that sooner or later the king discovered almost everything.

49. In 1755 he ordered the president of the Breslau chamber secretly to supervise Massow, the minister of Silesia. He promised to send the president duplicates of all the cabinet orders which were normally sent to Massow alone. The president was to report to him every instance of Massow's failure to enforce the cabinet orders sent to him. *A.B.,* X, 225. In 1768 he secretly instructed Brauchitsch, the president of the chamber in Cüstrin, to keep a watchful eye on Minister v. Brenckenhoff. The former was secretly to examine Brenckenhoff's accounts to make certain that funds were actually being spent for the purpose for which they were appropriated, and report his findings to the king. Minüten, October 1, 1768. Rep. 96, B. 70. *Geheimes Preussisches Staatsarchiv.*

50. Distrusting Auer, the president of the chamber in Magdeburg, who made some difficulties about buying up grain for the royal magazines, the king ordered a secret agent to canvass the region about Magdeburg to verify Auer's report. Minüten, November 2, 1766. Rep. 96, B. 69. Another case of this sort: Minüten, June 13, 1766. Rep. 96, B. 69. *Geheimes Preussisches Staatsarchiv.*

CHIEF BAILIFF FROMME

An Inspection Tour

In the summer of 1779 Frederick inspected districts along the Rhin and Drosse rivers, some thirty miles northwest of Berlin— marshland that had recently been drained and was now being cultivated by hundreds of new settlers. The king had last seen the area more than forty years earlier as a young prince, when he was stationed there with his regiment. For a part of his tour he was accompanied by a local official, Fromme, who later wrote down what he remembered of the king's words. Fromme's account agrees with records of similar trips: it shows Frederick's concern for economic improvement, as well as his limited knowledge of agriculture; the calculated manner in which he presented himself to his

From *Reisegespräch des Königs im Jahre 1779,* edited by J. W. L. Gleim. Halberstadt, 1784. Translation copyright © 1972 by Peter Paret.

subjects, especially his wish to impress them with his memory; his persistent suspicion of corruption and favoritism; but also the matter-of-fact, rather frank tone that marked the exchanges between the old monarch and his nobility and officials.—EDITOR.

TOWARD EIGHT in the morning His Majesty arrived in Seelenhorst. General Count Görtz was also in the carriage. While the horses were being changed, the king talked to the officers of the Ziethen Hussars, whose squadrons were put out to pasture in the surrounding villages; I was not noticed. Then the trip continued. Because the dams over which the road ran were too narrow I could not ride next to the carriage. In Dechtow, His Majesty caught sight of Captain von Ziethen, the owner of Dechtow, and since the road became wider, kept him at his side until the boundary of the estate was reached. Here the horses were changed again, and Captain von Rathenow, lord of Carwesee, an old favorite of the king, stepped to the carriage.

CAPTAIN VON RATHENOW   Your devoted servant, Majesty.

KING   Who are you?

CAPTAIN   I am Captain von Rathenow, from Carwesee.

KING (folding his hands)   My God! Dear Rathenow, he is still alive? I thought you had died long ago. How goes it? Are you well?

CAPTAIN   Yes, indeed, Your Majesty.

KING   But my God! You have become fat.

CAPTAIN   Yes, Your Majesty. I still like food and drink; only the feet won't work anymore.

KING   Yes, that's the way it is with me too. Are you married?

CAPTAIN   Yes, Your Majesty!

KING   Is your wife among the ladies over there?

CAPTAIN   Yes, Your Majesty!

KING   Well, let her come here! (Immediately takes off his hat.) In your husband I have met a good, old friend.

FRAU VON RATHENOW A great honor for my husband.

KING What was your maiden name?

FRAU VON RATHENOW Von Kröcher.

KING Ah ha! A daughter of General von Kröcher!

FRAU VON RATHENOW Yes, Your Majesty.

KING Oh, I knew him quite well. Do you also have children, Rathenow?

CAPTAIN Yes, Your Majesty. My sons are in the service, and these here are my daughters.

KING A great pleasure. Good-bye, my dear Rathenow! Farewell!

We took the road to Fehrbellin, and the local forestry official, Ranger Brandt, rode with us. When we came to a sandy area before Fehrbellin, the king asked: Ranger, why is nothing growing here?

RANGER Your Majesty, the area is not part of the royal forest; it belongs to the county. On parts of it the peasants have seeded various kinds of grain; here on the right they have planted pines.

KING Who had this done?

RANGER The Chief Bailiff here.

KING (to me) Well, tell my Privy Councilor Michaelis that the sand should be cultivated. (To the ranger.) Do you know how pine seeds should be sown?

RANGER Oh yes, Your Majesty.

KING Well, how are they sown? From east to west, or from west to east?

RANGER From west to east.

KING Right. But why?

RANGER Because the wind usually comes from the west.

KING Right!

Now the king reached Fehrbellin. There he spoke with Lieutenant Probst of the Ziethen Hussars (his father had already served as squadron commander with the regiment) and with the local postmaster, Captain von Mosch. When fresh horses had been harnessed the trip continued, and since the king immediately passed by my drainage ditches in the Fehrbellin marsh, which had been financed by royal funds, I rode up to the carriage and said: Your Majesty, these are two new ditches, which we owe to Your Majesty's kindness, and which keep the marsh dry.

KING I am glad to hear it. Who are you?

FROMME Your Majesty, I am the bailiff of Fehrbellin.

KING What is your name?

FROMME Fromme.

KING Ah! You are County Councilor Fromme's son.

FROMME Your Majesty's pardon. My father was county judge in Lähme.

KING County judge! County judge! That's not true! Your father was a county councilor. I knew him quite well. But tell me, has the draining of the marsh helped much?

FROMME Yes, Your Majesty.

KING Do you keep more cattle than your predecessor?

FROMME Yes, Your Majesty! On this farm I have forty more cows than he had; on all my land seventy more cows.

KING Good. You don't have the cattle pest in this area?

FROMME No, Your Majesty.

KING Have you had it here?

FROMME Yes.

KING Just keep using rock salt, then the cattle pest won't return.

FROMME Yes, Your Majesty, that's what I use: but ordinary salt is almost as good.

KING I don't believe it! Just don't crush the rock salt; hang the pieces in such a way that the cattle can lick them.

FROMME It shall be done.

KING Are further improvements needed here?

FROMME Oh, yes, Your Majesty. Here is Lake Kremmen. If it were dammed and drained, Your Majesty would gain about 1200 acres of meadows, which could be settled. The whole area would be opened to shipping, which would greatly benefit

Fehrbellin and Stettin; besides, many things could be shipped by water from Mecklenburg to Berlin.

KING   I believe it! But it would also help you a great deal while many others would be ruined, at least the owners of the shore land.

FROMME   Beg pardon, Your Majesty. The shore belongs to the royal forest, and the only things growing there are birches.

KING   Well, if it's nothing more than birches then go ahead. But don't be reckless; make sure that the costs aren't higher than the profit.

FROMME   The costs will certainly not rise above the profit. First of all, Your Majesty can count on gaining 1200 acres from the lake; that would make thirty-six farms, each of thirty-three acres. If, in addition, we levy a reasonable toll on the ships that pass through the new canal and on the timber floated down, the investment will bring a good return.

KING   All right, talk to Privy Councilor Michaelis about it. He understands these matters, and I advise you to turn to him for everything; for example, when you know where new farmers can be settled. I don't ask for a whole colony at once; if it's only two or three families, you can always arrange it with Michaelis.

FROMME   It shall be done, Your Majesty.

KING   Can't I see Wustrau from here?

FROMME   Yes, Your Majesty. There on the right.

KING   Is the general at home?

FROMME   Yes.

KING   How do you know that?

FROMME   Your Majesty, Captain von Lestocq and his squadron are quartered in my village, and yesterday the general sent him a letter by orderly. That's how I found out.

KING   Did General von Ziethen benefit from the draining of the marsh?

FROMME   Yes. He built the dairy here on the right and is keeping a dairy herd, which he would not have been able to do otherwise.

KING   I am glad to hear it. Who is bailiff at Alt-Ruppin?

FROMME   Honig.

KING   How long has he been at his post?

FROMME   Since the beginning of June.

KING   Since June? What was he before?

FROMME   Canon.

KING   Canon? Canon? How the devil was the canon turned into an official?

FROMME   Your Majesty, he is a young man of means, who seeks the honor of serving Your Majesty.

KING   But why didn't his predecessor stay?

FROMME   He died.

KING   Couldn't his widow have kept the domain?

FROMME   She fell into poverty.

KING   Through mismanagement?

FROMME   Beg pardon, Your Majesty; she was a careful manager, but a run of bad luck ruined her. Bad luck can set back the best managers. Two years ago my own herd was hit by hoof-and-mouth disease; I was given no remission of taxes, and I can't recover either.

KING   My son, today something is wrong with my left ear; I can't hear well.

FROMME   It's my bad luck that Privy Councilor Michaelis suffers from the same wrong. (I believed the king would react unfavorably to my answer, and fell back a few paces.)

KING   Now, Bailiff, move up! Stay by the carriage, but take care that you don't have bad luck. Go ahead and speak loudly; I understand you quite well. (The king repeated these words at least ten times during the trip.) Tell me, what is the name of that village over there on the right?

FROMME   Langen.

KING   Who is the owner?

FROMME   A third of the village is part of the domain Alt-Ruppin and belongs to Your Majesty; another third belongs to Herr von Hagen; and the cathedral chapter of Berlin also has dependents there.

KING   You are mistaken; it is the Magdeburg Cathedral!

FROMME Forgive me, Your Majesty; the Berlin Cathedral.

KING That isn't true; the cathedral chapter in Berlin has no peasants.

FROMME Beg pardon, Your Majesty; the Berlin chapter has three peasants in my own village.

KING You are mistaken; it is the Magdeburg chapter.

FROMME Your Majesty, I would be a bad official if I did not know the jurisdictions in the villages of my own district.

KING Yes, that's true. You are right. Tell me, here on the right must be an estate; I can't recall its name. List the estates on the right here.

FROMME Buskow, Radensleben, Sommerfeld, Beetz, Karwe.

KING That's it? Karwe. Who is the owner?

FROMME Herr von Knesebeck.

KING Was he in service?

FROMME Yes. Lieutenant or ensign in the guards.

KING In the guards? (Counting on his fingers.) You are right; he was lieutenant in the guards. I am very glad that the estate still belongs to the family. Well, tell me, the road running up this hill goes to Ruppin? And here on the left lies the highway to Hamburg?

FROMME Yes, Your Majesty.

KING Do you know how long it has been since I was here?

FROMME No.

KING Forty-three years ago! Can I see Ruppin from here?

FROMME Yes, Your Majesty. The steeple that peers over the firs on the right is the church of Ruppin.

KING (leaning over the side of the carriage and looking through his spyglass): Yes, yes, that's the church! I remember it. Can I also see Tramnitz?

FROMME No, Your Majesty. Tramnitz lies too far on the left, close to Kyritz.

KING Won't we see it farther along the road?

FROMME Possibly, near Neustadt; but I doubt it.

KING That's too bad. Will I see Bechlin?

FROMME Not from here, Your Majesty; it lies too low. Perhaps Your Majesty won't be able to see it at all.

KING   Well, keep an eye out, and when you see it, tell me. Where is the bailiff of Alt-Ruppin?

FROMME   Presumably in Protzen, where the horses will be changed.

KING   Can't we see Bechlin now?

FROMME   No!

KING   Who is the owner now?

FROMME   A certain Schönermark.

KING   Is he noble?

FROMME   No!

KING   Who owned it before?

FROMME   Ahrens from the chasseur regiment. He inherited it from his father. The estate has always been in bourgeois hands.

KING   I know it. What is the name of the village ahead?

FROMME   Walchow.

KING   Who is the owner?

FROMME   You are, Your Majesty. It is part of Alt-Ruppin.

KING   What is the name of the village ahead?

FROMME   Protzen.

KING   Who is the owner?

FROMME   Herr von Kleist.

KING   Which Kleist?

FROMME   A son of General von Kleist.

KING   Which General von Kleist?

FROMME   His brother was Your Majesty's adjutant, and is now lieutenant-colonel in the Regiment von Kalkstein, stationed in Magdeburg.

KING   Oh, that Kleist! I know the family well. Was this Kleist also in service?

FROMME   Yes, Your Majesty. He was ensign in the Regiment Prince Ferdinand.

KING   Why did he resign?

FROMME   I don't know.

KING   You can be frank; I have no ulterior motives. Why did the man resign?

FROMME   Your Majesty, I really don't know.

Now we had reached Protzen. I noticed that the old General von Ziethen stood before the manor house; I rode up to the carriage and said: Your Majesty, General von Ziethen is also here.

KING Where? Where? Ride up to the coachmen and tell them to stop. I want to get out.

The king stepped from his carriage and was exceptionally pleased at the presence of General von Ziethen. He talked with him and Herr von Kleist about any number of things: whether draining the marsh had helped them, whether their cattle had been infected, and recommended rock salt against hoof-and-mouth disease. Suddenly His Majesty left them, came to me, and called: Bailiff (into my ear): Who is the fat man in the white coat? I (whispering into his ear): Your Majesty, that is County Councilor von Quast, of Radensleben in the county of Ruppin.

KING All right!

The king returned to General von Ziethen and Herr von Kleist, and continued the conversation. Herr von Kleist offered the king some very beautiful fruit. His Majesty thanked him. Suddenly he turned and said: Your servant, County Councilor. The county councilor began to approach His Majesty, but the king said: Stay where you are. I know you; you are Herr von Quast.

The new team had been harnessed to the carriage. The king parted affectionately from the old General von Ziethen, paid his respects to the others, and drove off. He had not eaten any fruit in Protzen; now he took sandwiches for himself and for General Count Görtz from a carriage pocket and ate peaches with them. When we left Protzen he thought I was staying behind and called from the carriage: Bailiff, come along!

KING Where is the bailiff of Alt-Ruppin?
FROMME Presumably he is ill; otherwise he would have been in Protzen when the horses were changed.

KING Now, tell me: you really don't know why Kleist back there left the service?

FROMME No, Your Majesty: I honestly don't know.

KING What is the name of the village ahead?

FROMME Manker.

KING Who is the proprietor?

FROMME You are, Your Majesty; it is part of the domain of Alt-Ruppin.

KING Tell me, are you satisfied with the harvest?

FROMME Very much so, Your Majesty.

KING Very much? And I was told the harvest was poor!

FROMME Your Majesty, the winter wheat was partly frozen, but the summer wheat stands so high that the damage of last winter has been more than made up.

(Now the king saw rows on rows of sheaves in the fields.)

KING You are right; the harvest is good.

FROMME Yes, Your Majesty, and besides the people here put the wheat up in *Stiege* not in shocks.

KING What does that mean, *Stiege?*

FROMME A *Stiege* means twenty sheaves rather than a shock of fifteen.

KING Oh, the harvest is unquestionably good. But tell me, why did Kleist quit the service?

FROMME Your Majesty, I don't know. I believe he had to take over the estate from his father. I know of no other reason. . . .

We arrived in Garz. Herr von Lüderitz, lord of Nakel, oversaw the changing of the horses in his capacity as first deputy of the county of Ruppin. He wore a hat with a white feather. As soon as the new team had been harnessed to the carriage the trip continued.

KING Who owns the estate on the left?

FROMME Herr von Lüderitz; it's called Nakel.

KING Which Lüderitz is that?

FROMME Your Majesty, the one who supervised the changing of the horses in Garz.

KING (laughing) Ah, the gentleman with the white feather! Do you also plant wheat on your own land?

FROMME Yes, Your Majesty.

KING How much have you sown?

FROMME Eighty-four bushels.

KING How much did your predecessor sow?

FROMME Four bushels.

KING How is it that you sow so much more than your predecessor?

FROMME As I already had the honor of telling Your Majesty, I keep seventy cows more than my predecessor; consequently, I can fertilize my land better than he did and sow more wheat.

KING But why don't you plant hemp?

FROMME Hemp doesn't do well in this area; a cold climate suits it better. Our ropemakers can buy Russian hemp in Lübeck that is cheaper and better than the hemp I can grow here.

KING And what do you plant where ordinarily you would grow hemp?

FROMME Wheat.

KING But why don't you grow woad?

FROMME It wouldn't do well; the soil isn't good enough.

KING You just say that; you should have made the experiment.

FROMME I did, but it failed. And as an official I can't afford to make many experiments; if they fail I still have to pay the rent.

KING What do you plant where you would ordinarily grow woad?

FROMME Wheat.

KING Well then, stay with wheat! Your peasants must be rather well off.

FROMME Yes, Your Majesty. The mortgage register would show that they have about 50,000 Thaler capital.

KING Excellent.

FROMME   Three years ago a peasant died who had 11,000 Thaler in the bank.

KING   How much?

FROMME   Eleven thousand Thaler.

KING   You must keep them at that level.

FROMME   Yes, Your Majesty. It is good for the peasant to have money, but it also makes him presumptuous, as has happened to the peasants here who have now complained seven times to Your Majesty in order to be freed from compulsory services.

KING   Probably they had good reason.

FROMME   I beg your pardon. There was an investigation, which found that I didn't press the peasants, but was always in the right and only held them to their obligations! And yet it made no difference; the peasants were not punished. Your Majesty always supports the peasants, and the poor official is in the wrong!

KING   My son, I have no doubt that the local officials find you in the right. You probably keep your superior supplied with butter, capons, and turkeys.

FROMME   No, Your Majesty; that's not possible. Wheat doesn't bring in anything; if I wouldn't sell my other products, how could I pay the rent?

KING   Where do you sell your butter and fowl?

FROMME   In Berlin.

KING   Why not in Ruppin?

FROMME   Most people in Ruppin have as many cows as they need for their household. The soldier eats old butter; he can't afford the fresh.

KING   What do you get for your butter in Berlin?

FROMME   Four pence for the pound. Soldiers in Ruppin buy old butter for two pence the pound.

KING   But couldn't you sell your capons and turkeys in Ruppin?

FROMME   The entire regiment has only four field-grade officers. They don't consume much! And the bourgeois don't have refined standards; they thank God when they can eat pork.

KING   Yes, you are right; the Berliners like to eat delicate things.

Well, do what you will with the peasants, but don't press them.

FROMME Your Majesty, that would never occur to me, nor to any honest official.

KING Tell me, where is Stölln?

FROMME Your Majesty can't see Stölln. Those high hills on the left are the hills of Stölln. From there Your Majesty can see all the villages and settlements.

KING Really? Good! Ride along until we get there.

Now we came to a group of peasants who were mowing rye. They lined up in two rows, presented their scythes, and the king's carriage passed between them.

KING What the devil do these people want? Not money, by any chance?

FROMME Oh no, Your Majesty. They are overjoyed at your graciousness in visiting this area.

KING I'm not going to give them any money either. What is the name of the village ahead?

FROMME Barsikow.

KING Who is the owner?

FROMME Herr von Mütschefall.

KING Who is that?

FROMME He was major in the regiment that Your Majesty commanded as crown prince.

KING Good Heavens! Is he still alive?

FROMME No, he is dead. His daughter has the estate now.

We entered the village, and came to the ruined manor house.

KING Tell me, is that the manor?

FROMME Yes.

KING What a pitiful sight! Listen, the owners here must be having a hard time?

FROMME They are doing badly, Your Majesty; they are in extreme poverty.

KING I am sorry. Tell me, before this family a county councilor lived here. He had many children; can you recall him?

FROMME It must have been County Councilor von Jürgass from Ganzer.

KING Yes, yes! That was the one. Is he dead?

FROMME Yes, Your Majesty. He died in 1771 and it was a strange business. Within fourteen days after he died, his wife died, the daughters, and four of his sons. The other four sons came down with the same illness, which was like a violent fever. Although they served in different garrisons and did not see each other, all four caught the same disease and just barely lived through it.

KING What a desperate business! Where are the surviving four sons?

FROMME One serves with the Ziethen Hussars and one with the *gendarmes*. Another served in Prince Ferdinand's regiment, and now lives on his estate at Dessow. The fourth is the son-in-law of General von Ziethen. He was lieutenant in the Ziethen Hussars, but in the last war Your Majesty dismissed him on account of his health. Now he lives in Ganzer.

KING Oh? So that one belongs to the Jürgass family? Are you making other experiments with foreign grain?

FROMME Yes. This year I planted Spanish barley. But it won't take hold properly, and I am going to discontinue it. But I am satisfied with the shrub-rye from Holstein.

KING What kind of rye is that?

FROMME It is planted in the Holstein plain. My yield has never been less than ten grains per ear.

KING Now, now!

FROMME That isn't much! If Your Majesty asks General Count Görtz, he will tell you that in Holstein that is not unusual.

Now the king and Count Görtz talked for a while about rye. Suddenly, His Majesty called from the carriage: Well! stick to shrub-rye from Holstein, and distribute some to the peasants as well.

FROMME Yes, Your Majesty.

KING But tell me—can you give me a picture of the marsh before it was drained?

FROMME It was filled with tall stumps; between them stood water. Even in the driest years we could not take out the hay in wagons but had to pile it up in large ricks. Not until winter, when the water had frozen solid, could we cart out the hay. But now we have cut down the stumps, and the ditches have drained the water. Now, as Your Majesty saw, the marsh is dry and we can take out the hay whenever we like.

KING That's good! And the peasants keep more cattle than before?

FROMME Yes.

KING How many more?

FROMME Some keep one additional cow, others two, depending on their wealth.

KING But what would be the total number of additional cattle —approximately?

FROMME As many as 120 cattle.

The king must have asked Count Görtz how it was that he knew me, since I had said he should ask Count Görtz about the rye from Holstein, and presumably the general answered that he had met me in Holstein when I bought horses there, and that I had also sold horses in Potsdam. Suddenly His Majesty said: Listen, I know you fancy horses. But leave that and raise cattle instead; you will find them more profitable.

FROMME Your Majesty, I no longer trade horses. I just raise a few colts every year.

KING Raise calves instead; that's better.

FROMME Oh, Your Majesty, if one works hard, raising horses

can be profitable. I know a man who two years ago received 1,000 Thaler for a stallion from his stud.

KING It was a fool who paid that much!

FROMME Your Majesty, he was a nobleman from Mecklenburg.

KING He was a fool anyway.

Now we reached the royal domain Neustadt, where Councilor Klausius, who is the tenant of the domain, waited on the boundary as the carriage passed. But since talking was becoming very irksome to me, with the king always asking about the villages, which are numerous here, and I having to tell him the names of the landlords and who among them had sons in the royal service, I brought Klausius to the carriage and said: Your Majesty, this is Councilor Klausius, of the domain Neustadt, who is in charge of the new settlements here.

KING Fine! I am glad to know it. Let him come here.

[From now on, Fromme remarks, the king spoke mostly with Klausius, and I note down only what I overheard.]

KING What is your name?

COUNCILOR Klausius.

KING Klau-si-us? Well, do you have much cattle on the new farms?

KLAUSIUS One thousand eight hundred and eighty-seven cows, Your Majesty. It would be well over 3,000 if we hadn't suffered from hoof-and-mouth disease.

KING And is there a good increase in the population? Are children born at a good rate?

KLAUSIUS Yes, Your Majesty. We now have 1,576 people in the settlements.

KING Are you married too?

KLAUSIUS Yes, Your Majesty.

KING And have children?

KLAUSIUS Stepchildren, Your Majesty.

KING Why not your own?

KLAUSIUS I don't know the reason, Your Majesty.

KING (To me.) Listen, is the Mecklenburg border far from here?

FROMME Only a short mile. Only two villages still lie in Brandenburg territory: Netzeband and Rossow.

KING Yes, yes, I know them. But I wouldn't have believed that we are so near Mecklenburg. (To Klausius.) Where were you born?

KLAUSIUS In Neustadt on the Dosse River.

KING What was your father?

KLAUSIUS A parson.

KING Are the settlers good people? Usually the first generation isn't worth much.

KLAUSIUS They are not too bad.

KING Are they good farmers?

KLAUSIUS Oh, yes, Your Majesty. And His Excellency, Minister von Derschau, has given me fifty acres to show the other settlers what can be done . . . to serve as a good example.

KING (smiling) Ha ha! To serve as good example! But tell me, I don't see any wood here. Where do the settlers get their wood?

KLAUSIUS From the Ruppin district.

KING How far is that?

KLAUSIUS Three miles.

KING But that's very far! One should have seen to it that their supply was nearby! (To me.) Who is that man over there?

FROMME Building Inspector Menzelius, who was in charge of construction here.

KING Am I in Rome? All the names are in Latin! Why is this plot fenced so high?

FROMME It is a mule-stud.

KING What is the name of this farm?

FROMME Klausius Farm.

KLAUSIUS Your Majesty, it can also be called Klaus Farm.

KING The name is Klau-si-us Farm. What is the name of that other farm?

FROMME Brenken Farm.

KING That's not its right name.

FROMME Well, Your Majesty, that's the only name I know.

KING Its name is Bren-ken-farm-ius-farm. Are those the hills near Stölln ahead of us?

FROMME Yes, Your Majesty.

KING Must I drive through the village to get to them?

FROMME It's not really necessary, but a fresh team of horses is waiting there. If Your Majesty wishes, I'll ride ahead and move the horses from the village to the hills.

KING Yes, do that. Take one of my pages along.

I moved the horses to the foot of the hills, and then rode on so that I was at the top when the king arrived. He stepped from the carriage, called for his spyglass, and examined the country below. Then he said: It's true, that is more than I expected! It's beautiful. I must say that to all of you who shared in the work! You were faithful men! (To me.) Tell me, is the Elbe far from here?

FROMME Your Majesty, two miles from here. Over there is Werben in the Altenmark, close to the Elbe.

KING That can't be! Give me the spyglass again. Yes, yes, it *is* true. And that other steeple, what is that?

FROMME The town of Havelberg, Your Majesty.

KING Well, everyone come here. (To Klausius, Building Inspector Menzelius, and me.) Now listen, the marsh on the left must be drained and all the area to the right, as far as the end of the swamp. What trees grow there?

FROMME Alders and oak, Your Majesty!

KING Well, the alders can be rooted out and the oaks can stay; let the peasants sell them or use them in other ways. When the land has been cleared, I would estimate it will support 300 families and 500 cows: right?

No one answered, finally I began, and said: Yes, Your Majesty; perhaps.

KING Listen, you can safely tell me; it will be a larger or a smaller number. I know quite well that at the start you can't predict the number exactly. I haven't been down there and don't know the terrain at first hand; otherwise I can evaluate as well as you how many families can be settled on the land.

BUILDING INSPECTOR Your Majesty, the marsh belongs to a land-owners' collective.

KING That doesn't matter. We can make an exchange, or buy it—whatever is more suitable. I don't mean to expropriate it. (To Klausius.) Listen, write to the provincial administration that I want to clear this land; I'll provide the funds. (To me.) And you go to Berlin and personally report to Privy Councilor Michaelis that I want the other areas cleared.

His Majesty stepped into the carriage and we returned to the plain. There the horses were changed again. Since he had ordered me to accompany him just to the hills, I walked to the carriage and asked: Does Your Majesty wish that I accompany him further?

KING No, my son. Ride home with God!

[This is the end of Fromme's personal account. To it he added a few details about the rest of the King's trip, which he learned subsequently.]

Councilor Klausius accompanied His Majesty to Rathenow, where the king stayed overnight in the post house. At dinner with Lieutenant Colonel von Backhoff of the Carabiniers, the king was in an excellent mood. Lieutenant Colonel von Backhoff said that His Majesty told him: Dear Backhoff, you haven't been near Fehr-bellin for some time and should really see it. The area is much improved. It's been a long time since I have had so much pleasure on a trip. I decided on the tour because there were no maneuvers, and I liked it so much that I certainly will go on other such trips! Tell me, how did things go with you in the last war? Badly, I suppose. You couldn't get anywhere in Saxony either. . . . I would have been able to achieve something, but it would have cost more than half of my army, and I would have spilled innocent blood. Had I done that I would have deserved being tied up in front of a guard house and publicly punished. Wars are becoming terrible to fight.

Later His Majesty said: I am as well informed about the battle of Fehrbellin [in which the Great Elector defeated the Swedes in 1675] as though I had personally taken part. When I was crown prince, stationed in Ruppin, there was an old man—he was already ancient—who knew the battlefield very well and could describe the entire action. One day I took him in my carriage to the battlefield, and he showed me everything in such precise detail that I was very satisfied with him. On our way home I thought I'd have some fun with the old man, and asked: "Father, do you know why the two princes fought each other?" "Oh yes, Royal Highness," he said, "I'll tell you exactly. When our elector was young he studied in Utrecht, and the Swedish king—still prince then— was also there. And the two gentlemen fell out and fought until they had each other by the short hairs. And then their grudge led to this!"

GERHARD RITTER

Frederician Warfare

FREDERICK'S PERSONALITY and his historical significance come to life fully only when we understand his military
achievements and the nature of his system of warfare. What was
it that distinguished him from the traditional strategists of his day?
What enabled him to gain such brilliant victories, and what caused
him to suffer such serious—at times ruinous—defeats? Few aspects
of his life remain as much in doubt as these.

To the most knowledgeable military critic among his contem-

From *Frederick the Great* by Gerhard Ritter. Translated by Peter Paret.
Berkeley: University of California Press, 1968, pp. 129–148. Originally published by the University of California Press; reprinted by permission of The
Regents of the University of California and Eyre & Spottiswoode (Publish-
ers) Ltd.

poraries, Prince Henry, it was evident that the royal commander permitted his genius, his impetuous temperament, and his excitable imagination to seduce him into committing constantly new errors. According to this view, he owed his victories to the unusual courage and reliability of his troops—it was only their quality and the prudent strategy of his most eminent subordinate (Prince Henry himself) that prevented his faulty maneuvers and self-administered defeats from leading to disaster. This judgment was based on the conventional point of view of maneuver strategy. Napoleon, the military idol of a new era, showed a greater understanding of Frederick's passionate offensive spirit. He extolled the arrangement of certain Frederician battles—particularly Leuthen. He admired as Frederick's greatest achievement the ability to fight on regardless of circumstance. On the other hand he found much to criticize in Frederick's strategy. In the meantime Napoleon's own campaigns had brought about a complete revolution in the art of warfare and in military institutions, but a full understanding of Napoleon's strategy and tactics had to await the analysis of Carl von Clausewitz, whose insights were to contribute directly to the further development of German strategic theory. His experience in the Wars of Liberation led Clausewitz to consider traditional Frederician strategy and tactics as outdated, retarded by the thousand debilities of a primitive and ponderous military organization, incapable of pursuing the war to its climactic ideal: the destruction of the enemy. Like Napoleon he thought Frederick's strategic achievements admirable, but necessarily limited by the narrow constraints of their age.

In the patriotic historical interpretations of the nineteenth century, Clausewitz's insight into the fundamental difference between the two epochs was largely lost. Moltke's general staff sought the inspiration for its daring strategy not in Bonaparte, but in the great king, whose spirit after all continued to be cherished in the Prussian army. People were indignant—and not entirely without reason—when toward the end of the 1870's Delbrück took up Clausewitz's analysis and with doctrinaire exaggeration propounded a Frederician "strategy of exhaustion" in contrast to Napoleon's "strategy of annihilation." For several decades a debate raged between the Historical Section of the General Staff and the "academic strategist" Delbrück. As usually happens, it was never completely resolved, but it did bring about a certain mutual accommodation, and finally seemed to disintegrate into little more than a question of semantics. Actually, although the participants were not always clearly aware of it, a highly topical concern lay behind the scholarly dispute. Was the now classic "Napoleonic" method of seeking to destroy the main enemy army through the ruthless application of one's offensive potential the best in every circumstance—even against a greatly superior opponent who was pressing forward on several fronts at once? Or was another equally classic method available, that of exhausting the enemy through continued limited actions, pursuing the war with the least possible expenditure of force? And in a situation such as Frederick faced in the 1750's, might not this approach offer greater promise of success in the long run? Was the reckless offensive spirit a danger that could become fatal under such conditions?

The experience of the First World War lent additional weight to these questions, and stimulated even professional soldiers to renewed study of Frederick's strategy. We cannot follow them in their analyses. But we can learn from the previous dispute that the nature of Frederician war is clearly understood only if we first see how it differs from war in the Napoleonic era.

What Napoleon established was, in its general features, the now familiar kind of war waged by modern nation-states with the mass armies that universal conscription provides. The leadership of such armies may hope to achieve the highest goal of all strategy: breaking the enemy's will to resist by short, rapid, and destructive strokes against his main force. Napoleon's strategy, which derived less from theoretical studies than from the violence of his nature, from practical experience, and the instinct of his genius, can be outlined by mentioning a few simple principles. First, the resolute concentration of all available force on the decisive point, without anxious concern about such nonessentials as provinces that require protection, fortresses that must be kept under observation, and rear areas that must be secured—in short, no fragmentation of the main force. What matters above all is to have superior forces available or at least near at hand at the decisive moment. Second, a determined advance on the center of enemy power, the direction of attack masked by cavalry; whenever possible the opponent is outflanked by forced marches that cut his lines of communication. Third, on the day of battle itself, concentration of the attack against the key sector of the enemy's position; preparation of the assault with massive artillery fire; attack in deep columns, which can continue to commit new reserves into the fight. Fourth, immediately after the decision, ruthless pursuit of the enemy until horse and man drop. If such a major stroke succeeds, the end of the war is generally in sight. What is still lacking to shatter the opponent's self-confidence is provided by a purposeful and flexible diplomacy that is especially adept at constantly driving new wedges between the partners of an alliance.

Most of the major wars of the nineteenth century were waged according to this general scheme, not least the campaigns of Moltke, though his creative imagination was far too rich to be restricted by any particular pattern. This type of warfare completely surprised Napoleon's opponents, who were helpless so long as they lacked its political and social preconditions, which in France had been created by the great revolution.

The first of the new prerequisites was the mass and relative cheapness of the human material at the disposal of the post-revolutionary army, in contrast to the far smaller resources available to the professional forces of the previous periods. Frederick had been forced to finance most of his campaigns, especially the first two Silesian Wars, out of a painstakingly accumulated war chest; the largely agrarian Prussian economy could not accommodate major loans, and foreign credit was unobtainable. After the supply of money became almost limitless, war could grow far more encompassing. Until 1809 Napoleon never felt handicapped by fiscal concerns. His sizable armies enabled him to make deep advances, whose offensive thrust was scarcely diminished by the inevitable detachment of units for security purposes. The manpower now available permitted a more rapid replacement of disabled and wounded, which in turn made possible unheard-of improvements in march performance; it permitted attack in massive columns rather than in thin lines, and the ruthless employment of troops to pursue the beaten enemy.

A second factor was the national character of the revolutionary armies. They no longer consisted of mercenaries, foreign scoundrels that were kept in line by the corporal's rod, but of citizens defending their fatherland. To be sure, not too much should be made of this very obvious difference. France in the Napoleonic era was still far from having genuinely accepted the idea of universal military service. Usually the well-to-do bourgeois freed himself from this obligation by paying for a substitute, who then tended to remain permanently with the colors. Every year only a part of the able-bodied males were actually conscripted—far fewer than a third between 1799 and 1804—and of the conscripts a good number always managed to desert. On the whole France found it difficult to accustom herself to the concept of universal military obligation; she did so unwillingly and never completely. On the other hand, desertion in the Prussian army had significantly dropped since the days of Frederick William I. After the First Silesian War it often came to be a matter of pride even for a simple peasant's son to serve in the victorious army of the great king. Patriotism, at least in an early form of development, was awakening in the country. The French jest, that in Prussia one half of the garrison was needed to guard and whip the other, had long since lost its justification. The Prussian troops of the Seven Years' War, especially in the early campaigns, were something more than hordes of forced, rebellious mercenaries lacking any sense of public morality. If consciousness of Prussia as a state was still absent, the men nevertheless possessed traditional regional pride, which Frederick knew better than to discount. "The enemy has no Pomeranians," a grinning musketeer told him as he rode through the camp on the eve of Leuthen, "and you know how good they are!"

The discipline of the Pomeranians and the men from the Mark stemmed from local and regional comradeship, the patriarchal loyalty that the peasant owed to his squire, whose sons or brothers led him in the field, and of confidence in the great and victorious king. But above all it was formed by the strict religious obligation to obey, which Lutheranism had for centuries imposed on the north German peasant. Again and again we are told that on the march Frederick's soldiers sang the chorales that they had learned in their village church. The solemn "Now thank we all our God" rang out not only on the evening of Leuthen, but also after the triumph of Rossbach and on other victorious days. "We fight for religion, for you, for the fatherland," replied a veteran of the school of Leopold von Dessau to the king's praise after the battle of Liegnitz, and his words suggest the order of precedence of the ethical motives that animated the best elements in the army. Even in the revolutionary wars of the 1790's an intelligent observer still thought that for the Prussian mercenary faith took the place of the more developed sense of honor and military ambition found among the French.

In general, however, these moral obligations affected only native soldiers. They were scarcely felt by hired or forcibly recruited foreigners, by prisoners of war forced into Prussian uniform, least of all by the pillaging mob in the Free Battalions that waged guerrilla warfare or was used as cannon fodder to clear the way for the regulars' attack. It should be added that the number of foreigners in the Prussian army has often been exaggerated. Studies by the Historical Section of the General Staff have shown that foreigners formed a majority only in those regiments that lacked their own native draft districts—the so-called cantons. At Frederick's accession, the army contained 26,000 foreigners out of 76,000 men; his intention to raise the foreigners' strength to two thirds in each company was never achieved. In 1752 Frederick estimated that one half of his troops were foreign born, but the regimental rolls show that during the Seven Years' War the elite regiments were almost entirely made up of Prussians. In February 1763 the entire army consisted of 103,000 natives and 37,000 foreigners.

Even so, the admixture of foreign elements was not insignificant. It was far larger, for instance, than in the armies of populous France, even in the days of the monarchy. The changes the Revolution brought about in manpower procurement gave the commander an unaccustomed freedom of action, because he was no longer dependent on unreliable and laboriously drilled foreign mercenaries. How many possibilities had Frederick shied away from because they seemed to facilitate desertion: night marches, marching through forests, marching in open formations—especially through so-called *defilées*—camping near woods, sending out small detachments for water or straw. Everywhere he had to post hussar patrols, officer pickets, guards, and even fence in the camps to prevent his men from running away. With the disappearance of mercenaries, service in the field became far simpler. Above all, it was no longer necessary to march troops against the enemy in closely ranged lines, with officers to the front and rear; now men could be sent forward as *tirailleurs,* that is, in skirmish groups that could exploit concealment and cover. Casualties declined. The greater reliability of the rank and file made possible greater initiative on the part of the tactical commanders. Such initiative had in any case become essential since the great numbers and dispersion of the combatants precluded Frederick's close order of battle and firm central control.

March security, cooperation among separate units, the gathering of information—all were greatly facilitated once patrols and security detachments could be sent out over longer distances. One eyewitness of the Prussian campaign of 1745 reported that one did not dare risk sending patrols out for even a few hundred feet at that time. As a result, Frederick's army operated with a highly defective intelligence service; repeatedly the king found himself in situations in which he was for weeks cut off from communication with his distant corps, and learned of their fate only through rumor. Particularly during his early campaigns he lacked both reliable cavalry patrols and light cavalry that could be employed in small units—only after some time, and then never completely, was this weakness remedied by his hussars. His mounted troops were essentially battle cavalry, useful only for massed attacks in closed units. His infantry, too, lacked light troops that could disrupt the enemy's advance by fighting, as the Austrian Croats and Pandurs did, behind trees and hedges, in gardens, and other obstructed terrain. His Free Battalions were too poor, his *Jäger* numerically insufficient, to achieve much. His infantry was unmatched in the impetus of its closed linear attack, but it was not suited to fight in open order and in small formations. The battle of Colin was lost partly because the advancing Prussian infantry proved unable to clear Croats from a small stand of trees in its flank. The serried ranks were obliged to avoid, rather than seek, obstructed terrain. Forests, hills, sunken roads were considered dangerous because they afforded possibilities for desertion. Even today's commander must fear that some of his men will be immobilized in such terrain; but the danger was infinitely greater for mercenaries. Under certain conditions even a hundred-yard gap between two wooded areas counted as a *defilée* that inhibited the attack, because to negotiate it the infantry lines had to break up into marching columns. Only gradually did the Prussian troops learn to master such obstacles. In Frederick's early campaigns he considered unobstructed plains as the ideal field of battle; later the successful repulse of the surprise attack in the hills of Soor taught him that battles might also be won on irregular ground.

The use of mercenaries also contributed to that extreme slowness of the baggage train and of the supply services which constitutes a basic difference between Frederick's military system and that of the Revolution. The French revolutionary armies made no distinction between noble officers and plebeian troops; all were sons of the fatherland who could be called upon to suffer the same exertions and hardships. Keeping the men in good humor was no longer the concern it had been for Frederick, whose army enjoyed a particularly high reputation for its good rations (one pound of beef per man weekly), and therefore attracted many deserters. The defenders of the fatherland of a later age might sometimes go hungry; if things got too bad nobody hesitated to resort to requisitions. Had Frederick permitted this to his mercenaries there would have been no end to looting, deserting, and pillage—abuses that had horrified every responsible government since the Landsknecht era. Aimless destruction also conflicted with the new concept of the *raison d'état*. Wars were waged without national passion. So far as possible, occupied enemy territory was treated considerately, if only because wars could be expected to continue for long periods, and armies were not self-sufficient. But as we shall see, purchases in the zone of operations could only rarely satisfy the armies' requirements. The magazine system—which was to play a major part in shaping the warfare of the period—developed as a consequence of this.

In the zone of operations depots were established at easily accessible localities, at most five or six days' march apart, preferably near navigable streams. Saxony and Silesia were Frederick's favored bases because here the Elbe and Oder facilitated heavy traffic. Large quantities of grain, flour, and livestock could be accumulated in the depots, whose possession, together with control of the supply roads, came to be among the most important objectives of maneuver strategy. The fate of a campaign—or even, as Frederick once wrote from Moravia, the future of the state—might depend on the arrival of a great transport. But by no means all necessities could be stored and shipped to the troops. Particular difficulties were created by the cavalry's vast requirements of hay, straw, and oats. In order to have an adequate supply of fresh fodder, campaigns were postponed, if possible, until June. Often skirmishing broke out over stands of oats for the horses. Other needs, too, could not always be met without forced requisitions or the supplementary purchase on the spot of rations and spirits. But while Napoleon had enough men to garrison entire provinces, and to make the civil administration work for him, Frederician armies were rarely strong enough for an effective occupation. In Moravia and Bohemia Frederick's army remained limited to local foraging, which the peasants, especially in the Czech areas, could frequently evade. As they had for centuries when enemy soldiers approached, the peasants buried their valuables, drove off their animals and fled to the forests or to fortified towns and castles. It was in any case poor country; the standard of living of the serfs was miserable. Frederick thought Bohemia "not much better than a desert." The foreign invaders were hated, and the Prussians had to proceed with great circumspection to acquire any supplies at all. On the whole they remained dependent on their own transports, which were handicapped, especially during the wet season, by a lack of good roads and navigable streams. After the experiences of 1744 Frederick considered a prolonged occupation of Bohemia with Silesia for his supply base as highly dangerous: "A chain of mountains, created by nature to irritate us, separates these two areas—if you penetrate deeply into enemy territory, the aforementioned mountains choke off your supplies, the enemy cuts your lines of communication, and you risk having your army starve to death!" Saxony was thus essential to him as base of operations.

Napoleon possessed sufficient manpower and money to build military highways across Europe; Frederick's campaigns often became bogged down in the mire of country roads, which prevented any supplies from reaching the troops. In rainy weather the bread-wagons might take days to move a mile to two, and still they had to throw away half of their loads. To minimize the consequences of such conditions, military theory taught that an army should not move farther than five days' march from its depots.

The soldiers of the revolutionary armies camped under the open sky if they found no quarters; Frederick's mercenaries rarely did, except before battle. At other times they slept in tents taken along to protect the precious human material. This added enormously to the baggage train; on the march each infantry regiment was accompanied by sixty pack-horses that carried the tents. Another burden was the personal baggage of the still largely aristocratic officer corps. Every company commander was entitled to a carriage and two saddle horses, every lieutenant to a pack and a saddle horse; staff officers and generals took along five or ten times as much for their personal needs, as well as coaches and equipment carts. Wars were expected to last a long time, and sanitary conditions on campaign could be counted on to be very poor. The Prussians carried only a modest fraction of the baggage that the court generals and noble gentlemen of the royal French armies considered indispensable—but even so it was a mighty burden.

Equally ponderous was the artillery train, which Frederick did not seriously attempt to improve until the Seven Years' War. Prussian artillery consisted of heavy guns (pulled to the battlefield by requisitioned farm horses) and light battalion guns (used particularly with case shot) which the soldiers themselves dragged from position to position. To match the superior Austrian gunnery, Frederick augmented his artillery until there were seven guns for every thousand infantrymen, whereas in 1809 Napoleon at Wagram had only somewhat over two guns for each thousand. By introducing horse artillery, Frederick sought to raise the mobility of the army, and to lessen the danger that a cavalry charge might silence the guns. But to achieve the massive artillery fire which was often to prove decisive in Napoleonic warfare, significant technical improvements in carriage design and driver training were needed, as well as the reduction of calibers, an increase in range and accuracy, and better roads to assure the supply of ammunition.

The problem of pursuit perhaps most clearly demonstrates the limited mobility of eighteenth-century armies. It has always been particularly difficult to reorganize exhausted troops at the conclusion of battle and to set them in motion after a retreating enemy; but the reorganization of units was understandably far more essential with mercenaries than for a citizen army. To avoid uncontrollable flight, the defeated general frequently broke off battle while his command still retained a measure of cohesion—thus making it much easier for him to take up a strong position at the next obstacle, to disrupt the pursuer with his cavalry reserves, and to prepare other surprises. For these reasons, pursuit after victory rarely went beyond the next *defilée*. Frederick benefited from this limitation after the defeats of Colin and Kunersdorf; but in turn it prevented him from exploiting his successes. Among his major victories, only Leuthen and Rossbach led to energetic pursuits of the enemy.

All this suggests that the size of Frederician armies and their freedom of movement never sufficed to attempt the far-reaching strategic thrusts—aimed directly at destroying the enemy's center of power—that Napoleon was to undertake. In particular, Frederick condemned deep penetration into enemy territory without secure lines of communication and assured supply—actions that he called *pointes*. His *General Principles of War* of 1748 stated this clearly: "On the whole, those wars are useless in which we move too far from our borders. All wars that others have led in this fashion we have seen end in disaster! The glory of Charles XII vanished in the wastes of Poltava. Emperor Charles VI could not maintain himself in Spain, nor could the French remain in Bohemia. All plans that call for long advances should therefore be condemned."

This recognition resulted even more from experience than from theoretical studies. At times during the First Silesian War Frederick had considered a thrust to the gates of Vienna—only of course if it should be possible for the Prussians and Saxons to advance from the north while the French and Bavarians moved against the capital from the west. In practice he never attempted to execute such schemes, partly from suspicion of his allies, perhaps also on political grounds (as long as he acquired Silesia he was not at all interested in defeating the Hapsburg monarchy) but mainly because such a distant goal of Vienna soon proved to be unattainable. Even to advance on Vienna was much too dangerous; for the Prussians alone to isolate and besiege such a strongly fortified city was unthinkable. Although Frederick in later years also worked out schemes for marching on Paris in case of war against France, all invasion plans of this type remained pure theory. Not one of the campaign plans of the Seven Years' War aimed for more than the occupation of Saxony, and for thrusts into Bohemia and Moravia. The most daring among them was the plan of 1757, which with some reason has been compared to Moltke's offensive of 1866. But closer study shows that this plan, too, originally did not intend the destruction of the enemy, but only the disruption of his initial deployment, the seizure of stores, and, under the most favorable circumstances, the capture of considerable terrain. In short, a rapidly executed stroke, a *coup de main* of the first magnitude! That this surprise move almost decided the war was an unexpected success.

Frederick owed this achievement, at least in part, to the fundamental changes he made in Schwerin's and Winterfeldt's schemes, by means of which he turned an operation that ran the danger of being fragmented over separate areas into a concentric advance on the enemy's center. But it remains doubtful whether he made the changes with the conscious intention of bringing about a decisive battle or simply in order to reduce the danger of the whole enterprise. The background of this campaign shows more clearly than any other the barriers of military reality that constrained Frederick's energy and strategic imagination after the unpleasant experience of the 1744 offensive. Much as Winterfeldt's daring plan attracted him from the start, he found it difficult to accept. If it had not been for the counsel of the two generals he would have restricted himself to a strategic defensive with various limited advances; he would even have dangerously divided his forces to cover as many positions as possible against enemy attack. After Colin he risked a major offensive only in Moravia—in accordance with the arguments developed in his theoretical writings. But the enemy needed only to evade him, refuse to give battle, interfere with his supplies or capture them, for this undertaking, too, to end in failure before the walls of Olmütz.

It follows that Frederick's war aims had to be entirely different from Napoleon's. In the Silesian Wars the issue was the conquest and retention of Silesia, not the enemy's military and political destruction. We have seen how Frederick tried to achieve his aims through nearly simultaneous military and diplomatic actions. During the Seven Years' War when he fought on three or four fronts at the same time, a decisive blow that would end the conflict was no longer a serious possibility. Now it was a question of making oneself as formidable as possible in the strategic defensive by maintaining a tactical offensive, and—if this could be managed—to keep control of a piece of enemy territory as a pawn in the peace negotiations. Remaining passively on the defensive, simply awaiting enemy attacks, would have resulted in the loss of one Prussian province after another, until the strangulation grew unbearable. A simple defensive could never protect this monarchy of border zones. But to achieve the "destruction" of his enemies, to fight campaigns that forced a quick decision, was beyond Frederick's means. He was already aware of the fundamentals of the Napoleonic strategy of annihilation: force must be concentrated and superior power must be available at the decisive point—he repeatedly impressed this on his generals. But he was not in the fortunate position of Napoleon, who wished to seek a decision by battle only when he could count on a 70 percent chance for success. Prussia's geographical position, and all the limitations of strategy that have just been discussed, mercilessly forced him to divide his troops, to cover at least the key provinces, in order to secure his communications and supply. Consequently he often had no choice but to risk battle even when he faced a clear superiority.

Thus his strategy was not based on the great decisive stroke, but on reducing the enemy's will to fight by lashing out with repeated blows. Whether or not this is called "strategy of attrition" does not really matter if it is understood that in this position no other strategy could have succeeded. Daring *pointes* in Charles XII's fashion would soon have led to catastrophe. Prudent maneuvering, cutting lines of communication and overrunning depots in Prince Henry's fashion might perhaps have postponed the catastrophe for a long time, but such methods could never have sufficiently impressed his enemies and kept them from the center of Prussian power. Even waged in Frederick's spirit, this war remained a highly uncertain risk, and no one will deny that haste, impatience, and underestimating the enemy several times led Frederick into fatal errors. But the same temperament that caused these mistakes also made him superior to his opponents, not least to the most capable among them, the clever procrastinator Daun.

A defensive strategy that wears down the enemy with repeated blows—that was also the system which Germany was forced to adopt in the First World War, after the attempt to destroy the opponent on the Marne had failed. By then it was no longer only the cabinets that faced each other, but the peoples themselves, with their national passions, their immeasurable material and moral reserves. That rendered the task of hanging on even more difficult for Germany. Frederick could still expect that in the eyes of his enemies Prussia's struggle for existence was little more than another episode of cabinet politics. Disagreements among the allied governments and their generals, court intrigues, change in rulers, opposition of interests and war aims, limitation of his enemies' finances—all these could, indeed would, one day improve his situation. Without such fortunate incidents he would eventually have been lost. Not that the allies during the First World War were without their internal differences—certainly England's true interest in the complete defeat of Germany soon became doubtful. But the peoples' enthusiasm and passion—a political factor that was still unknown to the eighteenth century—in the long run overwhelmed all else.

Our analysis has attempted to expose the limitations that Frederick's epoch placed on his military policies. We can now see how his system differed from that of later wars, and that it cannot be turned into a direct model for modern strategy. What did constitute its greatness?

Frederick's military genius goes far beyond the unique moral energy that permitted him to fight on regardless of circumstances. We can most readily identify it by relating it to the military theories and commanders of his own age, not by measuring his achievements against those of later periods. The first characteristic that sets Frederick apart is the unflagging offensive spirit, pressing for rapid decisions, which we have already discussed. The limitations of its military means had led the Baroque age to develop a so-called methodical strategy. The commander risked as little as possible and left few things to chance; instead he carefully weighed all probabilities and tried to predict them rationally. The greatest achievement of the methodical strategist lay in outflanking enemy positions and winning territory rather than in destroying enemy forces. To gain limited successes by surprising the opponent and masking one's own intentions, by careful exploitation of the terrain when choosing field positions and encampments, by cutting off the enemy's lines of communication and capturing his depots and forage areas and thus forcing him to quit his strong points—that was the true purpose of this strategy, which was neither risky nor too costly. Decision by battle was to be sought only in certain well-defined emergencies, or under unusually favorable circumstances.

Frederick was familiar with all these techniques; their discussion is prominent in his military works, especially in the earlier writings. But in practice even more than in theory, he outgrew them. The location of his state and the character of his army, above all his own turbulent genius led him to counter the considerations of cautious methodicalness with the principle: "Our wars must be short and active. . . . Those who lead the Prussian armies must be clever and careful, but must try to bring the issue to a decision." He acted according to this rule, despite criticism by his brother and many of his generals, even in situations in which a cautious defensive appeared the only salvation. He knew that he could never win wars simply by maneuvering. For him the true purpose of maneuvering was not to gain ground, but to force the evasive opponent to give battle, if possible under favorable conditions.

The other important characteristic of Frederician war is the methodical cultivation of the offensive battle as the core of Prussian tactics, in contrast to the Austrians, and especially Daun, who developed the defensive battle to a high level of sophistication. In practice the scope of Frederick's strategic offensives remained limited; but he brought the tactical offensive to a state of perfection far beyond the standard of the day. He realized that the superiority of his small army rested almost wholly on its tactical drill, its ability to maneuver quickly and precisely, and on its spirited attack. He, too, was at his best in combat.

What is the nature of the Frederician battle? First, it differs from the battles of a later age in that there are relatively few participants. Rarely were more than 30,000 to 40,000 men committed in combat; only at Prague did the total reach 90,000. With the tightly ranged formations of the day the battle did not take up very much space. At Leuthen, the unusually extended Austrian front measured about four and a half miles, the Prussian attacking lines probably not more than half that distance. If the terrain was relatively open, the whole battlefield could be pretty well observed from one elevated point. Battles of such limited extent could be centrally directed even without the means of modern technology. The action developed from a pre-arranged order of battle, with landmarks designated to the wings of every battle line as guides for their advance. In crises, much still depended on the initiative of the subordinate commanders, especially of the cavalry leaders, whose actions not infrequently decided the outcome. The heavy cavalry with its massive attacks remained the most valuable support of the infantry. Despite all its improvements, artillery was still incapable of seriously weakening a strong position for the assault. At least in the early period of the Seven Years' War, its greatest contribution was made by battalion guns in close combat.

Infantry tactics had entirely changed since the end of the seventeenth century, when the flintlock with paper cartridges had replaced the old matchlock. The efficacy of fire had increased enormously; fire rather than close combat with the pike now constituted the true strength of the foot soldier. In the seventeenth century pikemen, in conjunction with musketeers, had still played a major role; they advanced in close squares, lances extended—a method of fighting that was very strong in the defense but possessed little offensive force. Subsequent development reversed this relationship. Frederick raised the offensive power of the infantry to the highest level of the age, while the Austrians could not entirely free themselves from the old defensive approach. The infantry's fire is best exploited by linear formation: the more rapidly the men load and fire, the thinner the line can be. The complex loading drill performed with the old musket had necessitated a formation of at least six ranks, one of which fired while the other five were recharging. The Prussian line had been reduced to three ranks and was correspondingly longer. On the drill fields firing was practiced with great ingenuity; each battalion line was divided into eight *Pelotons* which fired in turn with great speed, all three ranks at once, the front rank kneeling, the other two standing, so that an uninterrupted rolling volley resulted. In battle such artifices quickly broke down; an irregular flickering fire was generally all that could be achieved, and the more one tried to volley strictly according to command, the more the attack was delayed and the troops' impetus paralyzed. Frederick soon recognized this. He enjoined his men to advance on the enemy with long strides, fire a good volley into his face, and then as rapidly as possible shove the bayonet into his ribs. At the beginning of the Seven Years' War he even had his men shoulder their muskets during the advance, and forbade all firing in order to get them more quickly to the enemy. Already at Prague this proved to be impracticable, since it asked too much of the troops' courage and casualties rose dreadfully. But the offensive spirit and dash of the Prussian infantry remained the secret of its success.

The Prussian infantry attack ideally took place in the following manner: the men advanced in carefully aligned ranks, in cadence to the beat of the drums, led and surrounded by officers and NCO's. Volleys were fired on command, at the earliest 300 paces from the enemy—muskets being ineffective at longer range—more usually at 200 paces. Rather than striving for accurate aim Frederick wanted rapid and massive volleys at this point. Then bayonets were fixed for the final assault. Frederick thought he could guarantee that the enemy would rarely be able to withstand a bayonet attack executed by this human wall.

This scheme naturally varied considerably over different terrain. At Kunersdorf, for example, forests, swamps, ponds, and ravines narrowed the main offensive thrust to such an extent that the formation of an extended line was impossible, and there was no opportunity for supporting cavalry attacks. The Prussian army bled itself white in hopeless frontal assaults of limited width against the well-fortified and safely anchored Russian positions. On other occasions the commanders lacked sufficient time to arrange the order of battle: Hochkirch, for instance, degenerated into wild struggles of separate, disconnected units. But basically the method of attack was always the same: an advance in line without depth. It is true that the attack formations were arranged in two lines of battle, each of three ranks, the second line perhaps 150 to 200 paces behind the first. But the shortness of the distance between them indicates that the second line of battle was not really a tactical reserve and could be used for little else than filling the gaps caused by enemy fire.

Such thin lines were needed to stretch the front as far as possible, and thus prevent its being outflanked. The flank was the weakest feature of the linear order of battle. Even bending back the extreme wings or inserting additional troops at the flanks between the two lines could not completely solve the problem. This was especially true of the original type of Frederician battle, in which the attack unrolled as a frontal assault parallel to the enemy front. The main object of such attacks was to outflank the enemy. That could be done by quickly forming from the marching columns into the line of battle, and by rapid and accurate deployment of the attacking lines, so that the enemy had no time to take countermeasures. To this end the advance was commonly made in several columns marching side by side from which a solid attacking line was formed. The rapid execution of these two phases constituted a primary objective of Prussian training. But in theory the opponent could be outflanked only if one's own lines were longer than his. What could be done if the Prussians were merely of equal strength, or even numerically inferior to the enemy? Would this put them in danger of being themselves outflanked? How could this threat be avoided?

To meet this problem Frederick developed the oblique order of battle. The concept evolved from his experiences at Mollwitz and other battles of the first two Silesian Wars, from his studies of military history, and above all from his tactical experiments. It consisted of withholding or "refusing" one wing of the attacking line, while the other wing was strengthened with additional troops, assault units, a tactical reserve, massed guns, and cavalry. This reinforced wing closed with the opposing enemy units, and if possible outflanked them. Its local success could then provide the starting point from which to roll up the entire enemy front. Even a weaker force could thus overcome a far stronger opponent, as was brilliantly demonstrated at Leuthen.

In theory the oblique order of battle is simple, but its execution in the field leads to great difficulties and complications. If the enemy perceives the purpose of the attack he can take countermeasures: he can reinforce the threatened wing, or bend back his front—as happened at Colin, or he can counterattack the refused wing and attempt to outflank it in turn—as was done at Zorndorf. Everything hinges on the enemy's not recognizing the direction of the true attack, or being deceived about it. Both occurred at Leuthen: a feint induced the Austrian commanders to make false dispositions, after which the true approach march was hidden from them by a rise in the ground. At Colin, by contrast, the Austrians from their positions on the hills could observe the entire maneuver in time to take remedial action, though they did not go so far as to counterattack. It is also essential that the attackers' withheld wing keep the opponent sufficiently occupied without itself becoming too deeply involved in the battle—above all, it must not take the offensive prematurely. Otherwise the oblique battle turns into a battle of parallel fronts with unequally distributed forces, a situation which can have serious consequences and deprive the com-

mander of his last reserves. Frederick experienced this more than
once. The tendency of his generals to advance too soon, in line
with the main attack, was almost always intensified by the fact
that in oblique advances the solid front tends to break, so that
dangerous gaps can easily appear between the attacking battalions.
Frederick tried to diminish this danger and insure that the refused
wing was actually held back. At Leuthen his solution was to advance his attacking battalions not in an oblique line but in echelons
—a formation which later, in the years before Jena, was taught and
practiced with doctrinaire zeal, as if such methods, which might
succeed once, could guarantee victory. Frederick himself knew that
the battle should be shaped not by doctrine but by the intellect of
the general and his exploitation of the specific situation. He also
knew that complex maneuvers rarely succeed under fire. In his
eyes, drill simply served to give his troops the mobility and precision that enabled them to carry out any maneuver in any direction.

Early forms of the oblique order of battle were discussed in the
theoretical literature long before Frederick's time; the concept was
already known in antiquity. But Frederick first made its actual
employment possible. In general his achievement lay not so much
in inventing new complicated methods as in simplifying those that
were too complex, and in recognizing a few basic rules—his "General Principles"—which could guide the commander's decisions and
actions in the pressure of events. To be sure, he too attempted to
subject war to the power of rational analysis, and to restrict the
scope of chance and accident as much as possible. But he never
surrendered to the rigid demands of theory. He proved himself in
the rapid exploitation of the changing aspects of combat, in his
rich inventiveness, and in the promptness and decisiveness of his
leadership.

The advantages and flaws of Frederick's tactics are apparent.
Usually a well-planned and energetically executed attack soon led
to a decision. Because Frederick's opponents were not his equal in
quick and determined action, and because their troops were better
trained for the defense than for the attack, he was able to overrun
even a very much stronger enemy within a few hours. But his

system suffered from certain defects. The best troops were expended in the first attack, and sufficient reserves could not be retained—a weakness ameliorated but never eliminated by withholding one wing. Even though Frederick could support his infantry's first assault with cavalry charges, he was unable to bring additional infantry to bear and could not maintain the battle for long periods. Because of this inability he foundered at Colin and at Kunersdorf, where—as already mentioned—the terrain also ruled out effective cavalry attacks. Finally, the rigid Prussian drill could sometimes prove a handicap: battalions moving in line and firing volleys were easily thrown into disorder by difficult terrain; they were not trained for fighting in open formations. But these were limitations that sprang almost inevitably from the structure of the military institutions of his day; what his troops could do Frederick exploited to the fullest. The scope of his tactical and strategic inventiveness would become wholly apparent to us only if we could trace the design of his battles from one campaign to the next. The difficulties constantly increased, his attempts to solve them became steadily more daring. As his enemies learned to perfect their defensive methods, he further expanded his enveloping tactics. At Rossbach he attacked the flank of an enemy envelopment; at Zorndorf and Kunersdorf both armies reversed their positions in attempting to outflank one another. At Torgau the flank attack was raised to a dual attack: two separate corps simultaneously moved on the enemy from north and south; the main assault proceeded from an enveloping march that led in a semicircle about the Austrian right wing.

In the final analysis, what proved decisive for Frederick's success was that his practical genius matched the clarity and profundity of his theoretical understanding. The rationality of his thought neither handicapped the soldier's determination nor reduced the self-confidence of the political leader. And so it was possible for him to raise the art of war of his period to its highest potential level. After the Seven Years' War he occupied the same position among the generals of Europe that once had been Prince Eugene's: Frederick was now the universally admired, studied, and emulated preceptor of modern war. But in the military realm as in the field of political theory his efforts constituted an ultimate achievement, a high point from which there could only be a decline. Very soon after his death a new age dawned for the military institutions of Europe.

ERNST FRIEDRICH RUDOLF VON BARSEWISCH

The Battle of Hochkirch

In October 1758, one of the critical periods of the Seven Years' War, Frederick advanced against a superior Austrian army in Saxony, hoping to compel it to withdraw so that he would be free to return to Silesia, which was being threatened by other forces. In the night of the thirteenth to the fourteenth, the Austrians surprised him instead, and defeated him in a costly battle. This eyewitness account by a twenty-one-year-old participant is naïve and confused, but gives a good picture of the conditions under which Frederick acted as military commander—a part of his life of major significance to his personality and reign.—EDITOR.

From *Meine Kriegserlebnisse in den Jahren 1757–1763*, by E. F. R. von Barsewisch. Berlin, 1863. Translation copyright © 1972 by Peter Paret.

THE NIGHT was exceptionally dark. We heard a few musket shots, but since all soon was quiet again we thought it might have been our outposts firing on a patrol, which often happens at night, or that it had to do with deserters, who are not uncommon in camps that lie close to the enemy. But since our regiment was stationed next to the guards, that is to say in the center of the camp, and like the guards was especially alert and accurate in matters of the service, we were prepared to fall in as soon as we heard the shots—the more so since our excellent commanding officer had some days earlier on his own ordered us to remain in uniform at night so as to be ready for any eventuality. The firing had aroused the curiosity of officers and men; we left our tents to see what more would happen. While we were asking what these shots nearby could mean, what had caused them, we suddenly heard tremendous musket volleys, and even saw the powder flashes through the darkness. It was about three-thirty in the morning. We officers immediately shouted: "Fall in! Under arms!" In less than two minutes we had our men in rank and file. The firing increased in intensity, and a few guns from the village of Hochkirch joined in. This lasted until shortly after four o'clock. . . .

While we were standing in readiness in our assembly area, His Majesty the King came from his headquarters, which lay close behind our tents, and walked along the front of the regiment until he stopped by the second battalion. "Go back to your tents," he said, "those are only pandurs on a raid." We motioned to our men to step back a few paces. About this time the firing increased again, and His Majesty said to Captain von Troschke, who stood next to me in front of our unit:

"What do you think this firing means?"

Troschke said: "The imperial troops have taken the great redoubt on the right wing, and the fire is coming from Hochkirch."

"How can you believe that?" the king responded.

"It won't be long," Troschke said, "and they will fire on us with our own cannon."

Just then the enemy began to fire on the camp. . . . The cannonballs roared over our heads.

Now the king said: "Troschke, you are right. Men, shoulder muskets! Where is my horse?"

His Majesty mounted his horse. At that moment an adjutant whom he had sent to Hochkirch returned with the information that all battalions on the right wing had been surprised by the enemy, and now were completely disorganized. The enemy had already gained a foothold in Hochkirch itself. His Majesty at once ordered the regiments to march toward them. Our commander had us turn right. The Itzenplitz Regiment, which marched ahead of us, formed into platoons from battalion lines. The king rode ahead to direct it against the enemy. It was about six o'clock.

During this time the enemy had formed a new line near the village of Hochkirch, had moved up the captured cannon from the great redoubt, and had occupied all paths and streets of the village so that we could not enter. As the king rode closer he was met by wounded soldiers and men who had lost their units. He ordered the Itzenplitz Regiment to hurry to the assistance of the troops still holding in front of Hochkirch, and to recapture it. With us he marched farther to the right, past the village, toward the area where our dragoons had camped, so that we retained contact with the right wing. We were followed by the guards and Retzow's battalion. Then we wheeled left, and the whole line began to advance on the enemy.

The Itzenplitz Regiment, which consisted of brave and experienced soldiers, marched straight at the imperial batteries in Hochkirch, which fired case-shot at point-blank range from all cannons. Until it had deployed, the regiment could not protect itself against this massive fire, and it was wiped out except for a few hundred men. The village was burning. Now the guards and Retzow's battalion attacked. They caused many casualties and, in union with scattered soldiers and the battalions defeated earlier, recaptured the village; but the superiority of the enemy, who continually brought up fresh units, was too great to permit them to retain possession.

Our regiment enjoyed a more favorable situation to the right of the village, where there was enough open space to deploy properly, and to launch a regular attack. We didn't hesitate, and

advanced with determination; our light regimental cannon caused
considerable damage; we drove the enemy through the area where
the cavalry of our right wing had camped—some of the huts in
the center were still standing—captured ten guns, and pushed the
Austrians back into the forest. In the meantime it was growing
light. Now the enemy cavalry saw us advancing—we were already
firing on his third infantry line—and attempted a charge. But
the attack was repelled with heavy casualties, and the squadrons
had to withdraw behind their infantry. During this time our own
cavalry executed a second brilliant attack on the enemy infantry,
and before our eyes scattered four battalions, few of whose men
were not cut down.

It was also during this period that the king honored our regiment with his presence. He sat on his horse only a few paces from
me, behind our second battalion, where the three ensigns—von
Unruh, von Hertzberg, and myself—closed the formation. . . .
His presence contributed a good deal to the special steadiness and
courage of our men; the king saw with his own eyes how very
many brave soldiers and officers were killed by the enemy's mur-
derous fire, particularly at the beginning of the action, when enemy
troops were hidden in the huts to our front, but also later on. The
forest, which was in their hands, and the ground sloping up to it
afforded the imperial troops a very great advantage. Most of the
well-aimed musket shots that came from the edge of the forest
struck our men and our officers in the head or chest. Next to the
king Major von Haugwitz was hit in the left arm. The king's
horse, standing close behind me, was shot through the neck. Field
Marshal Keith leading Geist's Regiment toward the village was
torn from his horse by a cannonball, and died immediately. In
front of our battalion, our brigadier, the brave Prince William of
Brunswick, was killed by a bullet. After he had fallen, his horse,
a gray without any markings whatever, bearing the prince's ornate
saddlecloth, galloped at full speed for a good thirty minutes between the imperial troops and our lines without finding a refuge.
It was sad to see. What in the end happened to the horse I can't
say.

While the king was with us, fifty Austrian deserters reached our regiment, and shouted: "Victory! Long live the king of Prussia!" But the enemy was again taking hold of Hochkirch, and once more subjected us to heavy fire. We had to withstand a second cavalry attack, and our situation became very dangerous. Major von Schmelinski, of the Regiment Alt-Retzow, crossed to the king, next to me, and said:

"Your Majesty, I beg you with all my heart, protect your sacred person, and at least ride out of musket range. See how the men around you are being killed."

The king replied: "First I want to see how the battalions opposite us are being driven back."

"For God's sake!" Schmelinski said. "I beg you, guard your sacred person. Hochkirch is lost, and the enemy may soon take us in the rear." Now Schmelinski saw the king's wounded horse, and added, "Your Majesty's horse is hit."

"I am?" the king asked.

"The horse—it will bleed to death and collapse."

Now the king himself recognized the danger, and called: "Where are my horses? Another horse!"

I stepped forward, and said, "Your Majesty, I noticed them behind the defile."

Not until then did the king agree to turn his horse around and, accompanied only by Schmelinski, he rode back. When he reached his mounts and changed horses, the other one fell dead. It was a magnificent light brown charger. . . .

For my part at the beginning of the engagement I was paid the compliment of having a bullet pierce the front of my hat close over my skull; not long after, a second drilled through the left brim with such force that the hat fell off. I said to the Hertzberg brothers who stood not far from me, "Gentlemen, shall I put on the hat again, which the Austrians like so much?"

"Yes, certainly," they said. "The hat does you honor." The older Hertzberg took out his snuffbox, and said, "Gentlemen, take a pinch of *contenance*." I walked over to him, took some snuff, and said, "True, here we have need of courage." Ensign von Unruh followed, and then Hertzberg's brother, the youngest, took the last pinch. As soon as the older Hertzberg had taken his own pinch from the snuffbox and was putting it to his nostril, a musket ball struck him directly in the forehead. I was standing next to him, and looked at him. He cried out: "Lord Jesus!" turned around, and fell dead to the ground. . . .

By eleven o'clock we were in a bad way. For the second time our soldiers called for ammunition, but the reserve supply was gone; all our resources had been pushed to the limit. . . . By the time that the enemy realized that our fire was weakening we no longer needed to fear his infantry, who during the past five hours must have been repelled ten times, but it was a different matter with the household cuirassiers and the mounted grenadiers in their bearskins, who now boldly advanced, and at some distance took up a position facing us. Hoping that our cavalry would relieve us for a third time, we kept up a weak fire; but since no help came, and our unit was being decimated, I ordered a soldier to collect the three colors, whose bearers and guards had been killed, and told him: "Stay with me, we must save the colors." He was a Wend by birth, named Hukatz. Unruh and the surviving Hertzberg had assumed command of the platoons on the left or right whose officers had fallen. Since my captain, von Ingersleben, in command of the color company, had also been killed, and Major von Haugwitz had been forced to leave the field because of his smashed arm (he died of the wound shortly afterward) it was my duty as the only remaining officer of the company to make certain that the colors were saved. . . . I collected a group of about thirty men, and told Hukatz, who was carrying the three colors: "Go ahead, I will cover you." The other two regimental colors, which had been positioned farther down the line, had been captured, together with their bearers, during the first Austrian attacks. I formed my thirty men into three ranks, as well as I could, and said that the ranks should alternately fire and retreat—the men in one rank firing their few remaining bullets at will, while the rest slowly withdrew. I have the habit of always closely observing the terrain around me, and now I recalled a defile about three hundred paces to the back of us, and behind it a swampy meadow. I ordered: "Men, follow me!" and we managed to withdraw a hundred paces before the enemy horsemen noticed us with our colors. But then they galloped after us, and caught up with us before we had reached the provisional safety of the defile. They swung their sabers at our little group, and though we were still able to shoot a few from the saddle, there were too many of them; they attacked us from all sides at once, and yelled: "Surrender, Prussian! Give up the colors!" But my brave men gave up their lives rather than surrender the remaining colors. Hukatz hurried toward the defile, while the rest of us fought and drew back. The colors had not yet been saved, and I was still twenty paces from the defile, when enemy horsemen reached me. They yelled: "Stand, Prussian!" and immediately an Austrian cuirassier swung at my head. I noticed it in time, bent low, and all that happened was that the point of his saber pierced the hat that earlier had done me so much honor. The hat bounced into the air and frightened the cuirassier's horse, giving me time to retreat further. As I was running I decided to take off my new sash, which I had received from Berlin only a few days ago, and threw the glittering cloth at the nearest Austrians—a cuirassier and a mounted grenadier. As soon as they noticed the prize, they stopped, and the grenadier jumped from his horse to pick up the booty. By that time I had crossed the defile with the flags. I stopped for a second and collected the rest of my men—now about fifteen. Two Austrians entered the defile and shouted: "Give us the colors, or we shoot!" and waved their pistols. But at that distance we had no cause to fear them, and I took the time to form up my men again, and to see what the Austrians were doing. Among them I noticed the grenadier, my sash and hat in hand, just remounting his horse. As the horsemen prepared to cross the defile, we marched with all possible speed to the swampy meadow, which we reached just when our pursuit came near. When they saw that we were sinking over our ankles into the morass, they reluctantly let us go.

With the three colors and my fifteen men I marched toward the heights beyond the great meadow, where royal headquarters had been and where the king had again taken up his position. As soon as I reached His Majesty, he asked: "Where are the others?"

I replied: "I am bringing three colors which were saved, the others were captured; and these fifteen men are the only survivors."

But gradually a few officers and some men, perhaps 150 in all, arrived on the heights from the other side. They had reached us by fleeing through the camp.

The king said to me: "Hand over the colors to NCO's."

I said: "Your Majesty, none is left."

"Then give them to soldiers, and form up the men," was the answer. As the king seemed astonished at my appearance, I said apologetically: "Your Majesty, I lost hat and sash . . ."

We had reached the heights around noon, which means that we had been in action for six hours. The king remained near us, and when he saw that the Austrian infantry was beginning to advance across the battlefield toward the swamp, drums and fifes playing, he at once ordered the gunners to fire. We still had two howitzers and one gun; that was our entire available artillery. The howitzers could not reach beyond the swamp, and so the enemy was hurt only by our one cannon.

Now General von Saldern with a few battalions from the left wing reached the heights, and asked the king: "Your Majesty, shall I attack?"

"No," said the king, "we will withdraw to the right; you cover the retreat."

In the greatest imaginable order we marched back to a stone bridge. When the enemy perceived this, he opened an intense fire on the bridge. Fortunately for us, the bridge was very strongly built of quarry rock, and at that distance the enemy could not damage it. We crossed the bridge as rapidly as possible, and only a few men were killed by grazing fire. At the same time Saldern's energetic resistance slowed the pursuit.

The Austrians were moving up perhaps as many as 10,000 men, but then General von Retzow with 4,000 men arrived from Weissenberg, and defended the bridge with his guns and musket volleys until Saldern's troops, too, had crossed to the other side. When they were safe, Retzow followed with the rest of the army; the enemy no longer bothered us and was content to remain master of the battlefield.

FRIEDRICH MEINECKE

Ruler Before Philosopher

T HE LIFE WORK of Frederick the Great can be viewed in
many contexts that are significant for universal history. One
of the most important for the history of European thought is the
context in which we shall seek to view it here. If any man of the
eighteenth century had the vocation and the strength to solve the
problem for his time, and to confer on *raison d'état* the aims and
standards of universal human reason, then it was Frederick. It
can be said that his whole life was dedicated to this task. With a
heroism that was just as philosophical as it was political, he took

From *Machiavellism,* by Friedrich Meinecke. Translated by Douglas Scott.
New Haven: Yale University Press, 1957, pp. 275–310. Copyright © by Yale
University Press. Reprinted with permission of Yale University Press and
Routledge & Kegan Paul Ltd.

it upon himself from the beginning and directed upon it all the divergent energies of his mind (which was by no means either simple or unambiguous) and all the scientific means of his time. The solution which he found and which satisfied him was certainly one which, in the main, he succeeded in discovering relatively quickly and early; but he did not allow it to deteriorate into a useful convention, but was ever reconsidering it freshly and intensively, and so even latterly was able to add something new to it. So that, as will presently be shown, it was ultimately capable of leading on to new stages of historical and political knowledge. But he himself remained confined all the time within the limitations of his own time and its mode of thought. The weapons of the philosophy of the Enlightenment revealed themselves as still incapable of solving the problem in such a manner that reality and the ideal could be harmonized together. He was least capable of doing so during the period when he was most passionately occupied with the question—during his political and intellectual *Sturm und Drang* period on the eve of his reign. This very period is therefore all the more instructive with respect to the problems of his time and his personality.

Frederick prided himself on having been a man before he became a king[1]—and for him, being a man meant also being a philosopher. But the future ruler in him was developed earlier than the philosopher;[2] and from the very beginning this development followed the lines required by the ⌐*raison d'état*⌐ of a state that was strong from a military point of view, but from the point of view of territory was quite incomplete, indeed was incapable of completion. It is from the year 1731 that one dates his first great youthful dream of politics which envisaged consolidations of every kind for the dismembered territory of the state by means of West

---

1. *Réfutation, Oeuvres de Frédéric le Grand*, 30 vols. (1846–1856), VIII, 278. This collection of Frederick's writings is hereafter referred to as *Oeuvres*.

2. One may say this, although the first stirrings of a philosophical interest showed themselves much earlier—as early as 1728 he called himself *Frédéric le philosophe*. Cf. v. Sommerfeld, *Die philosoph. Jugendentwicklung des Kronprinzen Friedrich, Forschungen zur brand. u. preuss. Geschichte*, 31, 69 ff.

Prussia, Swedish Pomerania, etc.[3] The years of serious illness on
the part of his father, 1734 and 1735, which brought him very close
to the throne, did clearly stir up passionately his desire to rule. In
secret conversations at that time, he offered himself to the French
ambassador as a second Gustavus Adolphus or Charles XII for
the future use of French policy.[4] The fact that his father recovered
deceived his expectations and produced a severe internal setback.[5]
It is from then on that he first seems to have devoted himself to
more serious philosophic and scientific studies, but simultaneously
he showed an increased interest in the burning questions of power
politics of the day. This was the beginning of his conscious double
life as politician and philosopher, and as he grew to manhood it
was reflected in his enthusiastic correspondence with Grumbkow,
who gave him a feeling for Prussian politics and for the European
politics of power and the balance of power. And it is also reflected
in the two books which are now about to influence us as thesis and
antithesis respectively in a weighty problem: the *Considérations
sur l'état présent du corps politique de l'Europe,* which was produced at the turn of the years 1737–1738,[6] and the *Réfutation du
prince de Machiavel,* which was written in 1739 and (altered by
Voltaire into the form of *Antimachiavell*) became known to the
world in 1740.[7]

3. Koser, *Geschichte Friedrichs des Grossen,* 4th and 5th ed., I, 159.
4. Lavisse, *Le Grand Frédéric avant l'avènement,* p. 327 f.
5. Volz, *Die Krisis in der Jugend Friedrichs d. Gr., Histor. Zeitschr.,* 118.
6. See my analysis of the origin and aims of this work in the *Histor.
Zeitschr.,* 117. Rohmer's work of research (*Vom Werdegange Friedrichs d.
Gr.,* 1924), where it differs from my views, contains nothing that convinces
me.
7. The title *Réfutation du prince de Machiavel* was chosen by Preuss (on
the basis of a description used by Frederick himself—to Voltaire on November 6, 1739), when for the first time he published in its entirety this purely
Frederician form of the book, in the *Oeuvres,* VIII. Cf. v. Sommerfeld, *Die
äussere Entstehungsgeschichte des Antimiachiavell Friedrichs d. Gr., Forsch.
zur brand. u. preuss. Gesch.,* 29, 460. He demonstrates that even the text of
the *Réfutation* does not represent Frederick's very first plan of 1739, and
that the changes in the edition of the *Antimachiavell* worked on by Voltaire
go back, partly, to yet another version sent to Voltaire by Frederick himself.
For the sake of brevity, we refer to the book here by the title of *Antimachiavell* which has become traditional, but for obvious reasons we are using the
text of the *Réfutation.* Madsack, *Der Antimachiavell* (1920), pp. 62 ff., has
overlooked the important investigation by Sommerfeld.

Thus it is a basic fact about his youthful development that his political interests were already formed before the development of his philosophical ideas. The future ruler and statesman had a priority over the philosopher. But in order to arrive at a clearer understanding of this priority, we need to make a comparison now between the ideas of his youthful period and those of his maturity. The relation between them is that between the first fruit-bud and the ripe fruit.

It must first of all be observed that from the very outset the ruler (which dominated the philosopher in him) was not a ruler in the conventional and customary—one might almost say, in the natural and organic—sense. Certainly the most personal impulses of a great ruler—ambition on the grand scale, a passionate love of glory and pleasure in power—were all present in him in such an elementally vital, and to begin with almost excessive, form that our judgment might appear surprising. But the element of princely milieu in him was absorbed remarkably early by the princely individual in him. As part of the natural and organic personality of a ruler, one should find that all-suffusing consciousness of belonging to a select stock, a feeling which is nevertheless founded on a completely unconscious element, on the powerful and elemental instincts of blood, family, and consanguinity, which the centuries have helped to fashion into an absolutely natural tradition of thought and feeling. The dynasty was the first and most basic one in the development toward the modern state; and its sentiments, which were so peculiarly different from any sense of belonging purely to the state, remained alive right up to the very last Hohenzollern ruler (and ultimately proved so disastrous for the dynasty, and for our country). This family instinct that they were rulers—which embraced not only their own dynasty, but also all the rest of the princely stock of the Christian world, as forming a divinely blessed and elevated social sphere with common interests—was completely lacking in Frederick. In any case, it died early. He might perhaps have developed this sense, if he had married a consort who was his equal in feeling and intelligence. But the completely new and individual manner (so different from the normal custom among rulers) in which he handled his marriage, condemned the unloved spouse to living a separate and superficial royal existence, and himself to an almost ascetic bachelor life, indicates a fundamental weakness in him of the instinct for blood and family, and equally points to a fundamental strength of his purely individual will.

His *Antimachiavell* confirms this impression. It is quite free from any specifically dynastic feeling, from any solid respect for princely stock. It is founded on just this basic idea that a purely dynastic interest is of no value at all if it lacks the foundation of a real popular and national collective whole; it implies that Machiavelli's counsels were therefore of little value, because they were drawn from the *principini* of his time, those hermaphroditic crosses between sovereign and private individual. But even those smaller princely equivalents of his fatherland, who could pride themselves on a better quality of lineage than Machiavelli's *principini*, fared no better in his opinion.[8] It is scarcely necessary to recall his countless later expressions of contempt for mere pride of birth and his mordant criticisms of his princely counterparts. These remarks, which were inspired by philosophical theory or by a personal pleasure in contempt,[9] are less interesting than the manner in which he treated the dynastic questions of statecraft in the two political Testaments of 1752 and 1768. Here the ruler in him speaks out on the subject of the essential nature of princely rank in a more unequivocal, deliberate, and austere manner than anywhere else. One only has to read the passage about "hereditary rulers" in the first Testament:[10] "They form a species of individual that is neither sovereign nor private person, and is occasionally very difficult to control." The importance of their lineage gives them a certain pride, which they call nobility, and which makes obedience insupportable to them and every form of subjection hateful. One must load them with every kind of outward honor, but keep them at a distance from affairs; and, if one is sure of their talent and

8. *Réfutation, Oeuvres*, VIII, 208 f.

9. Cf. for instance the instructions to Major v. Borcke in 1751, regarding the education of Prince Frederick William, *Oeuvres*, IX, 39, and the satirical poem of 1770 on the rulers of his time, *Oeuvres*, XIII, 41 ff., as also the passages quoted in Zeller, *Friedrich d. Gr. als Philosoph*, p. 240 f.

10. *Die politischen Testamente Friedrichs d. Gr.*, edition of 1920, p. 33.

their reliability, they should be used for leading troops. Richelieu had already had the same ideas about this.[11] But it was easier for Richelieu to think in this way, than for a born ruler. The remarkable thing about it is that Frederick's instructions were entirely free from any kind of family feeling. During the weeks after the Battle of Kolin, he turned against his unfortunate brother, the Prince Augustus William, with a terrible harshness.[12]

And then there were the remarks about the education of princes in the two Testaments.[13] He laid an enormous importance on the question of the spirit in which the monarchs were to be educated, for he saw that the fate of the kingdoms depended on this.[14] It was precisely for this reason that he demanded a radical break with the existing method of education, which tended to envelop the young ruler in a cloud of bigoted prejudices of the court, and (we may add) fostered most strongly that dynastic and hereditary instinct. The ruler should be educated "as a private person"—but this phrase alone would be very misleading; for it did not have in view any democratic leveling of the future ruler, on the contrary it was directed toward a strictly rational education for the position of head of the state. It was intended to produce a ruler who would stand on his own feet and view the world in a critical and unprejudiced manner, and who would be sufficiently independent of the resources of princely majesty that "he would by himself be able to create his own happiness." This then constituted the sense of dynasty in his eyes: it produces human material, from among which the central person required to lead the state may be selected, in order then to undergo a pure form of cultural training for this vocation. In the process he ought to learn to treat his own brothers and cousins solely in accordance with their usefulness toward the state. Certainly, from an external point of view, the old historic dignity of a collective dynasty ought to be maintained, but with

11. W. Mommsen, *Richelieu als Staatsmann, Histor. Zeitschr.,* 127, 223. It may be recalled that Spinoza too, in his *Tractatus politicus,* Chap. 6, § 14, and Chap. 7, § 23, recommends general rules for rendering some of the princes of the royal blood harmless.

12. Koser, II, 513.

13. *Polit. Testamente,* pp. 102 ff. and 231 ff.

14. *Ibid.,* pp. 69 and 223 concerning France.

regard to its internal structure it ought to be stripped of its senti-
mental and traditional associations, and converted into a utilitarian
organization for the benefit of the state. Every irrational and natural organic element in it which did not contribute to this end was
to be suppressed as far as possible. A living historical growth thus
becomes rationalized—rationalized in exactly the same way as the
state system of Frederick the Great rationalized the (in many
ways so irrational and individual) growth of the domestic landed
nobility, and turned it into a forcing-bed for the officer corps,
which the army of that time needed in just this and no other capacity; it was to be done in the same way as the burgher and
peasant classes were rationalized and used for the financial and
military ends of state and power. Rationalization, for the purposes
of the state, of those social forces that had developed since the
Middle Ages—this was the sum of his domestic policy. Thus they
were indeed retained, but at the same time they were quite clearly
prevented from following the lines of their own individual development.

All these measures of rationalization were bound to succeed in
making the Prussian state into a real great power, and in raising
it above the class of German territorial states, ruled on purely
dynastic lines. But a peculiar inner antinomy was thereby introduced into the essential character of Frederick and his state. For
what great state was and continued to be—more than the Prussian
—both the creation and at the same time the inherited patrimony
of a dynasty? This original character could not be entirely effaced
by all these rationalizations. Indeed they only caused it to appear
all the more clearly, because one immediately perceived the heterogeneous past that lay behind this artificially and consciously fashioned state-form which stood in such an obvious contrast to all
the great powers that had grown up on a natural basis. Indeed
the very will to become something different and something more
than birth and origin really allowed, here impelled the inborn
character of a dynastic state to assume its clearest and most distinctive expression. "So must thou be, thou canst not escape thy-
self." Frederick's consciously undynastic conception of the state —
offers one of the most remarkable examples of the Hegelian proc-

ess of dialectical development, of the *coincidentia oppositorum* in history—the example of a historical idea being forced by internal pressure and growth to change into its opposite, while at the same time an intimate continuity is maintained between the two contrasting ideas.

Frederick rationalized even himself; he knew how to control those impulses in his nature that were light-hearted and pleasure-loving, and which he felt to be inessential and harmful for the task of ruling, in order to change himself into the "first servant of the state." This process of self-education and transformation was fully at work in him from the middle of the thirties. One finds already in his *Antimachiavell* the remark that the ruler is the first servant of his people, and that he must look upon his subjects not merely as his equals, but in certain respects as his masters.[15] This remark was not in any way an isolated or merely personal recognition. It was the ripe product of the course of ideas hitherto concerning the problem of *raison d'état*. The ruler is the servant of *raison d'état*, of state interests—this had already been taught by the Italians and by Rohan. But other thinkers of the seventeenth century had been able to give this idea of the ruler being a servant an anti-absolutist turn, by taking this ruler's master to be no longer *raison d'état* or the *salus publica*, but purely and simply the people. Frederick linked himself with them, and perhaps coined his phrase in memory of similar expressions which he had read in Fénelon or Bayle.[16] But (and this is not always recognized) it proceeded from a deep and personal living basis in Frederick himself. One may perhaps look upon the feeling of dependence on a higher power as a most intimate and personal emotion of his being. It was therefore of some significance that he grew up in an intellectual atmosphere, in which Calvinist ideas were able to exert an influence. As a young man he grasped eagerly at the doctrine of predestination, and, when he afterward changed into a worldly

15. *Réfutation, Oeuvres,* VIII, 168 and 298.
16. Madsack, p. 79. Fénelon says in *Télémaque* that the king is a slave of his people. Bayle, in an article which Frederick also uses elsewhere, mentions the opinion of Althusius and others, that rulers are *des valets, des commis ou des procureurs du peuple.*

philosopher, he defended against Voltaire Man's dependence on the divinity and the idea that the human will was not free. It was certainly possible then for his determinism to stiffen in a naturalistic fashion into a belief in some incomprehensible Fate which caused men to move like puppets.[17] But the living environment of his calling worked against this stiffening influence. At this profoundest point of his life, it was possible for philosophy, ethics, and politics all to join hands. For who can fail to perceive their mutual influence in his spirit, when one sees how strongly (as he developed into a politician) he felt himself dependent on the duty of his calling, and at the same time on the constraining force of *raison d'état*. It was "A form expressed, unfolding vitally" and his career now became (as Ranke says on one occasion)[18] not his choice, but his destiny.

Thus the spirit of pure and strict *raison d'état* came to assume the mastery in him—but certainly not with any of that abstract and impersonal objectivity which might have made the agent of *raison d'état* into a mere interchangeable instrument for a task; on the contrary it was penetrated and fused with the vital will of a proud personality, who in this very task discerned the lifeform allotted to himself and the possibility of developing his most personal qualities. During the terrible year 1761, he wrote to William Pitt:[19] "I allow myself to be guided by two principles. One is honor, and the other is the interest of the state, which Heaven has entrusted to my care. With these two maxims, my dear sir, one never gives way to one's enemies." This principle of "honor" certainly also covered all that personal pleonexia, which is unavoidably linked with action prompted by *raison d'état*. Who could fail to perceive it in the great decisions of Frederick's life? Nothing is more indicative of the degree to which both his kingdom and he himself were rationalized than the famous instruction, which he wrote, on January 10, 1757, to his minister Count Finck-

17. Paul-Dubois, *Frédéric le Grand d'après sa correspondance politique,* 1903, p. 295 f.

18. *Werke,* 27/28, 480.

19. Frederick the Great, *Politische Correspondenz,* 47 vols. (1879–1939), XX, 508. This edition of Frederick's official correspondence is henceforth cited as *Polit. Corresp.*

enstein, in case of disaster overtaking him: "If it should be my fate to be taken prisoner, then I forbid anyone to have the smallest concern for my person, or to pay the slightest attention to anything I might write from my place of confinement. If such a misfortune should befall me, then I shall sacrifice myself for the state, and everyone must then obey my brother; I shall hold him, and all my ministers and generals, responsible with their heads for seeing that neither a province nor a ransom is offered for my release, but that the war is continued and every advantage seized, just as if I had never existed in the world." [20]

Rohan (who had also grown up amongst Calvinist feelings of dependence) said that rulers commanded nations, but that interest commanded the rulers. Now, since his time, this state interest had not only become more acute, but also wider and deeper. It had become sharper in that it was now more precisely and consciously separated from the dynastic interest with which it had originally been united—and further in that it had pressed into its service the conduct of men in every social stratum, from the monarch down to the peasant, thereby in many ways diverting them from their natural course of development and changing them designedly and purposively. It had become widened and deepened in that it had come to include the humanitarian ideals of the Enlightenment; and the phrase about the "general welfare," which was to form the content of state interest, was now spoken with greater warmth and with a greater wealth of association. There arose at the same time the ideal of the modern state, which was to be not only a power state, but also a cultural state; and the inadequate restriction of *raison d'état* to the mere tasks of directly securing power, with which the theorists of the seventeenth century were in many ways still occupied, was now overcome. Frederick held it a very serious and sacred task to procure for his subjects the very highest measure, compatible with the requirements of his state, of earthly happiness, material welfare, intellectual awakening and moral vigor; and this determination sprang from a deep and original feeling which one can only perceive with difficulty beneath the mordant tones of his contempt for humanity. For icy coldness and inner

20. *Oeuvres*, XXV, 320.

warmth were always welling up in him simultaneously and in opposition to one another.[21] "To show sympathy with the weaknesses of men, and to have a feeling of humanity for everyone— that is the way in which a reasonable man should act." [22] This humanitarian idea of the state remained alive in him from the beginning to the end. It was certainly often assumed that, after the Seven Years' War, his feeling grew harsher and more inflexible, because his governmental practice subsequently took on a sharper fiscal character. There was some astonishment when his Political Testament of 1768 became public and it was seen that the humanitarian and philanthropic points of view were expressed more frequently in this later document than in the earlier Testament of 1752.[23] He did not intend to conceal, with decorative phrases, the harsher methods which he was now practicing, for he also expressed these sharply enough at the same time. It was rather that he felt a need to prevent himself losing sight of the guiding star of humanity, particularly now when he was letting himself be influenced by the stern necessity for using harsh methods to protect the existence of an insecure and continually threatened state.

Thus his path of action was always quite clear and unambiguous. The imperative command of state necessity, as he understood it, triumphed always, and on all occasions where there was any choice, over the demands of humanity, and even over the ideals of his philosophy of the Enlightenment. But because this latter also engrossed him in an intimate and vital way, there was a

21. This was clumsily misunderstood by Lavisse, *Le Grand Frédéric avant l'avénement,* when on p. 169 he made the judgment: *Non, il n'était pas bon.* Much more just and in many ways also more subtle was the judgment of Paul-Dubois; but even he (making use of the French psychological methods, which are certainly mordant, but also schematic) makes too sharp a division between the different aspects of Frederick's character, between the elemental basic nature and the contemporary ideas by which he was moved.

22. *Dissertation sur les raisons d'établir ou d'abroger les lois* (1750), *Oeuvres,* IX, 33; cf. his letter to Voltaire of January 8, 1739. Koser and H. Droysen, *Briefwechsel usw.,* I, 232.

23. Hintze, *Friedrich d. Gr. nach dem Siebenjährigen Kriege und das Polit. Testament von 1768, Forschungen zur brand. u. preuss. Geschichte,* 32, 43. Cf. also H. v. Caemmerer in the *Hohenzollern-Jahrbuch,* 1911, p. 89.

strong problematical element in his thought. The supreme task which he set before the ruler and the state did not only embrace what had hitherto been the narrower aim of *raison d'état,* namely the guaranteeing and strengthening of its physical power; it also embraced that other humanitarian ideal of educating the people and making them happy. Thus two ideas of the state dwelt in him side by side—the idea of the humanitarian state and of the power-state: one, which had been created anew by the Enlightenment or at least filled with new content, and the other, which sprang from life, from history and experience, and which was continually being freshly confirmed by daily experience and necessity. It is impossible to avoid seeing that the second was prior to the first. It is easier to overlook the fact that this priority never led to a disappearance of the humanitarian idea of the state. So there was eventually bound to occur in him a very special and problematical kind of settling of accounts between the two ideas of the state. Indeed, to begin with (as we are about to show), he himself was under the mistaken impression that he had not only harmonized the two heterogeneous ideas, but actually fused them together into complete unity with one another.

It was at first possible for him to believe this, because he himself had inserted part of the philosophy of the Enlightenment into the very idea of the power state. He did this by his conception of the ruler as the first servant of the state, by his suppression of the purely dynastic elements in his thought and action, and by emphasizing the universally human qualities and tasks of his position. It is true that there were two sides to this action. It certainly threw a bridge across between the old power state and the new ideal of the Enlightenment which tended to refer everything to what was universally human. But at the same time it sharpened the weapons of the power state by cleaning from them the rust of the bad princely tradition and of useless personal and dynastic motives, while it also caused the bearer of power to recognize new and purer duties toward the state as a whole; but this in turn strengthened the ruler's belief in the real justification of using his power methods, in drawing the sword and making use of all the great and small devices of statecraft. And this was, in the very highest degree, the case with the power politics of Frederick the Great. We shall find it confirmed by his conception of the interests of states.[24]

And moreover, even in the realm of domestic politics it was not so difficult to achieve a satisfying harmony between *raison d'état* and the ideal of the Enlightenment. The security of the state in the face of foreign enemies was the first elementary prerequisite for any kind of humanitarian domestic policy. All the sacrifices and burdens which he laid upon his subjects, every renunciation which he, as monarch, had to make in refraining from carrying out philanthropic reforms, all restrictions put upon the humanitarian idea of the state within the country, could immediately be justified to his conscience by the supreme law of this State, namely that of maintaining an unusually strong and strictly organized army.[25] But Frederick was also in a position where he could carry on his domestic policy on much more moral principles than was possible for the rulers of the Renaissance. The latter had to be on their guard against enemies not only abroad but also inside the country; and so Machiavelli had felt himself obliged to advise his ruler to use the discreditable arts of deception even in dealing with his own subjects. But in the military monarchies there now reigned deep peace, order, and discipline. To continue making use of those same Machiavellian methods within the state was now entirely superfluous, and therefore seemed hateful. And Frederick also knew that it was unwise to set his subjects a bad example.[26] He demanded complete purity, uprightness and honorableness in the relations between ruler, state, and people, and was in the main able

24. Regarding the rationalist element in Frederick's politics, cf. also Küntzel, *Zum Gedächtnis Friedrichs d. Gr., Marine-Rundschau,* 1912, 206 ff., and his presentation of Frederick in the *Meister der Politik,* published by Marcks and v. Müller.

25. He was certainly able to conceal this basic motive from his contemporaries, and to justify the maintenance of the "barbaric" agrarian system by a regard for the agreements between landowners and peasants and for the interests of agriculture based as they were on these. *Essai sur les formes de gouvernement,* 1777, *Oeuvres,* IX, 205 f.

26. *Histoire de mon temps* of 1746, *Publik. aus den K. preuss. Staatsarchiven,* IV, 299; version of 1775, *Oeuvres,* II, 22 f.; cf. also Madsack, p. 82 n.

to act accordingly.[27] His handling of the administration of justice
(at least in regard to its subjective intentions) has a flavor, not only
of a utilitarian, but even of an ethical approach; and this was all
the more true of his policy of tolerance. There is even (as has been
correctly observed) a certain element of the American and French
views on human rights in both of them.[28] In the weaker type of
state, threatened by inner dissension, which had existed in the
period of the Renaissance and Counter-Reformation, intolerance
had been a matter of *raison d'état*. But in the more secure military
state of the eighteenth century this principle had become old-
fashioned. State interest no longer needed to use religious unity of
the subjects as a guarantee of their obedience. It could now to a
certain extent release the burden, withdraw from this province
and leave it to develop in its own way. In general, as the state
grew more powerful, it was able to become more liberal and
moral, though certainly only in that province where its power was
now completely dominant, that is to say within its own frontiers.
But wherever its power was still insecure and threatened by in-
calculable oppositions, namely in the sphere of foreign interests,
Frederick was bound to recognize the validity of harsher and
cruder laws.

The very instrument of these interests, namely the armed forces,
was subject to this constraining power. The Frederician army was
created and trained for combat by methods that were in many
ways barbaric. And so far as one can see, Frederick never reckoned
this barbarism in his military affairs to be a problem worth considering; and he never attempted to introduce more ethical and
humane principles into the underlying ideas. In individual instances he was certainly capable of being humane and ethical toward his soldiers; he was even capable of trying, by means of
decrees, to restrict any ill-treatment of them. But the structure of
the army itself remained unaffected by this. He did not let the
light of his humanity penetrate to this obscure basis of state power.
Here he was caught himself in the dark naïveté of the man of

27. *La dissimulation devient réprouvable, quand le fort s'en sert envers le
faible, le prince envers le sujet. Polit. Testament* of 1768, p. 219.
28. Hintze, p. 54.

action. The barbaric elements in his military matters (most of all, the practice of enlisting the scum of society at the foreign recruiting depots) were so intimately and inseparably bound up with the whole closely calculated system of his policy for population, finance, and economics, that the entire edifice would have seemed to him in danger of destruction if he had so much as moved one stone from the foundations.

But the sphere of foreign policy seemed to him, and indeed was, more fluid and flexible. Here there was no question of a rigid institution to which a man of the Enlightenment could shut his eyes. On the contrary, one was concerned here with a daily business of acting and taking decisions; with a mode of action which, though it was conditioned by what lay outside, was nevertheless determined by what lay within; and in short with the sphere in which, at every other moment, a compromise had to be reached between freedom and necessity. In this sphere the requirements of morality and the claim of the philosophy of the Enlightenment to pass a critical judgment on the real world made themselves heard in an imperious manner. And Frederick struggled earnestly, and from time to time passionately, to find an answer to the obscure questions which were forced upon him here by his vocation.

He began (as we have seen) as a political practitioner of power interest, but the philosophical point of view was close behind. The two approaches are entwined in the most remarkable manner in the *Considérations* of 1738. In order to strengthen the threatened hereditary claims of his house to Jülich-Berg, he wanted to influence by means of a pamphlet those powers whose support was now important for Prussia, notably Bavaria and most of all the maritime powers; indeed even France, which was attacked by him in the book, might perhaps in the end (once he had disclaimed the publication) be influenced by it in some roundabout manner. A peculiar concealed ambition revealed itself in the allusions to the great future opportunity for important undertakings, an opportunity which would certainly arise after the death of the Emperor Charles VI. But from the very outset he fashioned his very deliberate and shrewdly calculated observations into a philosophy, which at once demanded to be accepted for its causal and not its ethical value. The most important point for our general argument is that Frederick linked together in this book the stimulating ideas he had received from Montesquieu's *Considérations sur les causes de la grandeur des Romains et de leur décadence* (which had appeared in 1734)[29] with the traditions of the doctrine of interest. It is not so much a question of whether he knew any of the writings on this subject dealt with by us, and if so which;[30] for their basic ideas were common property among the diplomatic chancelleries of Europe. In any case we recognize the familiar atmosphere when in the very introduction we read about the "true interests of the kingdom" and the "fixed principles" of the courts which have to be investigated under the cloak of diplomatic representation. And all the optimism of the philosophy of the Enlightenment, directed here toward the matter of causation, was now elevated into a grandiose claim: namely, that with its help the "transcending spirit" of a historical politician would be capable of explaining the mechanism of political history, of demonstrating the unbroken chain of cause and effect stretching down from the most remote centuries, and finally of predicting the future. "It is a matter of wisdom to be able to know everything, to judge everything, and to foresee everything."[31]

Characteristic words, full of the exaggeration of youth, but also rich with meaning! For suddenly there comes to life here (something which was brought to fruition by Montesquieu's energetic application of the method of causal analysis)[32] an understanding of the immense value of the doctrine of state interests to the knowledge of history, and for the significance of these veins running through history; but at the same time he also began to perceive a much closer and more intimate connection between uni-

29. Demonstrated by M. Posner, *Die Montesquieunoten Friedrichs II, Histor. Zeitschr.,* 47, 253 ff. Cf. also Koser, 5th ed., I, 148, and Küntzel in the *Festgabe für F. v. Bezold* (1921), pp. 234 ff.

30. Regarding this, *vide infra.*

31. *Oeuvres,* VIII, 3 f. He thereby anticipated the watchword of Positivism: *Savoir pour prévoir et prévoir pour pourvoir.*

32. Cf. Montesquieu, *De la grandeur des Romains,* etc., Chap. 18: *Ce n'est pas la fortune qui domine le monde . . . il y a des causes générales, soit morales, soit physiques, qui agissent dans chaque monarchie. . . . En un mot, l'allure principale entraîne avec elle tous les accidents particuliers.*

versal history and day-to-day politics than he had been conscious
of hitherto. In Frederick's hands, the boldly hoped-for insight into
the laws of world history and the history of states was bound to
become, first and foremost, a means directed toward his political
ends. And one fundamental tendency of his political thought and
desires revealed itself forcefully and imperiously: namely, that of
predicting the future, of calculating the probable course of events
as a whole, and of blending what he thereby arrived at, together
with the whole content of his experience, into a system, within the
closed framework of which his action then to a great extent remained confined. Later on, as a natural reaction due to his skeptical turn of mind, he frequently enough recognized drastically the
fallibility and questionable character of such predictions; and he
cautiously restricted his innate tendency to set in motion important long-term plans based on such calculations, at any rate in the
much too fluid sphere of foreign policy.[33] But this inclination to
divine and guide the future by means of intellectual power—and
that meant also the rationalizing of irrational things—is revealed
by the famous *Rêveries politiques* and *Projets chimériques* in his
Political Testaments. For even politics (so he says there)[34] has
its metaphysics; and the politician must be permitted, just as much
as the philosopher, to disport himself in this field and to recognize
goals which, veiled in the deepest mystery, would be capable of
guiding subsequent generations.

So once again the spirit of contemporary philosophy flowed into
the bed of the old national and historical forces and tendencies.
A new sense for empiricism and causality had already arisen in
the seventeenth century, and (as we have seen) it had perceptibly
aided Rohan's doctrine of interest. The progress made by science,
in giving a mechanical explanation of the connections existing in
nature, had promoted the tendency to look for laws exerting a

33. This has been correctly observed by Volz, *Die auswärtige Politik
Friedrichs d. Gr., Deutsche Rundschau,* September 1921, but he failed to
notice Frederick's natural inclination which he himself was holding in check
here.

34. P. 59; cf. also *ibid.,* p. 36: *Un politique ne doit jamais dire: Je n'ai pas
cru que telle ou telle chose arrivât; son métier est de tout prévoir et d'être
préparé à tout.*

mechanical influence in history too. The Enlightenment, filled with pride and self-consciousness, and referring everything to the Universal, now introduced into these attempts a joyous forward impulse, confident of making an important advance in knowledge. And henceforth all knowledge (this being an essential part of the strongly utilitarian philosophy of the Enlightenment) ought to serve the interests of life and practical affairs. Here, for instance, are the words of the young Frederick in the *Considérations* which he inserted into an investigation of the important new successes of French policy:[35]

"There is no better means of arriving at a correct and precise idea of events happening in the world than that of comparing them, choosing examples from history, placing them alongside the events happening today, and then observing the relations and similarities between them. Nothing is worthier of human reason; nothing is more instructive or more calculated to increase the sum of our knowledge." For the human reason was the same in every country and every century; only that the degree of the constantly recurring and similar passions was capable of being completely different in the different epochs. But in general, in the history of states, like causes and like effects were necessarily bound to recur.

This was also the teaching of Montesquieu;[36] Machiavelli too had thought so, only he was (as it were) like an early pioneer, laboring with difficulty. But now one trod these paths quite easily and on wings. And so, as an appendix to this line of thought, Frederick now added quite boldly and with certainty the judgment that: "The policy of the great monarchies has always been the same. Their fundamental principle has constantly been to grasp at everything in order to increase their territory continually; and their wisdom has consisted in forestalling the tricks of their enemies, and playing the subtler game."

The constant principle of rulers to increase their territory was in practice certainly subject to countless variations, according to the

35. "Considérations sur l'état présent du corps politique de l'Europe," *Oeuvres*, VIII, 18 f.

36. *De la grandeur des Romains,* Chap. 1: *Comme les hommes ont eu dans tous les temps les mêmes passions, les occasions qui produisent les grands changements sont différentes, mais les causes sont toujours les mêmes.*

situation of the states, the power of one's neighbors, and the state of affairs; but the principle itself was unalterable and rulers never departed from it. "It is a question of their ostensible glory; in a word, they *must* increase in size." [37]

Here there was an exact agreement between the universalism of the Enlightenment, trying hastily to explain everything, and the bitter naturalism of Machiavelli; for both drew on reality and experience. But the Enlightenment was not only hasty in explaining things, but also hasty in judging and condemning them. The little phrase about ostensible glory (*prétendue gloire*), interspersed in a ruthlessly naturalistic line of thought, strikes one as a note from a different, a quite different register. For what did the humanitarian department of the Enlightenment say to this crude conclusion reached by its causality department? Here one sees the complete helplessness and powerlessness of one with regard to the other. For it creates an almost comic effect when Frederick, at the close of the *Considérations*,[38] sheds the ceremonial dress of the politician and slips on the mantle of the philosopher and then, pointing to the permanent principles of state life which he has established and which rest on the iron law of causality and the iron constancy of events, brands them morally as "false principles." Now he admonished rulers to leave the path they had strayed into, where their subjects became the instrument of their improper passions, and return to the true path of the princely calling and live for the happiness of their subjects. "Their high position is only the work of the people," who had chosen from among themselves the person they considered most suitable to rule them in a paternal manner. Only one step further and he would have gone on, from this fundamental recognition of the sovereignty of the people, to reach Rousseau's revolutionary ideas. But often in history the final consequences of ideas can only be drawn when life is ready for the whole series. The vital power of personal interest, not consciously felt, but nevertheless self-evident, prevented him from taking this step. He could scarcely saw off the branch that bore him. But his verdict on the power politics of rulers now stood out

37. *Oeuvres*, VIII, 15.
38. *Ibid.*, p. 25 f.

as inconsistent and undefended on either flank—open to Machiavelli's naturalism just as much as to Rousseau's ethical radicalism based on natural rights. Never again, so far as we can see, are Frederick's humanitarian idea of the state and his idea of the power state so naïvely superimposed one on the other within the same intellectual sphere.

And he did also have some idea of the contradiction involved. Mindful of the Prussian interest in making sure of the Jülich-Berg inheritance (which was the thing that had caused him to take up his pen), he closed his book with the words: "It is a shame and a humiliation to lose parts of one's territory; and it is an act of injustice and criminal robbery to conquer lands to which one has no legitimate right." Thus he considered that power politics was only permissible and necessary when based on *droit légitime,* and not on *droit de bienséance;* this was the compromise by which he extricated himself from his dilemma. And it is interesting to see what pledges he sought for the preservation of this limitation. The ruler ought to rule personally himself, and ought to watch personally over the machinations of his neighbor-states, prepare for them shrewdly and wisely, and restrain the activity of greedy and restless spirits by making good alliances. It was the practice of blindly surrendering affairs to ministers that he considered was the chief reason for the excesses of power politics.[39] And altogether was not the very nature of his whole grandly conceived enterprise—that of ennobling and reforming the idea of the power state by means of the humanitarian idea—was it not one that demanded the intense concentration and most acute watchfulness of a unified will? For completely new paths had to be trodden here, paths which were not yet a familiar part of the routine of the ordinary type of minister. And with an intense and passionate desire he wanted to serve both at the same time, not only the peaceful happiness of his people, but also the power and glory of his state. It was only himself alone that he trusted to find the narrow path on the razor's edge that made both possible.

39. Concerning the probable actual occasion for these conclusions, cf. my essay on the *Considérations, Hist. Zeitschr.,* 117, 56, n. 2.

It was then that the decision to *gouverner par lui-même*[40] was taken, and afterward carried through right to the end of his life with an iron consistency. From the very moment when he began to rule himself this resolve was strengthened and hardened by the special situation of his state, whose needy natural resources could only be maintained in a sound and healthy condition by means of a quite deliberate economy. Such decisions usually proceed in the first place from the pressure of real conditions, and only afterwards succeed in acquiring an ideal sanctity. But when the young crown prince, against the wishes of his father's negligent ministers, wanted to seize the helm himself, this was an event that also partook of a great idealistic conception. He was hoping to unite interest and idea in a masterly manner. Out of the bitter experiences undergone by Prussia after 1735 (owing to the unscrupulous Machiavellian statecraft pursued by the Great Powers) and out of the humanitarian ideals conceived at this very time, there grew up in 1739 his *Antimachiavell*, stemming from interest and idea simultaneously. For the contradiction between interest and idea, which had destroyed for him the inner connectedness of his *Considérations*, left him no peace. Now this contradiction would be removed altogether from the world; the wicked Machiavelli would be finally banished from the world—and from his own spirit. For who could fail to perceive that here he had arranged a secret dialogue with himself, and with the passionate impulses inside him.

He wanted to defend himself securely against himself. He was undoubtedly thinking about himself when (in the *Avant-propos* of his book) he spoke of the young ambitious man, whose personality and powers of judgment were not yet fixed, and in whose hands Machiavelli's dangerous book might be capable of causing the very greatest harm. Moreover, since he detected the criticism which the modern public imbued with the Enlightenment were making about the practice of the courts,[41] he also wanted to offer a general de-

40. Regarding this, cf. also *Réfutation, Oeuvres*, VIII, 272 f.
41. Cf. *Réfutation*, p. 282, and P. Wittichen, *Machiavelli und Antimachiavelli, Preuss. Jahrbücher*, 119, 489; one of the few useful observations in an essay that is otherwise entirely superficial and erroneous.

fense of the princely calling; and he wanted to show that an enlightened and moral ruler could still be a practical ruler, and that
his "true interest" was in harmony with virtue.[42] Whereas in the
Considérations he had mixed a large dose of Machiavellian politics
with a small dose of moral antidote, in the *Antimachiavell* he mixed
a large dose of moral principles with a considerable reservation on
the part of the sober realistic politician. For the very reason that he
thought he could see in Machiavelli a diabolical caricature of what
he himself was practicing, it was possible for a righteous anger to
blaze up in him; and so he was bound to feel obliged to attack
him with the strongest ethical weapons his period could offer.

The unhistorical method used in this coming-to-terms with the
greatest political thinker of the Renaissance has often enough been
remarked on. People still felt themselves to be, as it were, on a level
with past events; and they tended rather to consider the eternal
significance of these events than to ask themselves what the importance of these events was in the period when they occurred.
Frederick only knew Machiavelli's *Principe,* and even that only in
a French translation of 1696.[43] Whether the *Discorsi* would have
brought him to take a more favorable view of Machiavelli is certainly doubtful; for even they contained much of the poison which
he abhorred, and by the contrast of their republican patriotism they
might perhaps have aroused all the more his anger at the lack of
character shown by Machiavelli in the *Principe.*[44]

But the unhistorical element in Frederick's method must be distinguished more precisely. Frederick was very well aware of the

42. Letter to Voltaire, May 16, 1739, Koser and H. Droysen, *Briefwechsel Friedrichs d. Gr. mit Voltaire,* I, 271.
43. Cf. *Oeuvres,* VIII, xiv, and v. Sommerfeld, *Die äussere Entstehungsge-schichte des Antimachiavell Friedrichs d. Gr., Forsch. zur brand. u. preuss. Geschichte,* 29, 459.
44. A few years earlier, the Leipzig Professor Johann Friedrich Christ, relying essentially on the *Discorsi,* had undertaken to cleanse the image of Machiavelli from the reproach of immorality, and to prove that he was a moderate monarchomach, a pioneer of political freedom (*De N. Machiavello libri tres,* 1731). This book, which attempted to save the honor of Machiavelli and was undertaken with considerable talent and understanding for the in-tellectual greatness of Machiavelli (even if also with inadequate resources), was apparently unknown to Frederick, and in any case, owing to its scholarly Latin form, he would have been unable to enjoy it.

different times and political relationships amongst which Machiavelli lived, for he believed that progress in culture and morality had been made since then, and he looked upon Machiavelli's century as being in a condition of barbarism which had since been happily overcome. He realized that Machiavelli had only written for the small rulers, the *principini* of Italy; that at that time there had still not existed any *miles perpetuus* under strict discipline, but that on the contrary there was nothing much more than a mere rabble composed of bandits; that therefore Machiavelli's warnings about the unreliability of auxiliaries were a result of the times—as also that his warnings against the rebelliousness of subjects could no longer be considered valid with reference to the profound tranquillity of present-day peoples. Machiavelli's whole world, he had to admit, was hardly recognizable today.[45] But this was an essential weakness in the contemporary conception of history—the fact that, while it did indeed study (and with an intensive interest) the changes in the external world, it was only superficially and in the most general terms that it considered the changes in the inner world, the real modes of thought pursued by men. And even the simple consideration, that the completely different external relationships of that time might perhaps demand from men a different type of action, was for the most part left out of account. For, in the opinion of the Enlightenment, the Moral Individual now passed as having an absolute importance which could justifiably be considered as valid for every period. It was from these sources that the misunderstandings of Frederick arose which we must now illustrate by means of a few examples.

Frederick was judging from the point of view of the well-ordered conditions of a state which had already begun to become a constitutional state in the modern sense. Machiavelli's state on the other hand was still at the stage of a crude authoritarianism, both from above and below; and it had enough to do to try and create for itself a reservoir of power which was universally respected, and not respected solely out of pure fear. Cesar Borgia's conduct (as recounted by Machiavelli) toward his representative in the Romagna, Ramiro d'Orco, who had become hated by the people, offers an

45. *Oeuvres*, VIII, 175, 206, 215, 222, 243.

example of this. He caused him to be executed in a horrible manner which simultaneously satisfied and dumbfounded the people. A state of law and order was thereby restored, and the subjects were won over to it by brutal illegal means. But Frederick's comment was: What right had the arch-murderer Borgia to punish this guilty criminal, who was indeed nothing but a copy of himself in miniature? [46] He was unwilling to admit to himself that even in this instance a ghastly kind of *raison d'état* was at work, and was struggling up out of the darkness into the light.

But most of all the special mode of thought pursued by Machiavelli and his period was unintelligible to Frederick. The eighteenth century had become too abstract to understand properly the more concrete concepts of the sixteenth century. There was need first for a synthesis between the conceptual mode of thought and the art of sympathetically understanding the life of others—the kind of synthesis which the historicism of the nineteenth century succeeded in creating—before one could come anywhere near understanding it. The eighteenth century was now engaged in creating general concepts and broad ideals, such as humanity, virtue, justice, the general welfare, the spirit of nations. It accepted these without any concrete content, and enthused over them. Whereas the ethic of Machiavelli's period held much more firmly, in cases where it made use of the same words, to their concrete content and their application in individual instances. The objects it had in mind were more limited, but at the same time more plainly visible; and it still had fewer expressions applicable to the higher types of universal entity. Take a proposition such as the following one, used by Frederick in opposition to Machiavelli: "Today everything is subordinated to the cause of justice, and the strength and military capability of a conqueror are hateful if they bring misfortune upon the human race." [47] In Renaissance times such a statement would scarcely have been possible, not only by reason of its content, but also on account of its intellectual approach. Moreover when Machiavelli was thinking of something universal—and he certainly did so to a very great extent

46. *Ibid.*, p. 192.
47. *Ibid.*, p. 170.

—he always preferred to express it by means of living comprehensible examples. His thought was also suffused by the spirit of the artistic advances of his day, whereas at the same time the greatness, beauty, and charm of this art are founded on the special mentality of that period. But this was how it came about that Machiavelli's conceptual language—useless if one judges it by abstract logical terms, but splendid if one feels it in an individual manner—was no longer intelligible to Frederick. When, in the *Principe,* Machiavelli wanted to suggest his supreme aims, directed toward the complete regeneration of his fallen fatherland, he could find no better means than to refer to the sublime examples of Moses, Cyrus, Theseus, and Romulus. The young Frederick took this to be mere *mauvaise foi.*[48]

Even those general concepts and ideals which Machiavelli certainly made use of were generally still rooted firmly in the soil of concrete fact. Out of the sensuous element of reality, full of contradiction and mingled with filth, there struggled up in him the higher element, still completely interwound with all that was lower. Nature and spirit were still so closely connected in him that even what was spiritual in him seemed to be a natural force. Most of all, this was true (as we saw earlier on) of his concept of *virtù.* How completely different—purer certainly, but also emptier—was the Enlightenment's conception of *vertu* which Frederick professed. It was, first and foremost, an ideal, a command, something that ought to exist. Machiavelli's *virtù* was a force, something that existed. As an ideal, *vertu* was eternal and timeless; Machiavelli's *virtù* was something earthly, but certainly also something which, with an obscure longing, he felt and believed to be imperishable in humanity. But he caused it to wander from nation to nation, vanishing here and then blazing up there. Virtue perishes, he said, when the opportunity to implement it is lacking. This criminal, Frederick commented on this, talks about virtue, and yet only means by it the skill of a rogue, who needs a favorable moment to demonstrate it.[49]

48. *Ibid.,* p. 185.
49. *Ibid.,* p. 188.

It is quite curious and remarkable that Machiavelli's strictly inductive and empirical method, which refused to let itself be blinded by any illusions about "that which ought to exist," made so little impression on Frederick, who even as a young man already had in him the basis of his future sober sense of reality. Frederick even reproached Machiavelli with it. Why, he asked,[50] does he begin by describing the differences between monarchical states, instead of going back to the original source of things and investigating the origin of royal power and the reasons which could have caused men to subordinate themselves to a master. In his actions Frederick was at that time an empiricist and a realist, but in his thought he was influenced by the universalism of the Enlightenment, and he never fully got over this duality. And since the causal, just as much as the ethical, thought of the Enlightenment was dominated by this abstract universalism, he had no attention to spare for modern man's strongly felt desire for causal analysis, which was already breaking through in the naked empiricism of Machiavelli. So it came about that the latter seemed to him paltry and of secondary importance. Swept up by the Enlightenment toward the highest principles, he conceived man as he ought to be according to the ideal of humanity; and he demanded of the ruler that he should even look upon true glory as being simply "a puff of smoke," and he became angered by the bestial element in man, which in the case of Machiavelli appeared to be very closely interwoven with his *virtù*. He was even wounded by Machiavelli's remark: "Whoever believes that good actions on the part of great rulers will cause their old evil deeds to be forgotten, is only deceiving himself." [51]

All this has to be said in order to make it possible to understand why the forceful political basis of truth in Machiavelli's *Principe,* the discovery of the element of necessity in political conduct (and this is nothing else, succinctly expressed, than the essence of *raison d'état*), remained invisible to the very ruler in whom this *raison d'état* was due to find its most complete embodiment. He certainly realized very well that Machiavelli was trying to demonstrate the

50. *Ibid.,* p. 167.
51. *Ibid.,* p. 194. In the process however (misled by the translation) he confused *personnaggi grandi* with *grands hommes.*

existence of this kind of coercive force which could serve as a great general all-explaining principle in the political sphere. "Everything is achieved by interest in Machiavelli, just as whirlwinds signify everything in Descartes." [52] Interest was his sole god, his demon. But in Machiavelli this interest was clothed in too unfamiliar and too dirty a dress for him to be able to recognize it. The unfamiliarity of the conceptual language and the crudity of the period which enveloped it, we have already assessed. But there were two other things that made it distasteful to him in the form in which Machiavelli presented it. First, that in Machiavelli there still seemed to be no distinction between the interest of the ruler and that of the state. It could not very well have been otherwise, because the modern state in Italy developed out of the *stato,* the power apparatus of the ruler, and because the specifically dynastic interest here seemed to be particularly sharp and egotistical where one was not concerned with old and hallowed dynasties, but with new ones that had arisen by usurpation. And secondly, it was only the interest of small rulers and states, not great ones, which Machiavelli seemed to be expressing in his *Principe,* and for which he seemed to be claiming dominion over all moral values. But from the very beginning Frederick had despised the small princely states,[53] because he thought in an undynastic manner and purely along the lines of the state itself. And what he saw of the small states in Germany could only strengthen this disdain in him. At the very least, he held it to be a fundamental rule of all politics that large and small states had to be treated according to very different rules. All his life he was really only interested in the relations and vital conditions of large states.

At the same time there was also a link joining him to Machiavelli —not to the instructor of the *principini,* with all the limitations of his period, but rather to the timeless advocate of the idea of the power state. And there was also another invisible link between Frederick's humanitarian idea and his idea of the power state. Only a large state could promote the happiness of humanity on a grand scale. And he even said in the *Antimachiavell,* that today only im-

52. *Ibid.,* p. 168; cf. also pp. 181, 232, 241.
53. Cf. *ibid.,* pp. 209, 222, 235 f.

portant rulers were capable of making war! [54] In the first instance,
he considered this to be based only on material and technical causes.
But, once the fact had been recognized, he found himself forced
back again further into the sphere of considerations of power politics, a sphere which he had already handled with great skill in the
Considérations. And if, in the *Antimachiavell,* he tried to narrow
this sphere as much as possible, he still had no intention whatsoever
of following in the footsteps of the Abbé St. Pierre and of banish-
ing it from the world altogether.

One almost has the impression that, during the course of working on his book, it brought him once again more strongly under
its spell. The word *intérêt,* which at the beginning is used chiefly as
a term of contempt for the petty egoism of Machiavelli's *principini,*
often reappears in the later chapters in a good sense, as applied to
truly national and universal interests.[55] This reminds one of the
fact that Frederick's ethics in general, both then and later, derived
virtue from interest, from a properly controlled and correctly understood self-love.[56] His own moral conduct came to extend beyond
this somewhat exiguous foundation, but his sensualist theory un-
mistakably created a new link with Machiavellism. Moreover at the
beginning of the book the important and difficult concept of "necessity" also appears, as the "evil necessity" of political action, the concept that had formerly produced Machiavelli's doctrines; then in
the later parts of the book he uses it more frequently.[57] He distinguished between the conqueror "from necessity" and the conqueror
by temperament, and conceded true glory to the former, if he
made use of his talents to maintain true justice. He compared him
with surgeons, who by means of their "barbaric" operations save
men from a danger that threatens them. In short, he sought for and
desired "just grounds" for war and power politics.

This was the old doctrine of the *bellum justum* and the compromise between ethics and *raison d'état,* with which he had reassured

54. *Ibid.,* p. 210.
55. Cf. *ibid.* with the passages quoted above (in the *Antimachiavell*), pp.
266, 274, 275, 291, 297.
56. Zeller, pp. 70 ff. *"Le principe primitif de la vertu est l'intérêt,"* to
Voltaire, December 25, 1737, Koser and Droysen, I, 120.
57. *Antimachiavell, Oeuvres,* VIII, 172, 249, 295, 297.

himself in the *Considérations*. He had in view his own future
conduct when he spoke of the glory of that type of ruler who
"maintained by means of firmness, wisdom, and the warlike virtues
those rights, which someone wishes to wrest from him by injustice
and usurpation." [58] For (so he argued, with a sense of reality unaffected by any ideal of the Enlightenment) kings were not judged
by any tribunals that were capable of deciding their differences,
their rights, and the importance of their claims. And it was not only
in the case of conflicting claims of right or (as was self-evident) for
the defense of one's own country that he considered it permissible
and just to draw the sword. The importance of the European balance of power was capable, in his opinion, of justifying even offensive wars: "preventive wars, if an overpowering increase in the
strongest European powers threatens to overflow and swallow up
the whole universe." He expressly recognized the maxim that *prae-
venire* was better than *praeveniri*. "Great men have always done
well, when they made use of their power before their enemies
reached a position where they could tie their hands and destroy
their power." [59]

And how did it stand with the central problem of Machiavellian
politics, the doctrine that treaties were only to be kept just so long
as they served the interests of the state? Frederick asserted that this
was indeed basically a bad and villainous policy, "for one only has
to make one deception of this kind, and one loses the confidence
of every ruler." And yet he felt himself obliged to add (impelled
by an obscure and strong premonition of coming events) that unfortunate situations of necessity (*nécessités fâcheuses*) did occur, in
which a ruler was forced to break treaties and alliances. In any
case, this had to be done in a proper manner; the ruler must immediately inform his allies, and it was only permissible for him to
do it "if the safety of his people and a very great necessity obliged

58. *Ibid.*, p. 218.
59. *Ibid.*, pp. 296 and 139. On the basis of v. Sommerfeld's assertions in
Forsch. z. brand. u. preuss. Gesch., 29, 468, it was already seen to be highly
probable that the more subtle grasp of the doctrine of the preventive war
in the Voltairean version of the *Antimachiavell* did not proceed from
Voltaire (as is assumed by Heydmann, *Histor. Vierteljahrschr.*, 1922, 70),
but on the contrary was produced by Frederick himself.

him to." [60] This was the first attempt (and in the young Frederick
it seems a surprisingly naïve and useless attempt) to solve this
problem which was to occupy him through his entire life. All the
different answers to it which he gave both now and later were
swings of the pendulum between Machiavellism and Antimachia-
vellism, between the ideals of the Enlightenment and the reality of
the power state. With a genuine naïveté the author of the *Antimachiavell* even expressed that very dualism which was already
inherent in the life of the state itself: namely, that while the inner
part of him was already striving toward the constitutional state
with its moral associations, the external part of him was still tied
to the natural laws of the struggle for existence. When he came to
speak of choosing servants for the state, he noted without contradiction the practice of wise rulers in making use of respectable
characters for the internal administration, but using the more lively
and fiery personalities for diplomatic dealings; for in this latter
sphere, where it was necessary to use intrigue *and often corruption
too,* skill and spirit were obviously more useful than uprightness.[61]
He certainly also acknowledged similar principles later, in his
Political Testaments;[62] but there they have the appearance of cautious maxims of experience, as if he were taking a severely wide
view, whereas in the *Antimachiavell* on the contrary they seem like
a separate element adrift among thought-processes which are really
of an entirely different character.

But this did succeed in marring the basic idea of the book, which
was to demonstrate the possibility of meeting the demands of morality over the whole sphere of state life. His program, which was
to act as wisely as a serpent and as innocently as a dove,[63] was one
that he did not dare, even in theory, to carry out completely.

60. *Oeuvres,* VIII, 248 f; cf. 208, 282, 292, 297. In 1735 he had already
written to Grumbkow: *Conserver son honneur et s'il le faut, ne tromper
qu'une fois de ses jours, et cela dans une occasion des plus pressantes, c'est
la fin et le grand art de la politique.* Koser, *Briefwechsel Friedrichs d. Gr.
mit Grumbkow und Maupertuis,* p. 124; cf. also p. 121.

61. *Ibid.,* p. 274.

62. *Polit. Testamente,* pp. 54 ff. and 216 ff.

63. *Oeuvres,* VIII, 246: "The world is a game of cards, where cheats and
honest players are sitting side by side. A ruler must get to know the tricks
of the cheats, not in order to use them himself, but in order not to be duped
by them." So too on *ibid.,* p. 294.

In the last resort, the difference between him and Machiavelli was thereby weakened from one of principle to one of degree; so that the measure of cunning and deception which had flourished during the Renaissance was greatly lessened by the more civilized and morally sensitive spirit of the eighteenth century, but not entirely removed. This danger inherent in his point of view, by which the tiger of Machiavellism could be changed into a pleasant domestic cat, was apparently not fully appreciated by Frederick at that time.

Nevertheless Machiavelli also offered a whole series of rules of statecraft which were morally unobjectionable and which Frederick found altogether illuminating. His advice to the prince, to rule personally, to act as his own commander in the field, to accommodate himself to the situation, to despise flatterers, to ascertain the secret intentions of other rulers, and so forth, entirely coincided with his own ideas and certainly helped to bring his political thought to fruition at that time.[64]

Thus the *Antimachiavell* as a whole, taken together with the *Considérations,* reveals in its symbolism the interplay of two streams of quite a different color, that of a constraining destiny and that of his own inner inclination, both forced to flow in the same bed, where they gradually have to accommodate themselves to one another.

Frederick was soon to experience that the man of action may be led beyond the boundaries which the man of thought has set up for himself. If one were to take his move to conquer Silesia, to the *"rendez-vous* with glory," the territorial claims which he presented to Maria Theresa, the attitude he took up toward his allies at the conclusion of the Convention of Kleinschnellendorf and the two Peaces of Breslau and Dresden, and if one were to measure these by the standards which he himself laid down at the close of the *Considérations* and in the *Antimachiavell,* then a number of objections could be raised. It is true that he was entirely convinced of the justice of his claim to the greater part of Silesia. But was it really this conviction of right that actually determined his decision?

64. Cf. Zeller, p. 94 f., and Madsack, pp. 99 ff.

Was it not much more the knowledge that (as he himself expressed it) this acquisition was also "very useful to the House of Brandenburg"? [65] It must be admitted that here Frederick—as in all other instances where he relied upon the "rights" of his house, which derived from inheritances, privileges, and so forth—was making use of parts of that dynastic and territorial system which he had really banished from his mind, and which his own idea of the state had left behind.[66] He was giving himself moral reassurance by invoking these "rights" and (in accordance with the practice of the time) was using them to cover up the motive which really impelled him and which he himself described as *droit de bienséance*. The complicated legal question had not been studied by him with any care when he began the enterprise. This (as he remarked on November 7, 1740) was the concern of ministers: it is time to work on the matter secretly, for the troops have been given their orders. This was the commanding voice of *raison d'état*. Henceforth it ran right through his whole political correspondence. If one had nothing but this correspondence, then one would know very little about that other world of his spirit or about the cleavages and contradictions of his inner will. Once he had taken his place by the humming loom of politics his hand was guided by nothing else but the power interest of his state and the heroic ambition of protecting it. And yet, on drawing breath for the first time after the chaos of the First Silesian War, he wrote to his friends on June 18, 1742, from the camp at Kuttenberg: "You might cure all the ills of war, but I tell you candidly that you will not have achieved anything, if you can-

---

65. *Polit. Correspondenz*, I, 90. In the first version of the *Histoire de mon temps* of 1743 (of which only fragments remain) it says: *L'ambition, l'intérêt, le désir de faire parler de moi l'emportèrent, et la guerre fut résolue.* H. Droysen, *Beitr. zu einer Bibliographie der prosaischen Schriften Friedrichs d. Gr.*, II, 30. Cf. also Koser, 5th ed., I, 253. In the *Histoire de la guerre de sept ans (Oeuvres,* IV, 25) it says later: *Quand les souverains veulent en venir à une rupture, ce n'est pas la matière du manifeste qui les arrête; ils prennent leur parti, ils font la guerre, et ils laissent à quelque jurisconsultelaborieux le soin de les justifier.* Cf. also *Oeuvres*, IX, 81 f.

66. This has already been suggested by Fechner, *Friedrichs d. Gr. Theorie der auswärtigen Politik, Programm des Breslauer Johannisgymnasiums*, 1876, pp. 11 ff.

not banish two frightful things from this world—interest and ambition." [67]

Here, as so often happened with him, a passionate feeling broke through the phraseology of the Enlightenment. As a functionary of the Prussian state interest, he felt himself bound, and perhaps even really carried away, by the demonic spirit that drove him on. For this demon was certainly dualistic itself, and signified not only something quite objective and material, not only the need for life on the part of his state, but also something subjective and personal —ambition, the desire for glory, and pleasure in power—in fact all the things which as a philosopher and a man of intellect he was obliged to condemn, and had indeed condemned so violently in Machiavelli. Now he was forced to perceive that the man of action loses his conscience. It remained true at the same time that "interest" was a living force, in which clean and unclean constituents were blended together; and that all attempts to purify it, though not indeed quite ineffectual, can never be crowned with complete success. A residue of human and egotistical motives is left in everything, even the most matter-of-fact state conduct.

Frederick was indeed obliged to express this realization rather differently, in accordance with the thought of his period and his own personality. Honest with himself and a "born enemy of lies," [68] he found no other way of expressing it than by giving himself up to the moment, and (exactly as he had done in the *Considérations* and *Antimachiavell* when he was crown prince) surveyed his own conduct now from this, now from that point of view of his divergent world of ideas. This was how it was in the Confessions of 1742 and 1743, in a letter to Jordan of June 15, 1742, and in the *Avant-propos* written a year later for the first printing of the *Histoire de mon temps*.[69] The first Confession was intended for con-

67. To Jordan, *Oeuvres*, XVII, 229; and also to Voltaire, June 18, 1742; Koser and Droysen, II, 130. Many similar observations in Fechner, pp. 20 ff. Cf. also Paul-Dubois, *Frédéric le Grand d'après sa correspondance politique*, p. 134.
68. *Réfutation, Oeuvres,* VIII, 277.
69. *Oeuvres*, XVII, 226, and especially Küntzel, *Polit. Testamente der Hohenzollern*, II, 85.

temporaries, in order to justify himself for having left his French ally in the lurch, when he made the separate Peace of Breslau. The second was intended for posterity, and therefore expressed his inner duality in a manner that was more direct and less obscured by arbitrary prejudice. The first went further along the lines of the *Antimachiavell*, but in a more mature and practical way. I am vindicated (he more or less says here) by the necessities of the situation, in which I am bound to fear that at the first failure I shall be forsaken by the most powerful of my allies, and by continuing the war I shall lose my conquests and plunge my people into ruin. And for the first time he distinguished sharply between the ethic of the private individual and the duty of the ruler, which was to subordinate his personal advantage to the welfare of the community—"he must sacrifice himself." At the same time, with his simile of the gambler hastily retiring from play after making a big win, he certainly revealed that his own conduct actually partook of other more natural motives.

But is it really possible to separate in his conduct the motives of sacrificial feelings for state morality on the one hand, and the ordinary shrewdness of a gambler on the other? They coalesced to form that obscure constraining force of political action which is chiefly nourished by the elemental impulses of self-preservation, the strongest roots of *raison d'état*. The solution here was that one had to choose between being the hammer or the anvil. If I refrain from duping others, then I shall be duped by my ally who is physically superior to me and will have no compunction about ill-treating me —this was the strongest of the considerations that impelled him to conclude the Convention of Kleinschnellendorf and the separate Peace of Breslau. We need not consider now whether his actions then, when measured by the standard of pure utility, were politically expedient and did not perhaps in some respects cut both ways; for we are concerned here with the essential nature of his *raison d'état*, and not with its direct results. But this resolve of Frederick's —to behave in a Machiavellian world in a Machiavellian manner himself—sprang forth complete and instantaneously under the hammer-blows of this world, like Minerva from the head of Zeus.

Soyons donc fourbes, he wrote to his minister Podewils,[70] with a real contempt for this world that forced him to act in this way, and yet also with a bitter decisiveness.

And this was also how he wanted at that time to be viewed by posterity. "I hope," he wrote in the *Avant-propos* to the *Histoire de mon temps* of 1743, "that the posterity I am writing for will distinguish the philosopher in me from the ruler, and the respectable man from the politician. I must confess that it is very hard to maintain purity and uprightness if one is caught up in the great political maelstrom of Europe. One sees oneself continually in danger of being betrayed by one's allies, forsaken by one's friends, brought low by envy and jealousy; and ultimately one finds oneself obliged to choose between the terrible alternatives of sacrificing one's people or one's word of honor.

"Of all states, from the smallest to the biggest, one can safely say that the fundamental rule of government is the principle of extending their territories. This passion is as deeply rooted in every ministry as universal despotism is in the Vatican.

"The passions of rulers have no other curb but the limits of their power. Those are the fixed laws of European politics to which every politician submits. If a ruler were to tend his own interests less carefully than his neighbors, then the latter would only grow stronger; and it would leave him more virtuous but also weaker. . . . To tell the truth, treaties are only affirmations of deception and faithlessness." [71]

With this he returned to the naturalistic point of view of the *Considérations,* abandoned the attempt of the *Antimachiavell* (which had not been entirely consistent even then) to subordinate power politics to the ideals of the Enlightenment, and quite simply recognized the uncompromising duality of both worlds, the auton-

---

70. *S'il y a à gagner à être honnête homme, nous le serons, et s'il faut duper, soyons donc fourbes,* May 12, 1741. *Polit. Corresp.,* I, 245. Similar remarks at this period: *Trompez les trompeurs* and *Dupons les plutot que d'être dupe.* Cf. Koser, in the *Sitzungsberichte der Berliner Akademie,* 1908, p. 66.

71. Cf. also the proclamation to Podewils in the Hague, February 28, 1745, *Polit. Corresp.,* IV, 67 ff., and Koser in the *Histor. Zeitschr.,* 43, 97 ff.

omous character of power politics. With a sublime honesty he confessed himself guilty of the same things that he had condemned in the *Antimachiavell* with an indignation that was just as honest. The sun of the Enlightenment—as he was now obliged to admit to himself—had not yet succeeded in overcoming the night of barbarism in politics. He now said (though not with any excess of confidence) that it would be able to sooner or later. He remarked with an undertone of resignation, and as a man who wishes rather than believes: "One *must* believe that a more enlightened time will one day come, when *bonne foi* will receive the glory to which it is entitled." The actual historical presages on which he based this hope (of which he made a duty) were confined to the perfectly correct, but not very important observation that such crude and obvious methods of power politics as had been customary in earlier periods would today arouse fierce indignation among civilized contemporaries.

The same youthful radicalism suffuses the writings of the period when he was crown prince, and the *Avant-propos* of 1743. The latter also contained the remembered trepidation of the first war full of disturbing decisions and changing circumstances. This mental disturbance led to an extreme ruthlessness of confession. Precisely through this he now also revealed that he had no thought whatsoever of withdrawing from the moral world. Its laws were valid for him more widely, not only in this one sphere which seemed to him to be separated from it by an unbridgeable gulf. And because he felt and wanted to act in a moral manner on a wider basis, the sentiments underlying the *Antimachiavell* were also capable of blazing up in him again from time to time.[72] But, in spite of the very deliberate and reflective manner in which he later came to treat once more the question of keeping treaties, his fundamental position with respect to the phenomenon of power politics never altered. It was, and henceforth remained for him, something unalterably elemental and natural, which from a practical point of view left one no other course but to howl with the wolves. In his Political Testament of 1752, he even broke expressly

72. Cf. with this *Oeuvres*, XV, 138 (1760), and XXIV, 322 (Letter to the Electoral Princess of Saxony, May 29, 1779).

with the fundamental thesis of the *Antimachiavell*.[73] Machiavelli says that a disinterested power which finds itself in the middle of ambitious powers will be bound to come to grief sooner or later. This has troubled me, but I am bound to confess that Machiavelli is right." And sixteen years later, after his great struggles for power and existence were ended, he advised his successor: "Keep it firmly fixed in your mind, that there is no great ruler who does not cherish the idea of extending his dominion." [74]

His words of 1752 were of course followed by the further statement: "Rulers must of necessity possess ambition, but this ambition must be wise, moderate, and enlightened by reason." One may perhaps discern here a certain ethical tendency; but in the main it was intended more as a rationalization of power politics than as an attempt to make it ethical. It was not the Reason of the eighteenth century (which he professed as a philosopher) that he was thinking of here, so much as the "Goddess Reason" whom Richelieu had already raised to the place of mistress of politics[75] and who really signified nothing else but the principle of the highest expediency. Frederick had entered upon the First Silesian War with the ambition of joining battle with the masters of cabinet politics, and playing a more skillful game than any of them. This shows itself chiefly in the complications of the very different lines of thought which led him to conclude the Convention of Kleinschnellendorf in 1742 with the Austrians and thereby free the House of Austria from serious danger. But this very Convention and the two separate Peaces of Breslau and Dresden had also weakened his political credit as a reliable ally. They produced the very result which Frederick himself, in the *Antimachiavell,* had already predicted as a probable consequence of breaking treaties. Frederick inferred from this that the method of breaking treaties must only be used very sparingly and with extreme caution. In the two *Avant-propos* to the *Histoire de mon temps* of 1743 and 1746 (quite bluntly in

73. *Die politischen Testamente*, p. 59.
74. *Ibid.*, p. 200. Cf. also his remark to the Electoral Princess of Saxony, December 2, 1763; *La jurisprudence des souverains est ordinairement le droit du plus fort. Oeuvres*, XXIV, 56.
75. Meinecke discusses Richelieu's concept of reason in politics on page 167 of *Machiavellism.* [ed.]

the first, and somewhat more moderately in the second) he had been content to justify breach of agreement in general as an indispensable method of statecraft; whereas in later discussions of the question, in the Political Testaments of 1752 and 1768, and in the *Avant-propos* to the third edition of the *Histoire* in 1775, he had striven hard to limit this dangerous method and to restrict its use to definite cases of necessity. He was rather like a doctor, who to begin with had made use unthinkingly of a certain remedy, and then, being taken aback by its two-edged effects, would only continue using it afterward subject to definite precautions and reservations.

"It is only permissible," he remarked in 1752,[76] "to break treaties for important reasons. You may be led to do it, if you fear that your allies will conclude a separate peace of their own, and if you have the time and means to anticipate them; or if lack of money prevents you from continuing the war; or finally if important advantages are to be derived from it. But strokes of this kind can only be made once, or at the most twice, in one's life; they are not remedies to which one can have recourse every day."

"It is a very important question," he said in 1768,[77] "that of deciding when it is permissible to carry out a so-called great *coup d'état*—I am watering down the expression. I really mean when it is permissible to deceive others. Those who consider this legitimate base their opinion on the view that, since one had only made one's agreements with knaves and scoundrels, it is permissible to pay them in their own coin. But others believe that scoundrels do in fact discredit themselves, and that even Cardinal Mazarin made a serious political mistake by playing the rogue in small matters as well as in great. In my opinion, one ought to depart as little as possible from fair dealing. When one sees that another ruler has left the path of Right, then one is undoubtedly justified in serving him in the same way; and if there are cases where it is excusable to neglect one's obligations, then those are cases where the safety or greater welfare of the state demand it."

76. *Die politischen Testamente,* p. 76.
77. *Ibid.,* p. 212.

And finally, in 1775:[78] "The rulers must always be guided by the interest of the state. The instances in which alliances may be broken are the following: (1) If one's ally neglects his obligations, or (2) If he is thinking of deceiving you, and you have no course but to forestall him; (3) If you are obliged by *force majeure* to break your treaties, and finally, (4) Lack of means to continue the war —for accursed money influences everything in a fatal manner. Rulers are the slaves of their resources, the interest of the state is their law, and this law may not be infringed."

For the moment we need not consider the gradual but significant variations and increasingly subtle modifications in this casuistical reasoning. It has been said,[79] that to a certain extent Frederick finally returned here to the point of view of the *Antimachiavell;* that in the last resort he believed the wisest course was to recognize the validity of moral obligations in principle, but to lay down certain exceptions based on necessity. Certainly in these three later discussions of the subject, in contrast to the almost completely naturalistic approach of the *Avant-propos* of 1743, there is a re-appearance of the moral demand that loyalty to treaties should basically and in general be maintained, but in a different context and on different grounds. In the *Antimachiavell* the moral demand arose from a broad moral basis; and even the limiting reservation of necessity, which the politically versed heir to the throne cautiously included, was still provided with a marvellous and very unpractical moral garment to cover its nakedness. But the three discussions of the subject in 1752, 1768, and 1775 were based on grounds of state utility. The moral requirement to abide by treaties is recognized as a basic rule because it is wise and expedient, and because *raison d'état* itself demands it. In the *Avant-propos* of 1743, the philosopher and the politician in him had resignedly parted company and gone their own ways. Now the politician could offer the philosopher his hand once again, and assure him that his own reasoned needs would keep him in the vicinity of the philosopher;

78. *Oeuvres, II,* xxv–xxvi. Cf. also Meusel, *Friedrich d. Gr. als historisch-polit. Schriftsteller, Preuss. Jahrbücher,* 120, 505.
79. Hintze, 32, 26; cf. also Meusel, 512.

and that he would be only too glad to remain there, but that he would have to leave at once if *force majeure* or a greater advantage for the state should call him over to the terrain of Machiavelli.

If one compares once again the three stages in the development of his doctrines of treaty faith and treaty breach, then one certainly sees that they are governed by something of Hegel's dialectical law. Each of the earlier stages is "neutralized" in the following one; that is to say, it is not overcome but continues to operate, and the third stage (though not, by any means, simply returning to the first) does however approach it once more, impelled by the forces of the second stage itself. But the pleasant feeling of having at last reached a harmonious sense of "for itself" in the idea will not be produced; for even here the old conflict between morality and power politics seems only to have been solved in a superficial and utilitarian way, and not really solved.

There is however one other line of development in the different discussions of the matter by Frederick which we have reproduced; this is a line which up to now we have left on one side, but we must now bring it forward in the hope that it will help us to penetrate to the inner sphere of the problem. In this line of development too there is a compromise between the elements of power and of the Enlightenment, of the ideal and the elemental; and they seem to be in such close contact with one another that it is here that one generally thinks to find the point of harmonious union in Frederick's world of ideas—that point of union which seems to be within reach at every stage of Frederick's development. He did indeed always try to find a more profound basis for breach of treaty than that of the merely naturalistic motive that it was necessary to howl with the wolves. In the *Antimachiavell,* besides the indeterminately obscure, but forceful concept of a "very great necessity," which would justify the ruler in breaking treaties, he also emphasized a regard for the "safety of his peoples" which might oblige him to do so. In 1742, after the deed was accomplished, he cried: "Ought I to plunge my people into misery?" The basic principle, which he now laid down, that the ruler "was obliged to sacrifice" himself and his private ethics for the sake of

his people, was interwoven with the otherwise entirely naturalistic
Avant-propos of 1743, and was given a calm and basic discussion
in the second *Avant-propos* of 1746. A private individual, it says
here, must keep his word under all circumstances, "for honor
comes before self-interest. But a ruler who binds himself under
an obligation does not bind himself alone, otherwise he would
be in the situation of a private individual. It is much more true
that he exposes great states and great provinces to a thousand
dangers of misfortune. It is therefore better that he breaks his
agreement, than that his people should perish." [80] He attempted
to make this evident by means of an image he had already used
in the *Antimachiavell*:[81] Would a surgeon not seem to be acting
in a laughably scrupulous way if he thought of hesitating about
cutting off the gangrened arm of a man? In the *Avant-propos*
to the *Histoire de mon temps* of 1775, which was carefully re-
fashioned and adapted to his more mature mood, he did indeed
omit this crude comparison, but he repeated the question: "Is it
better that the nation should perish, or that the ruler should break
his agreement?" The ruler must "sacrifice his person for the safety
of his subjects." [82]

Curiously enough, no one has so far taken into account the fact
that these formulations bear a tinge which is specifically humanitarian and characteristic of the Enlightenment, nor has anyone
considered the critical questions arising out of this. The purpose
of the state, as laid down by the Enlightenment and conceived by
it in the spirit of individualism—that of promoting the human
happiness of its subjects—was indeed utilized in this respect to
justify a serious breach of individual ethics. Thus, the thesis which
had to be proved and the foundation on which the proof rested
each sprang from heterogeneous spheres. Was this not capable of
destroying the internal validity of the argument? In other words,
taking everything as a whole, was it really possible to prove the

---

80. *Histoire* of 1746, *Publikationen aus den K. preuss. Staatsarchiven,* IV,
155.
81. *Oeuvres,* VIII, 172.
82. *Oeuvres,* II, xxvi f.

breaking of treaties—that keystone of pure and absolute power policy and *raison d'état*—was an indispensable means for securing the human happiness of one's subjects? And particularly, moreover, when restricted to those rare instances of emergency which Frederick was from time to time concerned with working out?

In many instances this was certainly possible. The conclusion of a separate peace, made possible by breaking a treaty, such as those of Breslau and Dresden, certainly spared one's own subjects further war losses and untold miseries—though in these and similar cases it would always remain doubtful whether it actually was this humanitarian motive that gave the first impulse toward the decision to break the treaty. Moreover Frederick was able to plead (and in fact frequently did plead)[83] that power policy, by virtue of the fact that it ensured the territorial stability of the state, did also ensure the physical means for making the subjects happy. "If the ruler loses certain provinces, he is no longer in the same position as before to help his subjects." This was also felt very strongly and personally by Frederick, who in domestic affairs was trying to carry on a patriarchal policy of welfare. Indeed, humanitarian motives could even become valid as a reason for acquiring new provinces which were indispensable for the material well-being of the state as a whole. But, in the process, was that pressing necessity always paramount—that necessity which ought always to exist as a *conditio sine qua non* of any breach of treaty? Was it not possible (if the humanitarian motive were really being given the preference) for the provinces that were being threatened or claimed to live just as peacefully and happily under the rule of a different scepter? To a pure representative of the Enlightenment it ought to be a matter of complete indifference which state this or that province belonged to, inasmuch as he would be concerned solely with the welfare of his subjects. Thus in his *Antimachiavell* Frederick had conceded throughout that it was not permissible to base the acquisition at least of new provinces on humanitarian aims. "The new conquests of a ruler do not make the states already in his possession either more opulent or more rich; his peoples do

83. *Essai sur les formes de gouvernement, Oeuvres,* IX, 200; *Lettres sur l'amour de la patrie* (1779), *Oeuvres,* IX, 221.

not profit in any way from these conquests." [84] One might well have asked him whether his old original provinces and his Silesia could not have flourished just as well under Saxon and Austrian rule. As a great ruler, it would have been permissible for him to deny the suggestion with all the force of historical truth. But as a thinker who had at his disposal only the intellectual methods of his own time, he would have been placed in an embarrassing position. In 1793 Fichte, whose political beginnings belonged entirely to the Enlightenment, demanded sarcastically whether it was of such great importance to the German artist or the German peasant, that in future the artist and peasant from Alsace and Lorraine should find his city and his village listed in geographical textbooks under the heading of the German Empire. In short, the individualistic and essentially unpolitical ethic of the Enlightenment was of no use whatsoever for the purpose for which Frederick sought to use it when he based the *raison d'état* of breach of treaty (and hence also power policy, as a whole) on the welfare and happiness of the subjects. At least, it was only by introducing inconsistencies that they could be made usable for this purpose. Their real implication was toward the pacificism of St. Pierre.

It is therefore noteworthy that Frederick himself, in his later remarks on the subject of breaking treaties, in addition to the mode of expression still current from the Enlightenment—the mode that spoke of the happiness of the people and of the subjects as the supreme value—also found another different, better, and more meaningful expression for what he felt so strongly. Now indeed it was simply the state itself that appeared in places where he would hitherto have spoken of the peoples or the subjects. "The safety and greater good of the *state*" demands (so says the Testament of 1768) "that treaties should be broken under certain circumstances." The *Avant-propos* of 1775 has an even sharper ring. "The interest of the *state*," it says in the opening of the passage

---

84. *Ibid.*, VIII, 171. This idea, which was characteristic of the Enlightenment, that lawful territorial claims could not by themselves constitute a morally justifiable motive for war (since it in no way affected the happiness of the subjects whether they belonged to one ruler or another) was in fact very widespread at the time. Cf. de Lavie, *Des Corps politiques,* 1766, II, 136.

concerning treaty breach, "must serve as a rule for those who are governing. . . . This law is sacred." Thus was discovered the only possible basis that was capable of justifying both the right to break a treaty, in case of need, and power policy. The state, as an individual living entity, was able to claim the right, in order to preserve itself in a case of emergency, to make use of measures which were condemned by the ethic which applied to the separate individual. The state, moreover, was something different from what the Enlightenment had understood by "people" and "subjects." At this time it still stood (and this again was different from the position it held in the nineteenth century) beside and above the people; but nor was it any longer the mere power apparatus of a dynasty, on the contrary it was a great living unity which, even if it had been created by dynastic means, had grown up above it. Once again we must recall the characteristic fact that Frederick had very largely eliminated the dynastic idea from the conception of the vocation of a ruler. From the very outset he instinctively felt himself to be the instrument of a higher greatness. In the *Antimachiavell* he still called himself the "first servant (*domestique*) of his peoples";[85] later there also appeared the phrase "first servant of the state." [86] At first sight the earlier draft may strike one as being more modern and national in tone than the second; but in fact, as we now see, it was not. For this "people" was nothing more than population; it did not yet stand for any real people or nation; as a concept it was not yet felt in any individual or historical manner, but on the contrary only as being purely humanitarian and rationalist. This very transition from "people" to "state" in Frederick's mode of thinking and expressing himself

85. In Voltaire's second edition of the *Antimachiavell* this was changed to *magistrat*. Cf. Heydemann, *Friedrichs d. Gr. Antimachiavell, Histor. Vierteljahrschr.*, 1922, p. 66. It is possible (see p. 131, n. 7) that Voltaire did not make this alteration on his own authority, but that on the contrary it was based on one of Frederick's own manuscripts.

86. This was first, in 1747, *premier serviteur et premier magistrat de l'Etat* (*Oeuvres*, I, 123); in 1752 it was *premier serviteur de l'Etat* (*Polit. Testamente*, p. 38); in 1757 *premier ministre* (*du peuple*) (*Oeuvres*, XXVII, part 3, 279); in 1766 *premier magistrat de la nation* (*Oeuvres*, XXIV, 109); in 1777 *premier serviteur de l'Etat* (*Oeuvres*, IX, 197 and 208). Cf. Zeller, p. 241 f.

does indicate a movement in the direction of modern thought, and also toward the modern national state. It represents a movement toward modern thought, because it led on to a recognition of one of those great vital unities which were no longer capable of being conceived in a rationalist manner but had to be grasped historically: the ability to understand such unities is one of the chief characteristics of the modern mind. On the other hand it represents a movement toward the modern state, because it was Frederick's state that first created the fixed and definite form within which it was possible for a mere population to become welded together into a real people and nation with its own vital will.

The Enlightenment's ideal of humanity had grown up as the ideal of the rational individual, which looked upon the reason inherent in the individual as universally valid; it embraced the whole world universally with this reason, and was consequently incapable of understanding completely the historical and political intermediate power of the state entity, and was only able in practice to let it operate and pass as valid. It was this that gave rise to the former harsh dualism in Frederick between the philosopher and the ruler. But life and experience taught him more and more to recognize the state as a pre-eminent and constraining vital force, a collective entity which not only guided the ruler but also conditioned and embraced the happiness of the subjects, of the people. It was life and experience, rather than rational thought, that led him on in this way to the threshold of the nineteenth century. His discernment sprang from the innermost essence of *raison d'état* itself, from a sense of what was necessary.[87]

87. Compare Ranke's fine remark (*Werke*, 29, 154): "His opinions themselves, deeply rooted as they were in him, were nevertheless not the pure outcome of his own reflection; they were at the same time necessitated by the situation he was in of being threatened from all sides, by the need for action which was *immediately necessary*."—Dock, *Der Souveranitätsbegriff von Bodin bis zu Friedrich d. Gr.* (1897), spoke of him in tones that were much too modern, when he wrote (p. 142): "Frederick the Great was the first to grasp the idea of the personification of the state, and consequently also that of state sovereignty." Cf. on the other hand Heller, *Hegel und der nationale Machtstaatsgedanke in Deutschland* (1921), p. 165, who correctly points out that a monarch had seldom advocated so forcefully, both in word and deed, the doctrine of the sovereignty of the ruler. The curious thing

The transition from "people" to "state" thus signified the transition from a humanitarian and moral ideology of power policy to that other historical and political ideology of power policy which afterward came to be developed chiefly in nineteenth-century Germany. But together with it, as we have observed, the former humanitarian ideology still remained alive in Frederick right up to the end of his life. We have come to know well enough the shortcomings and discrepancies in this ideology. But one must not on this account overlook the historical force and significance that it bore. This ideology was very far from succeeding in making the state completely moral, but it did succeed in giving it a very much more moral tenor than hitherto. The victory of Machiavelli over Anti-Machiavelli in the political thought and conduct of the king, which we have had to depict, was only one aspect of the historical process. There was also another aspect in which Anti-Machiavelli triumphed over Machiavelli. For Prussia did not become a pure power state; on the contrary, owing to Frederick it was also put on the road to being a civilized and constitutional state. Henceforth it harbored within itself both Machiavelli and Anti-Machiavelli.

The warmth of feeling which in his later years he was anxious to introduce into the concept of the "Fatherland" [88] shows how he himself was also emotionally inclined toward that which his will had created. The marble statue, which his *raison d'état* had fashioned, began to come alive.

But serious problems resulted for the Prussian state, and later for the German nation, on account of this dualism between Machiavelli and Anti-Machiavelli, which Frederick had implanted there. And if previously we declared that an appeal to the interest of the "state" constituted the only possible basis for the right to break treaties in case of need, then we must now add that even this did not lead on to a complete harmony that was ultimately satisfying to the human mind; on the contrary, it led on to conflicts and deep abysses.

about Frederick however is that he does indeed already have a vital perception of the personality of the state, but that, in spite of looking on himself merely as an instrument of the state, he nevertheless holds fast to the sovereignty of the ruler.

88. *Lettres sur l'amour de la patrie* (1779), *Oeuvres,* IX, 213 ff.

PART THREE

Frederick and the Enlightenment

WILHELM DILTHEY

Frederick and the Academy

ANY SERIOUS STUDENT of the history of Frederick will realize again and again that there is something that makes it difficult to understand and describe this life, yet that also accounts for the fascination of such an attempt. This life, even less than others, cannot be reduced to a simple formula; behind Frederick's every act and utterance, there is the whole complex and mercurial personality we have come to know. At every turn, various aspects

From "Friedrich der Grosse und die deutsche Aufklärung," in *Studien zur Geschichte des deutschen Geistes,* Vol. III of *Gesammelte Schriften,* by Wilhelm Dilthey. Leipzig: B. G. Teubner, 1927. Translation copyright © 1972 by Peter Paret.

crystallize or else dissolve in rapid change: his eagerness to enjoy
life in pleasant company, in conversation, music, reading, and his
own literary endeavors, and the consciousness that the state demands the sacrifice of the prince; the ambition of the commander-
in-chief who yearns for military glory, and the philosopher-king
who wants to make his people happy and further the progress of
mankind; the cult of friendship and friendly association with literary figures on a footing of equality, and the imperious self-assurance in the solitary heights of genius and absolute power; yielding to momentary impulses to the point of abandon, and heroic
courage in the face of adversity which has parallels and examples
only in the classic days of Rome. It was these dichotomies which
filled . . . all who approached this personality with enthusiastic
admiration, attracted them, yet also kept them at a distance and
even repelled them; something in this personality always remained
enigmatic and awe-inspiring. The Seven Years' War almost destroyed this richness; after that time everything threatened to become colorless, hard, centered upon reason, duty, and renunciation.

This constant interplay of the many facets of Frederick's attitude
must be kept in mind if we are to follow the steps he took in order
to make his capital and court the center of the intellectual culture
which he desired. The new *Académie des sciences et belles-lettres,*
which was to be the successor of Leibniz's near-defunct foundation,
was a leading factor in these endeavors. It was on behalf of the
Academy that the king and his agents negotiated with scholars
and writers who were to be attracted to Berlin; and all who came
were assigned a place in it. This fact constitutes a natural framework for the present study. It is certain that, from the very beginning, the Academy was a powerful, independent ingredient of
Frederick's cultural policy. Even as crown prince he had repeatedly
mentioned it in his correspondence with Voltaire, and it was one
of his first official acts as king to ask for a report on the state of
the old society and to begin its reorganization. In his day, the new
intellectual movement considered the Academy the organizational
framework *par excellence* for the propagation of a new human
civilization. Furthermore, it was part of the brilliant image of a

monarchy in the style of Louis XIV which Frederick always strove to emulate. Nonetheless, the king expected those whom he appointed to do more than fill their positions in the Academy usefully and properly. He also counted on them for his other organizational plans and purposes, such as his *Académie des nobles* and the constantly growing number of institutes serving the technical needs of the economy and the bureaucracy. He was keenly aware that he must bring the greatest increase of intellectual resources to his nation and his state. The first step, therefore, was to win such persons; how to make use of them could be left to experience and circumstances. Intellectual greatness in itself attracted him. He sought to attach it to himself wherever he encountered it. Nor did his respect for such greatness falter when it was manifested in areas with which he was personally unfamiliar. He might make fun of people who could think only in terms of numbers and curves, but he let them go their own way, confident that even such rivulets would eventually join the great stream of the intellectual and moral progress of mankind. He appointed the mathematician Euler and the logician Lambert, even though they lacked all the qualities that he personally appreciated in Maupertuis and d'Alembert. But then, who was safe from his mockery? After all, he did not except even himself. He only demanded one thing, and that was that every man know his craft, have the courage to stand by his convictions, and be too proud to stoop to sham and superstition. This freedom of the spirit was what he really sought in people. Whenever he found it in a person's entire bearing, in his talent of serenely accepting life with all its joys and sorrows, linked with the ability to give adequate expression to every thought and feeling in words, music, or color, he believed that this was the best mankind had to offer. It made him feel that he could tolerate mankind. This personal motivation, the yearning of his own spirit for a freer, happier, more beautiful world, was always an element in his other plans on behalf of the state, the nation, and mankind; and we should not attempt to separate feelings and ideas that are fundamentally one. And it matters little whether Voltaire, Maupertuis, Lamettrie, d'Alembert, and others came or not, whether they kept their promises or not—the many facets of this unique man were made to shine and sparkle by his association and correspondence with them.

In short, the history of the new Academy is first of all a history of Frederick, of his plans and experiments for a new cultural policy, as well as of his personality. It was a role that had been played in the original academy by the universal philosopher Leibniz who founded it. The history of such an organization also illustrates the significance of those great intellects who at the same time direct the life of their nation.

II

Great institutions which mankind has formed for its common ends have an indestructible vitality that permits them to adapt to changing circumstances. Even when the fundamental laws of such an institution have proven inadequate, even if certain aspects of its purpose have become obsolete, its roots, reaching down to these common ends, continue to live; its legal foundations, its financial means, and the manifold relationships in which it has become involved guarantee its continued existence. The function it has served in one cultural situation is replaced by a new one in keeping with new needs.

This is what happened with the Prussian Academy of Science. It could not even claim to have made any significant contributions in the forty years of its existence; but since it possessed the monopoly of publishing calendars in the Prussian state, it had continued to vegetate. Now began a new phase of its development, as it faced new tasks.

In the *Histoire de mon temps* Frederick wrote: "The progress of philosophy, political economy, the art of war, taste, and morals no doubt constitutes a more interesting field of study than the character of crowned madmen, charlatans wearing a tiara, and those second-rate kings called ministers, of whom but few deserve a place in history." In political life [he said], the same things happen over and over again, and only the actors change, while the discovery of new, hitherto unknown truths and the enlightenment of the mind should occupy the interest of all thinking men. This was the sum of the philosophy of history of the age. Guided by the power of reason, mankind will necessarily proceed from barbarism to refinement, tolerance, and autonomous morality. From this it follows that rational thinking is of absolute value, and that scholarly work is international in scope. Leibniz's aims had been more modest. He could only envisage scholarly endeavor in direct relations with other values of civilization; in fact, he almost lost sight of it in the multitude of practical tasks, especially when he sought to demonstrate the usefulness of scholarship to the state in his organizational proposals. For him, academies were always also technological institutions, in the widest and in the narrowest sense. For Frederick, the reign of reason and its propagation represented the highest good for the human race itself. He felt that by cultivating the arts and sciences, the state becomes the embodiment of values far beyond its own ephemeral existence and serves the absolute, highest end of human society. By performing this function moreover in a disinterested manner, the state will also stimulate man's highest faculty, namely the power of reasonable thinking, and thereby further its own ends. This is the general sense of Formey's preface to the first volume of the *Transactions of the New Academy* (1745)—the ideas and, in part, the very words of the king. A first change in the function of the Academy made at Frederick's behest was therefore the following: henceforth it was no longer to weigh or to justify its existence in terms of the use of its accomplishments for public utility, economic or technological progress. Every discovery was to be considered valuable in itself because of its inherent power to further the progress of reason. This was a new ideal for the Academy, and one that was pregnant with future developments.

For this reason, the work of the Academy had to be accessible to all civilized nations. In the past, this was accomplished by the use of Latin; now French had taken its place. It was the language of the courts and of diplomatic exchange and had become *the* international language. Thus the reasons which led Frederick to make French the official language of the Academy were primarily of a practical nature. Written in any other language, the transactions of the Berlin Academy simply would not have been read beyond the frontiers of Germany in the eighteenth century. Or, as Maupertuis put it: the use of Latin for the concepts of modern science would result in a strange and ridiculous jargon. It is only in French that one can discourse on every kind of subject in an exact and elegant fashion; the logical perfection of that language has given it universal currency. "For this reason, a monarch whose taste is the arbiter in such matters and who speaks and writes it with such elegance has prescribed it for his Academy."

Only a more detailed history of literary German will be able to ascertain accurately to what extent the dominant position of the French language in the middle of the last century—even further enhanced by Frederick and the Academy—wrought changes in the language and affected the style of a Lessing, a Mendelssohn, or a Wieland.

The third and most important change in the function of the Academy was proclaimed in its new title: *Académie des sciences et belles-lettres*. This expansion too had roots in the spirit of the French literature of the age. It followed from the new concept of the writer as represented by Voltaire, Diderot, and Frederick himself, which eventually found its true German embodiment in Lessing. Undoubtedly a decisive advance in the intellectual history of Germany was here taken under the auspices of French literature. The encompassing unity of literary endeavor, exemplified in its highest form by Schiller and Goethe in his later years, is the continuation of Voltaire's achievement for France. For the first time in Germany, Frederick's Academy gave expression to this unity: the Academy used literary form as a means for bringing together all of its work, from the most abstract scientific investigation to literary criticism and the exposition of philosophical ideas to the general public.

Frederick felt that the proper spokesmen for these new functions of the Academy were the French writers. This was the consequence of his ideas which we have already discussed, as well as of circumstances. If he sought the company of French courtiers and literary figures, it was the normal thing to do, and was also practiced at other courts. In addition, there was the intellectual influence of the French colony. At that time, it still constituted a considerable fraction of the population of the [Prussian] capital. But their energy, logical training, and eloquence—legacies of French Calvinism—even more than their number, made these descendants of the Huguenots an important factor in the life of Berlin. . . . The king also maintained personal relations with the spokesmen of the Enlightenment; he marched, as it were, in the ranks of that advancing European movement and had given it a new rallying point in the north. And if the modern writers' freedom of the pen were restricted in Paris, if life were to become difficult for them, all free minds could find asylum and a safe existence under the wings of his eagle. For such a purpose, the Academy offered itself as a natural gathering place. It was to be the stronghold of the Enlightenment; the king felt that it could rival the Paris academies, perhaps even surpass them. "I am really most obliged to Louis XIV," he wrote to d'Alembert, "for the Revocation of the Edict of Nantes; if his grandson were to follow this august example, I should be filled with gratitude; and especially if he should seize the opportunity of ridding his kingdom of the rabble of *philosophes,* I should be kindhearted enough to receive the exiles."

Here we still find the old opposition between the Catholic system which, ever since the days of Descartes, had demanded reverence for the pope and the Jesuits from every thinker, and the freedom of thought which was the basis of the Reformation and had motivated the Great Elector to grant the Huguenots asylum in his territories. Frederick meant to extend this freedom of thought to the entire range of intellectual heresy, without any restriction. If he brought Lamettrie to Berlin, it was in order to show the world that toleration was absolute in his state. It was not his fault that in this endeavor he usually had to make do with freethinkers of the lesser sort. He was engaged in a quiet, prolonged battle with France for that country's great writers. Strange as such an undertaking may seem to us today, it was the logical consequence of his deepest convictions in the philosophy of history, convictions which he shared with Voltaire. Not only abstract scholarship but literature as well is part of an exalted ideal whose values and norms dwell, as it were, above nationalities in the realm of pure

humanity and universality. The golden ages of Pericles and
Augustus, Lorenzo de' Medici and Louis XIV, though separated
by centuries, form a unity. Such golden ages appear when the
same pure and classical taste is transferred from one nation to
another; they are unified by virtue of the universally recognized
canons of genuine art. The forms of the various literary genres
are defined once and for all by firm laws and constitute an im-
mutable natural system. To these ideas Hamann and Herder were
later to oppose the distinctive characteristics of national literature,
springing from the inner vitality of a people.

III

In June 1740, the young king sent out the first invitations to
the scholars and writers who were to help him reform the
Academy. Not all those who were expected appeared. Among the
scientific celebrities, Vaucanson of Paris and s'Gravesande of
Leyden declined. But Euler, the greatest mathematician of his day,
was persuaded, and for the next twenty-five years he was, as it
were, the backbone of the mathematic-scientific section of the
Academy. Among the writers in the grand manner, Voltaire was
waiting in the wings, even though, for the moment, he did not
want to leave "the divine Emily." A poor and temporary replacement was found in the Italian windbag Algarotti. He came and
proved a disappointment. The king was especially anxious to offer
a position to Christian Wolff. Seventeen years earlier, his father's
brutal hatred for the new philosophy had driven Wolff, the most
influential of the German thinkers of the time, from Halle.
Frederick owed his first acquaintance with the philosophy of the
century to Wolff's writings, and he was determined to make
amends to him. At the same time he hoped to use his extraordinary,
if somewhat pedantic, teaching ability for the benefit of the
Academy: ". . . our Academy must not be for ostentation, but for
learning." Therefore "qualified men from outside should lecture
on all aspects of philosophy, so that young noblemen and others
can have solid instruction." Thus this Academy also might have
become a kind of modern university for the ruling classes of the

country; but the project for such an unusual expansion of its activities was eventually dropped. Wolff, for his part, would rather be "professor generis humani" (as he proudly put it) at Halle than "académicien" at Berlin; especially since he soon discovered that a Newtonian, Maupertuis, was to be the head of the Academy and that French was to be its official language. This was the first instance in which the aspiring universities came into conflict with the academy.

Then, in September 1740, there was the memorable interview in which Frederick met Voltaire and Maupertuis for the first time. "Ever since my accession to the throne"—these were the words with which he had invited Maupertuis—"my heart and my tastes have inspired me with the desire to have you here, so that you might give the Academy of Berlin the tone you alone can give it. You have enlightened the world as to the shape of the earth; may you now teach a king how sweet it is to be with a man of your stature." Maupertuis had become world-famous following his expedition to Lapland, which empirically confirmed Newton's theoretical postulate concerning the oblateness of the earth. But even at this early stage, Maupertuis' overbearing attitude had already provoked opposition against him in the scientific milieu of Paris. He was therefore glad to accept the flattering invitation of the Solomon of the North. In this interview, the young king took an immediate liking to Maupertuis, which was to last all his life. "The most morose face I have ever seen," but Maupertuis was a man of complete integrity, and a thorough scholar of great intuitive powers whose conversation the king preferred to that of Voltaire in the long run. But what a meeting between Voltaire, who remembered certain vague, nebulous prospects for the presidency of the Academy, and Maupertuis, that personification of scholarly arrogance, who was assured of the president's chair— Maupertuis whenever he spoke of his polar expedition, took a tone that sounded "as if he had personally oblated the poles." Under these circumstances, Voltaire went back to his marquise and Maupertuis followed the king to Berlin. "When the two of us," Voltaire wrote, "left Cleve, you going to the right, and I to the left, I felt as if I were at the Last Judgment where God separates the elect from the damned. The divine Frederick said to you: 'Sit at my right hand in the paradise of Berlin,' but to me he said: 'Go, damned soul, to Holland!' "

Then the First Silesian War began, and Frederick had to deal with a "mathematics" that left him little time for other things. He tried to keep up the morale of Maupertuis, who had stayed behind in Berlin, with the most gracious messages. But in the long run, there was nothing he could do for this president without an academy. Maupertuis returned to Paris before the year 1741 was over. There he became director of the *Académie des sciences* and, a year later, he was chosen as one of the forty immortals upon the recommendation of Montesquieu. Frederick left things as they were, but the situation demanded action.

The circle of like-minded persons who had gathered more or less closely about the king had already become a power. Some of them had been members of the company at Rheinsberg; others had only awaited his accession to the throne to acknowledge their allegiance to the new master or to seek his service and his favor. Then there were the French literary men who had appeared, invited or uninvited, but always welcomed. There were also the reliable friends of the French colony, which had always had a personal attachment to the Reformed dynasty to which it owed its religious freedom. Above all, the example of the crown prince, now the young king, had formed or attracted a new type of officer, very different from the God-fearing and uncouth companions of Frederick William and his *Tabakkollegium*. The ideal of these men was Julius Caesar, who had combined military genius with the gifts of a statesman and writer; and they saw Frederick as a new embodiment of their ideal. Today they might command their battalions under his eyes on the parade ground or in battle; tomorrow they might speed to Paris, London, or Vienna on a diplomatic mission; they might also be called upon to reorganize some branch of the government or to settle some complicated question of administration; but they would always return to gather around their hero, whether it be to receive new orders or to share in happy sociability. Full of enthusiasm, they were open to everything that spoke of the mind or of beauty, and some of them were writers and artists in their own right. And they, rather than the other literary figures—even those who had achieved greatness—were Frederick's intimates, the companions of his life. He felt complete solidarity with them, loved them, celebrated them in his odes, and mourned when he lost them.

All of these elements needed an organization for their common intellectual pursuits. Field Marshal Samuel von Schmettau assumed leadership. One of the last representatives of that international officer-caste which had by now become rare in the Prussian army, he was also an *homme d'esprit*. Conversant with the new scientific and literary culture, he knew how to express it in the sparkling conversation the king loved so much. He found allies in the ranks of the old Academy itself headed by the newly appointed Euler. In the summer of 1743 the first steps were taken with the founding of a *Société littéraire*. It showed how quickly the new intellectual movement had found adherents in all milieus. Sixteen honorary and twenty regular members were brought together in a few short weeks. Among the former were important personalities of the court: Schmettau, the minister of state Kaspar Wilhelm von Borcke, one of the first German translators of Shakespeare, and three other ministers, as well as Gotter, Pöllnitz, Keyserlingk, Knobelsdorff, Finckenstein, Stille, Duhan de Jandun; among the latter, the regular members, ten members of the old Academy in addition to Frenchmen of the colony and of more recent immigration: the two Achards, Formey, d'Argens, Jordan, Francheville. The motive for this foundation was "The desire of some residents of Berlin who have a taste for science and literature to broaden their knowledge and to become more and more useful to the public," and its aim was "the cultivation of every interesting and useful aspect of the various branches of philosophy, mathematics, physics, natural history, political and literary history, as well as literary criticism." Such a program was narrower, and at the same time broader, than that of the old Academy. Philosophy was the most important subject, and literary history and criticism were included. On this occasion Francheville presented his project for a history of the arts, which he planned to write under the auspices of the Academy, and the Academy expressly stated its satisfaction with such a project. It was also consistent with the idea that the literature of the Enlightenment had brought about the unity of all intellectual endeavor that no division into sections was envisaged. The statute of this *Société littéraire* provided only for plenary sessions; these were to be used for lectures, discussions, and correspondence in easy informality.

The new club met regularly and pursued serious scholarly work. The session of October 8 was glorified by the presence of Voltaire who had come to Berlin for a few weeks in the autumn of 1743, but this time as a representative of France. This was a new role for that versatile man, and one the king took less seriously than his literary friend. But the old Academy also stayed alive; after all it was the representative of scholarship, chartered and financed by the state. For this reason, Schmettau and Euler were determined from the very beginning to do away with it. They applied for a merger of the two institutions, and the king, feeling that the right moment had come, agreed. A commission was appointed, a lengthy battle between the old and the new ensued, and, as usual in such cases, the result was a compromise. To be sure, the new "Royal Academy of Science" made certain concessions to the new ideas. It expressly excluded positive theology, jurisprudence, and medicine from its concerns and abolished the special German section of the old Academy by assigning its subject matter to the literary section. Furthermore, it no longer required the latter section to focus its interest on Oriental languages and Christian missionary activity. Above all, it instituted a completely new section, that of philosophy. Yet it by no means gave philosophy and history the central position they now claimed for themselves. Rather, it was felt that all work should be done within the sections, as in the past. In a general way, the sections preserved their autonomy. Thus the oligarchical character the governance of the Academy had assumed when Leibniz was supplanted remained unchanged; authority was placed into the hands of a *collegium* consisting of the vice-president, the directors of the sections, and four curators. How powerful the old ideas still were can also be seen from the fact that the statutes were once again written in German; and this language in its impurity, its prolixity, and its patriarchal, schoolmasterly tone, was still what it had been forty years before. Characteristically, French was only the third language authorized for use in publications, along with Latin and German.

This was not the academy Frederick had had in mind. When the new institution was inaugurated on January 24, 1744, the king's birthday, he did not attend. He was still hoping to persuade Maupertuis. Finally, the latter informed the king that he was willing to return to Berlin. The king received this news during the euphoria after his victory at Hohenfriedberg.[1] He replied enthusiastically, in the most charming and accommodating terms, which no one could employ as well as he when it came to dealing with such sensitive individuals: "You are making a great sacrifice for me; what can I do to compensate you for your country, your family, your friends?" Maupertuis did indeed come, and again it was the king's task to keep that difficult man in good spirits until the end of the war. This time, love came to his aid: Maupertuis became engaged to a lady of Prussian nobility. Frederick sent his compliments, not without the obligatory reference to the northern expedition: "May the same good fortune that smiled upon you during your scientific expeditions in Lapland be yours also in love. Urania and Newton are singing your wedding hymns."

As soon as the king returned from his campaign, work was begun. From the outset, Maupertuis insisted that for him the office of president be restored to the preeminence it had when Leibniz held that position: it was to be above all directors or curators. The king had no objection to this condition; it corresponded precisely to his own views. Then Maupertuis drafted a new set of rules—a model of brevity and precision. This constitution of the *Académie royale des sciences et belles-lettres* of May 10, 1746, placed the government of the Academy into the hands of its president, to be appointed by the sole authority of

1. On June 4, 1745, over the Austrians. This battle and the subsequent victories at Soor and Kesselsdorf decided the Second Silesian War. By the Treaty of Dresden, on December 24, 1745, Austria confirmed Prussia's possession of Silesia. [ed.]

the king. Indeed, Frederick did not feel that Maupertuis' demands
in this respect went far enough and added the proviso that nomina-
tions for salaried positions, which were also to be filled by the king,
should come not from the plenary assembly, but from the president alone. Thus the latter was virtually given the right to make
appointments; the Academy became an instrument in the hands of
the king and of the president who was in full agreement with his
views. This was also the time to abolish the sections once and for
all. Henceforth, they no longer had any independent field of
activity; they no longer held their own meetings, no longer were
a first forum for resolutions or elections, no longer even elected
their own directors. There were only plenary sessions, and they
were used for lectures, discussions, resolutions, and elections. This
innovation in the constitution is another indication of the character
of the Frederician Academy: it expressed the unity of its purpose
by tying together all of its various activities. And it was almost a
matter of course that henceforth all publications of the Academy
were to appear in French.

Maupertuis directed the Berlin Academy for a decade. His
addresses on ceremonial occasions show his complete agreement
with the views of the king. Now at last, the European reputation
of the new president made it possible to realize the program that
was dear to both of them. Maupertuis' solemn sense of the dignity
of scholarship, his very French, abstractly scientific pathos, his
Parisian familiarity with all that was necessary for presenting
scholarship in the most effective light soon conferred upon the
Academy the outward style and the distinguished forms which it
needed if it was to equal the two Parisian academies. The elite
of European scholarship now formed the core of its corresponding
membership. It was considered an honor to belong to it, and outstanding foreign scholars gladly offered to collaborate in its publications. But of course it was even more important to bring new
regular members of established reputation to Berlin. In this endeavor, the king gave a completely free hand to his president. To
be sure, the material means remained limited, so that many
desirable appointments could not be made. It was unfortunate,
especially for the strengthening of the German element in the

Academy, that two men declined, since, as rare exceptions among their compatriots, they represented that alliance of rigorous scholarship and elegant form which was the ideal pursued by Frederick and Maupertuis: they were Haller of Göttingen and Kästner of Leipzig. By this time, a new factor had to be reckoned with in negotiations with German scholars, and it proved as great an obstacle to the development of the German side of the Academy as Frederick's French predilections: it was that the German universities were becoming increasingly open to great European scholarship; Göttingen, in particular, set a shining example in this respect.

The scholarly prestige of the Academy now rested with the names of Euler and Maupertuis, Pott and Marggraf, Lieberkühn and Meckel. In the mathematical and scientific disciplines, in chemistry and anatomy, these men made the Berlin Academy the equal of any. The two other sections, philosophy and literature, which, according to the king's intentions, were to serve the purposes of the Academy directly, failed to achieve the same rank. Among its members only the German—Süssmilch—in the science of population, and the Swiss—Beguelin, Sulzer, and Merian—in philosophy, are still honorably remembered. Viewed from a historical perspective, however, even a Formey, a Francheville, and the numerous other French or partly French members of the Frederician Academy had their importance for Germany's intellectual development. The pleasing elegance of their conversation and their writings as well as the self-assured universality with which they applied deductive reasoning to all problems of life and scholarship contributed to the propagation of enlightened ideas and graceful literary forms in Germany. The characteristic intellectual atmosphere of the Prussian capital in particular goes back, to a large extent, to the time when Frederick and his Frenchmen set the tone of society.

Frederick was proud and happy to watch the rise of his Academy. He now liked to refer to himself as its protector, even its member, and had some of his papers and articles read in its sessions. That he never personally attended meetings had to do with his notions of royal dignity and solitude. As for his president, he continued to treat him with gracious consideration; but not even he was able to prevent the fiasco of the "pope of the Academy." Maupertuis' quarrel with König and with the terrible Voltaire, for whom the time of revenge had come, made his position untenable. Frederick had long suffered from Maupertuis' "extreme ambition, which was incommensurable with his genius" and from his brusque manner; he also felt that Maupertuis "made a spectacle of himself by his gigantic opinions." Now Frederick descended into the arena of the mathematicians and fought, chivalrously and daringly, just as he exposed himself in battle, to defend his friend and servant with his pen. It was no use. The story of that fiasco has often been told; the judgment of posterity in the great Maupertuis quarrel is now available to the public in Helmholtz's classic study, edited by Harnack.[2] In short, the reputation of the president was ruined. Furthermore, it is true that his precarious health suffered from the North German climate. So he left Berlin, originally for a year and then, in the summer of 1756, forever. Frederick's sympathetic, consoling, and amusing letters followed the incurably ill and broken man until he succumbed to his suffering in a foreign land.

IV

During the year in which Maupertuis took his last leave of absence, the Seven Years' War began. The Academy remained without a president, and Euler became caretaker. In the meager circumstances of this period of war, we find one strange piece of information. The Academy proposed nine non-Prussian members to the king, among them three Germans, one of whom was the greatest German writer of the age, Lessing. Frederick confirmed this appointment, but he was so dissatisfied that later when Gellert

2. Maupertuis' claim of having discovered the mathematical principle of least action was challenged by another member of the Academy, König, who asserted that a more accurate version of the theory could be found in Leibniz's unpublished writings. H. v. Helmholtz treated the background to the dispute in his essay "Über die Entdeckungsgeschichte der kleinsten Aktion," which A. Harnack printed as an appendix to his *Geschichte der Kgl. Preussischen Akademie zu Berlin*, 3 vols. (1900). [ed.]

and Lambert were proposed, he refused to confirm their elevation and autocratically assumed the right of appointment until a new president could be found.

After the Maupertuis disaster, the king began to think of d'Alembert and made discreet overtures. Now the Seven Years' War was over, and the Academy became again one of the king's important concerns. To d'Alembert's enthusiastic letter of felicitation, Frederick replied with a renewed invitation. D'Alembert spent three months at Sans Souci in the company of the king. They formed a friendly relationship which was to shed a quiet light over Frederick's later years.

D'Alembert was one of the leading figures in that mighty movement of the French genius which had crystallized around the Great Encyclopedia. He was a mathematician, but he was not like Euler, "that devil of a fellow" who loved to hunt in all the preserves of mathematics in order to test his prodigious analytical powers against all kinds of problems. D'Alembert, too, was adept at using the tool of mathematics for solving problems of physics; but the unique greatness of this thoroughly clear thinker showed itself in the elaboration of a new, positivistic basis of mechanics. D'Alembert was a philosopher, though not a *philosophe,* despite his solidarity with the Enlightenment in every other way. He occupied a special position among them, with his skeptical, superior smile. In the "Introduction to the Encyclopedia," he had laid the methodological foundation of empiricism, which became the cornerstone of the great science of the age. As his work attracted the attention of all of Europe, it also inspired Frederick with the desire to have him as president of his Academy. It is touching to see how the king took an active interest in the vicissitudes of that eventful literary life; how he granted d'Alembert a pension that permitted him a more independent life style when he was neglected in his own country; how he generously provided him with the means for traveling, thereby restoring his faltering health; how he cared for him like a father—and it was d'Alembert himself who felt moved to use this intimate word. There was in this care an element of gentle scheming, an attempt to use every favorable situation in order to win d'Alembert over. Sometimes there were discreet overtures and subtle hints, sometimes open and cordial proposals, or else vehement pressure and annoyance at the philosopher's consistent reticence, even scathing remarks, until at last the king resigned himself to mocking the geometer's inflexibility. A vivid impression of the king's graciousness toward his friend is found in d'Alembert's letters to Mademoiselle de l'Espinasse. They describe how, on one occasion, Frederick walked with him in the gardens of Sans Souci after a concert, picked a rose, and gave it to d'Alembert, saying that he "should like to give him something better" or how, ushering him into his library, he asked whether he "did not feel sorry for his poor orphans."

What was it that motivated d'Alembert's consistent refusal? After all, later he was perfectly willing to accept the post of perpetual secretary in both Parisian academies. The main objection he advanced against Frederick's brilliant offers, which assured him of a great position and seven times the income he had in Paris, was that he felt he could not give up the association with the circle of his friends in Paris. And this no doubt was largely true. Later, when Laplace was considering a move to Berlin, Lagrange advised him against it. It was, he said, a good place for a retiring, scholarly life, but one had to do without the stimulation of Parisian society and the pleasures of friendly association. And d'Alembert had a keen appreciation for the charms of this Parisian social life in which he was deeply involved ever since the editorship of the Encyclopedia had propelled him out of his quiet garret. Soon he found himself tied to that society by a new bond which changed his existence and was to become the tragedy of his life: his lasting attachment to Mademoiselle de l'Espinasse. But there were other and deeper reasons, which the philosopher did not mention to the king. The treatment Voltaire received toward the end at the hands of the king had never been forgotten in Paris. And even though d'Alembert was secretly awed by the demonic side of Voltaire, he took it to heart when the latter wrote to him: "Do not go to Luc, do not trust that beguiling exterior; even d'Argens could not get on with him for long"; whenever Voltaire took that scoffing tone—and he never failed to do so when the subject of d'Alembert's appointment was discussed—d'Alembert felt threatened in his love of freedom. "Do not fear," he wrote, "that I will be foolish enough to do such a thing, I am resolved never to serve any man, but to remain free, just as I was born free." Generous, warm, and touching though their amity was, d'Alembert never lost sight of the fact that Frederick was the king whose equal he felt himself to be in the autonomy of his thinking mind, but who was nonetheless separated from him by an insuperable barrier. He knew that a free person could candidly face Frederick and speak his mind, but never without an ultimate restraint, lest the imperious royal will suddenly come to the fore. There was something in d'Alembert's quiet, superior nature that led him to view all men from a certain distance. For him the king was an object to be observed; he studied him and wished to influence him, but he did not wish to be influenced himself. "No one should ever let d'Alembert know," he said of himself, "that he intends to guide him; he loves his freedom to the point of fanaticism, to such a degree, in fact, that he will forego things that would be to his advantage if he foresees that they might become the source of the least constraint." Once, after a presumable indiscretion, the king simply ignored a number of his letters; another time, when d'Alembert again used his weak health as an excuse, he [the king] replied scornfully: "Your mind is as sick as your body; that makes a twofold illness. I will not become involved in the cure."

Yet d'Alembert had promised the king at Sans Souci to "take an active interest in the welfare and the reputation of the Academy." And Frederick, for his part, always kept the presidency open for him, despite his friend's very definitive refusal. This created a most peculiar situation in the direction of the Academy after 1763. The king himself was its president; the Academy only informed him of the importance of any scholar it was considering and then awaited the king's decision. Though living in Paris, the French philosopher deployed considerable activity on behalf of the Berlin Academy. Certain procedures of communication were developed, especially after Lagrange came to Berlin, and these depended upon the integrity of the men involved, their firm and unstrained mutual relationships. But d'Alembert's influence only extended to matters of appointment. In the internal affairs of the Academy the king usually rejected d'Alembert's suggestions, even though they were offered with all due discretion.

D'Alembert surveyed the elite of contemporary scholarship with the most disinterested objectivity where positions in the exact sciences were concerned. Lagrange, the greatest mathematician of the next generation, was brought to the Academy through his efforts; he was involved when Laplace was considering a move to Berlin; he proposed the eminent chemist Scheele as a successor to Marggraf; and it was not his fault that his twice-repeated reference to Michaelis and his recommendation of Johannes Müller did not lead to an appointment. D'Alembert's influence did not extend to the philosophical section; it was here that the profound differences between the German metaphysicians and the positivist d'Alembert became most obvious. "I have the impression," wrote Lagrange with uncharacteristic maliciousness, "that almost every country has its own metaphysics, just as it has its own language." Thus d'Alembert had nothing to do with the appointment of the greatest among the philosophers of the Academy, Lambert, a rival of Kant, who had been "practically forced upon" the king. Yet d'Alembert acted justly and generously when, accepting the judgment of Lagrange, he came to the defense of Lambert, whose rather unprepossessing behavior was repulsive to Frederick.

D'Alembert's position regarding the volatile race of literary men in the milieu of the Encyclopedia was most complicated. This was his weak point. After the death of Maupertuis, when the king established a closer relationship with d'Alembert, when he sent him the poem against the enemies of the Encyclopedia,[3] when the two men were matching their wit, grace, and *esprit* in a friendly skirmish between poetry and mathematics—at that time d'Alembert wrote to Voltaire: "I do not know what will happen between him and me; but it would be a great pity if philosophy were to lose his protection." Then, in the Potsdam days, when he had become sure of his position with Frederick, he was happy that he could be useful to his companions in arms, and positively jubilant when he had

---

3. *"Epître à d'Alembert, sur ce qu'on avait défendu l'Encyclopédie et brulé ses ouvrages en France,"* written in February 1760. [ed.]

established Helvétius and Jaucourt as corresponding members of the Academy. On behalf of philosophy, he thanked the king for setting this example to all rulers. But as the relationship continued, Frederick's perceptive intelligence did not fail to discern the game that was being played in the background. Even though Frederick never said anything explicitly, d'Alembert could sense his awareness in the gently mocking tone the king sometimes employed when commenting on a glowing account of some persecuted literary man. Having taken a glance behind the scenes in the correspondence between Voltaire and d'Alembert, we realize that Frederick's guarded attitude was indeed justified.

FRIEDRICH GUNDOLF

Frederick's Essay on German Literature

AMONG THE MEN of action of world history, Frederick the Great has been the most prolific writer, and none has taken intellectual endeavor and commerce with the Muses as seriously as he. A long life of joyless toil, of active involvement in terrifying events, and of relentless service to the state forms the background to his epistles, verses, essays, and sundry treatises—and they were as numerous as if he had been one of the idle *abbés* of the salons and boudoirs in the world of Louis XV. Nor were his literary works much more weighty in content or mood except where they

From *Friedrichs des Grossen Schrift über die deutsche Literatur,* by Friedrich Gundolf. Zurich: Rascher Verlag, 1947. Reprinted with permission of Rosemarie Ostwald. Translation copyright © 1972 by Peter Paret.

touched upon matters with which he meant to immortalize his
own true concerns, statecraft and politics. His historical writings
are worthy of their author, not only by virtue of their subject matter, with which no other writer was as thoroughly familiar, but
also by the manner in which they are presented. Standing in the
tradition of the Greek and Roman classics and of Voltaire, they
bear witness to his imperious will and his clearsighted understanding of reality—despite the use of the foreign language and despite
a pretentiously elegant or overly direct style. His nonpolitical writings, especially those in verse, are less likely to reflect his moods at
any given moment than are his letters; they usually served to
give standard form to enlightened or stoic commonplaces, at best
to the permanent convictions that were dear to him. They must
be looked upon with the indulgence or the reservation with which
Goethe appeased those who questioned the value of the poetry of
the Bavarian king Ludwig: "In [the writings of] a king, art is
less important than opinion." Frederick's writings, of course, are
better in content and still more in form than those of the good-
natured fool Ludwig, not so much because they express his gigantic
personality, as because he was unable to suppress it altogether; but
they suffer from the use of the foreign language in a manner
similar to those of the great Neo-Latins, such as Hutten and even
Dante, whose true power comes to light only out of the depths of
their native language, where it is freed from the more artful conventions of a cultural vehicle instilled by learning.

Among the European rulers who were really rulers (rather than
schoolmasters, such as James I of England, or bluestockings, such
as Christina of Sweden) Frederick remains a miracle of true
thoughtfulness—which goes hand in hand with his prodigious activity—by the number, variety, and keenness of his contemplative
writings. (I purposely wish to exclude here the political and historical documents, such as inscriptions, decrees, and memorabilia,
which great men of action have used since classical times to further their purposes and immortalize their actions.) In classical
history Frederick found a model for his contemplative bent in
Marcus Aurelius, and he was more than pleased to be compared

to this saintly and energetic stoic; probably even secretly proud that, all things considered, he had achieved even more in word and deed. (In the East, we know of at least one sage, in the true sense of the word, who was an absolute prince: the grand mogul Akbar, a genuine philosopher-king, who made that proverbial glory come true.) By contrast to the Latins or the Anglo-Saxons, whose thinking was almost always propelled or carried along by will power, the Germans—especially since Luther—permitted almost all their values, including the very core of politics, to be shaped by teachers rather than by men of action—a vexation or an embarrassment to the few geniuses of power to appear among them. For this reason, even an intelligent and aware prince of Prussia found it easier to focus the still unformed, unstructured, and vacillating fantasies of his imagination upon an intellectual rather than a warlike ideal. His horrible childhood, in which he was so often constricted by the demands of the state, as well as the only happy period of his life, the leisure of Rheinsberg where he basked in the rays of that European universal genius, Voltaire (and Voltaire, for all his restlessness, was a contemplative mind, and as such the most persuasive master of the word since Petrarch, or at least Erasmus, for cosmopolitan amateurs of culture), were bound to make the reputation of a *bel esprit* appear in a rather more seductive light than the bloodstained and dirty toil of a conqueror. Like every true man of action, Frederick realized his strength and, above all, his true vocation only when called upon to act. Unable to remain idle, he filled his period of waiting communing with the Muses who were to teach him, the disciple of Voltaire and of the Enlightenment, how to be a king when the time came, or else with accumulating and choosing useful and agreeable knowledge whose eventual application he could not know, but only dimly foresee. But crown prince and pupil of the Muses, "effeminate fellow" and secretly demonic spirit—the fact is that in the decisive period of his coming to maturity in a barbaric land with a veneer of French civilization, as he and Voltaire saw it, Frederick found no other outlet for his supple intelligence than writing. Even in those dreams where he saw himself as Alexander or Caesar, he knew that it would be incumbent upon him to bring

the civilization of Pericles, of the Medici, and of the Sun-King to
the presumptive field of his future activity by means of the humanities. The talent—part blessing and part curse—of his entire
life, which made him the very personification of the enlightened
despot, namely, the will to do everything himself, even the things
that cannot be done but must be allowed to happen, his own creativity, and the school of Voltaire, misled him into writing his
French book about German literature soon after he had accomplished his first successful acts of statesmanship.[1] His twin motive
was the literary pretension of a German outsider and the desire
of a presumably expert lord and master to chart the course of his
cultural policies. This book remains a monument to his all-encom-
passing paternalism even where he was stricken with blindness;
it is also a warning that even the most talented minds have little
of value to contribute outside the sphere of their expertise. Napoleon's judgment of Shakespeare and Bismarck's rather average
taste in novels do not debase these eminent men, both of whom
had a certain literary culture—any more than Plato's *Laws* taint
the vision of the state of this seer of ideas. But where complete
faith in authority exists or a hero-worship that swallows everything emanating from the revered authority, it is only proper to
speak of such folly. The greatest men are not those who err least,
but those who, without impairing their stature, may, indeed must,
commit the greatest errors.

The essay on German literature in its published form is a work
of Frederick's old age, published by the splenetic, sick, and world-
famous king, who, as a conscientious administrator, felt duty-
bound to give his attention not only to welfare institutions, military security, and armaments for his state, but also to cultural
matters; and who did so with almost inhuman single-mindedness,
with his customary ponderous swiftness and spasmodic buoyancy.
It has been thought that the contents of this book date back a
generation, and that they were originally meant as a reply of the

1. *De la Littérature allemande, des défauts qu'on peut lui reprocher,
quelles sont les causes, et par quels moyens on peut les corriger* (Berlin,
1780).

young king to a book by a Baron Bielfeld, *Über die Fortschritte der Deutschen in Künsten und schönen Wissenschaften* (1752). Bielfeld was a French-educated nobleman who had the patriotic ambition of showing that from the time of Opitz to Gottsched the dominant influence of various foreign powers had brought about a flourishing of the German language, and his book is interspersed with proud or wistful references to the foreign models that were supposedly surpassed.[2] Frederick the Great had already attempted an outline of European intellectual history in the *Histoire de mon temps* (1746), a work he revised stylistically and completed or amended in 1775. From the Rheinsberg period until his death his general conception of world history remained virtually unchanged, though the fundamental ideas he had formed in conversation with Voltaire were justly strengthened and clarified by Voltaire's great study, the *Essai sur les moeurs* (1756). What did change was the *mood* in which Frederick later expounded the ideas he had formed early in life. (Development, becoming, metamorphosis of inner resources, complete change of form, as we understand and conceive them since Herder, especially through the example of Goethe's entire life and work—these are things that no author of the Enlightenment of the seventeenth and eighteenth century has experienced—"experienced" to be taken in the double sense of "lived" and "perceived." In this area as in others, Lessing, with his *Erziehung des Menschengeschlechts,* surpassed the Enlightenment, binding though its tenets still were for him. Beyond English and French aims and ends [beyond the *Esprit des lois* and the *Essai sur les moeurs,* beyond Bossuet's *Discours sur l'histoire universelle* and the Church Fathers upon whom the latter was based, and who felt that the course of history is fixed by a divine *telos,* a guiding Providence] Lessing believed in the possibility of perfecting the human race by virtue of an unexplained, unrevealed, but ultimately explicable *sense* of existence.) As for Frederick, it is true that he amplified and clarified his thinking over the years and placed the emphasis differently, but

2. The poet Martin Opitz (1597–1639) and the writer and editor Johann Christoph Gottsched (1700–1766) were inspired by foreign models in their efforts to cleanse and codify German literary style. [ed.]

he did not develop it, as a bud becomes fruit. For the understanding of his books as intellectual, rather than diplomatic documents, it is highly important to know in which decade they appeared. The unquestioning enthusiasm of this sensitive and impetuous crown prince and victorious conqueror who shared the faith in progress of the Enlightenment—despite the Voltairean pretense of doubt and scorn and despite the profound knowledge of human nature of this man of action—had yielded after the Seven Years' War to disappointment, disgust, and misanthropy. Yet his fundamental commitment to action, to service to the state, to power, the mainspring of all his activities, was salvaged from his youth and remained unbroken. He clung almost desperately to the principles he had learned, because he considered them the imperatives of his existence, hardened as he was in defiant fatalism, in ascetic terror, as if he were to lose the meaning of his life if he were to demur against the dictates of fate. What had been deeply pleasurable to him in his youth now congealed into joyless duty, holloweyed defiance in the face of all odds, and the sublime obstinacy of a man possessed who has become impervious to any soothing illusion. Napoleon once called himself the slave of implacable necessity, of the nature of things, comparing himself to the menace of divine scourges, to the horsemen of the Apocalypse, or to the makers of a new age. *Der alte Fritz* was filled with a similar grating arrogance, but his arrogance lacked this swelling pride, this love of adventure, this sense of awe; and rather than enjoying his own exuberance—in the joyful or in the sinister sense of the word —he delighted in the severity of the inescapable servitude of which he would be both victim and creator. In later years, he incorporated even his pleasures into that servitude; what he had cultivated in his youth because it had challenged the surplus of his imperious powers he later pressed into the routine of the wise tyrant. The *bel esprit* of Rheinsberg is to the philosopher of Sans Souci what the horseman is to the animal trainer, what the strong man is to the prize fighter: in his calling he possesses, uses, and enjoys the same skills he once practiced for pleasure, and replaces his lost cheerfulness with the dignity of responsibility. Not that Frederick lost all cheerfulness, any more than his wit and humor. But all the subsidiary powers of his genius were now made to serve his main endeavor, to which he devoted himself without the heedless gaiety of youthful self-sufficiency. His very fame now became prestige; it was no longer a brilliant image, but a menacing means of power.

If the reply to Bielfeld about German literature was probably an act of patronizing benevolence, an equally important ingredient of the publication of 1780 was without doubt the despot's irritation with the increasing noisiness of the awakening German literature. Its best-known passages about Goethe's Götz von Berlichingen and about Shakespeare's aberrations were only outbursts of a vexation that gives a sour tone to the entire book; but this vexation almost certainly had not disfigured the earlier version, any more than the outbursts. Even in Frederick's conversations with Gottsched and Gellert during the Seven Years' War we sense a certain good-natured condescension of a soldier for these more or less respectable schoolmasters, we see the mocking but friendly smile of one who deals with the cultural concerns of these advocates of the Muses amidst the thunder of great events; but we also sense that, for all his blindness, he still is willing to listen and to understand.[3] If Gottsched bored him, if Gellert elicited only a lukewarm response, they did not anger him as the unfolding of the mysteriously budding creativity of great German poetry angered him. Under his eyes in Berlin, Doebbelin's German actors had performed *Romeo and Juliet, Othello, Macbeth, Hamlet,* and *King Lear* between 1768 and 1778. They had used Schröder's questionable prose-versions, and while these gave no idea of Shakespeare the poet, that magician of the word and interpreter of the heart, they made a great deal of noise on the stage. Of all this, the king heard no more than the noise, and all the things that spoke, indeed screamed, against his classicistic attitudes and desires; in

3. In 1757 Frederick had several conversations on literature with Gottsched, after which he composed a brief poem, calling on Gottsched, "Swan of the Saxons . . . to sweeten in your songs the hard and unpleasant sounds of a barbaric tongue." In the dedication Frederick erroneously replaced Gottsched's name with that of Christian Fürchtegott Gellert (1717–1769), whose agreeably poetic treatment of fables and religious topics he preferred to Gottsched's professorial muse. [ed.]

short, the barbaric ranting of a mob. That his taste was violated in this fashion, in his own capital, in his very presence, made him angry, because he was in charge but obviously not in control of literature. He did not even take the trouble to distinguish between Goethe's *Götz,* a German innovation, and Schröder's Shakespeare-libretti. For him it was sufficient that these fellows neglected the three unities and talked some noisy gibberish unfit for polite society. For it was the transgression of the law that struck the giver and servant of the law; and, being an old man, he did not listen to the source of the transgression.

As enlightened ruler he renounced the use of political terror and assumed the attitude of the scornful but magnanimous misanthropist who ordered hostile pamphlets to be posted lower so that they could be easily read, and permitted shoemakers' apprentices to laugh at him. Authoritarian suppression would have been beneath the dignity of a crowned sage. This is why his royal displeasure in cultural matters was incorporated into his essay *De la Littérature allemande.* As a patron and founder, he did not want to censor, but hoped to improve. As an adherent of the Enlightenment he had faith—as a matter of duty rather than of joyful optimism—in the healing power of the right teaching and, possibly even more than thirty years before, in the impression of his public admonitions. But by now, these were much less attuned to the situation, and therefore much less effective, than they would have been in 1750. At that time, German literature—despite Luther's and Hutten's use of language, despite the church hymns, despite Grimmelshausen, Gryphius, Fleming, and others—could not compete with the universality of the rest of European literature. Even Klopstock's Odes and his *Messias* promised, rather than produced, a flourishing of literature. But when Frederick actually launched his broadside, he laid hands on two creative geniuses—one dead and one living—who made the whole classicistic splendor look pale: Shakespeare and Goethe. Now he looked foolish not because he lacked a sense of the future, but because of the backwardness of old age. But his book, by its very wrongheadedness, which was part and parcel of Frederick's powerful mind, is emblematic of the tragic struggle of the greatest German king against the powers of the German spirit. Let us briefly interpret it as the scene of the battle between the old Enlightenment and the new feeling for Nature.

Even the genre of Frederick's manifesto is part of an intellectual tradition that—at least since the days of Romanticism, and that means since Herder's revelations about individual creativity, about the Bible, Shakespeare, Homer—is as alien to us as the belief that the citing of a Biblical passage, a verse of Virgil, or a sentence of Aristotle constitutes conclusive proof. Our reverence for Dante's works is in no way impaired by the fact that his rationalistic apparatus no longer has any power over us; his visions will endure because he was the first to receive them, and receive them in this form. Frederick's political, military, and autobiographical writings affect us in a similar way, because his extraordinary personality still pervades them beyond their specific concern and beyond their message. Ever since Plato (who was the first to attempt the intellectual fixation of the visions of the mind, that is, who wanted to make them binding by way of proofs, and tried to change insight into knowledge by arranging and ordering it) all ages have considered certain intellectual operations as leading to conclusive proof and have attempted to press their indispensable values, needs, dreams, and ideals—whatever their origin—upon their respective audiences by supposedly conclusive chains of reasoning. For Plato, mathematics was already a temptation, and his great new system of proofs, dialectics, was mathematics in a different guise applied to a different intellectual field. The age of science to which Frederick's teacher, Voltaire, felt indebted for his entire intellectual formation—an age that had freed itself of the absolute rule of scholasticism, of the magic hold of the Bible, and of the Aristotelian straitjacket—this age of experiment, of eager receptivity, of Kepler, Galileo, Newton, Leibniz, and Descartes, had also attempted to "prove" the universe mathematically, i.e., to apprehend it through its laws. To subordinate God's commands, as they are given by theology, to mathematics, or to replace them by mathematically controllable proofs, as Spinoza did, was the main endeavor of the European thinkers in whose milieu Voltaire ripened to his mission. The quasi-superstitious reverence of his acute mind for everything that can withstand the scrutiny of mathematics, the pious belief that everything that can be understood can be proven, the distrust for mystery and the unprovable forces of change, the determination to transform cognition into processes of reasoning, the desire to shape even taste, pleasure, and enjoyment by teachable precedents, namely rules and models—all of these questionable virtues of the cleverest of Frenchmen, Frederick had learned to admire, love, and practice. But since he had less leisure for cultural endeavors than Voltaire, since his conscience as a ruler was a heavier responsibility, and since he had found (or created) a more severe master in the Prussian state than Voltaire had found in the French-European society of cultural amateurs, he expressed his cultural opinions, wherever they seemed binding to him, in much stricter rules and regulations than Voltaire needed to do in his pliable and adaptable curiosity for everything. Constantly standing at the periphery of dangerous activity, Frederick's imperious mind could never afford the leisure or the mood of enchanting play, whether it be for studying or for applying what he had learned. And he never placed delight above usefulness, power, and effectiveness.

Although he was no schoolmaster, the lack of vivacity, of playfulness and lightness makes even his treatise on taste very different from Voltaire's scholarly essays. The king did not feel that delight with his own intelligence, his own capability, his own knowledge, which not only excuses but positively glorifies Voltaire's famous vanity. If he sometimes displayed unnecessary bits of information, he did not wear them, as Voltaire did, like so many alluring ornaments, but rather used them as imposing uniform accessories, as parts of his professional attire. Witness his passing stab at the German pedants who, when discussing the customary law of Osnabrück, brought in the Egyptian system of law, or his scathing remarks about the genealogists and chronologists. Such sallies expressed genuine scorn, but they also implied: I know about such esoteric matters. He was rather like a general who dutifully wears his decorations at a parade, but at times also displays them on social occasions in order to show that he has earned such honors. Frederick had derived almost all of his factual knowledge, all of his value-judgments and his entire outlook in matters of cultural history and natural philosophy from Voltaire's works. Once they were formed, he used them either summarily, like a commanding officer who is perpetually pressed for time, or else in a humorously clumsy way like an old soldier who is making light conversation with the ladies and brings in some civilian knowledge as if he did not really care about it. This was the case when he discussed Spinoza's system or the barbaric dialect of the Italians at the time of Charlemagne. They were meant as perfectly serious disciplinary hints to the German intellectuals, but they were also an authoritarian, yet somewhat bashful, display of knowledge. These discrepancies were aggravated not only by Frederick's character—for he had taken up writing from inclination and from a sense of duty and was determined to achieve victory and influence in this domain as in all others, and as soon as possible—but also by his lack of intimacy with the language in which he was writing, despite his artistic use of it, and despite the fact that he was Voltaire's pupil. Unlike Voltaire himself, he had not assimilated the treasures of learning with natural facility, but had appropriated them. He marshaled knowledge as possessor, not as an inventor or even a finder. In cultural matters a comparison with Voltaire makes him look like a good pupil next to an authoritative teacher —powerful master though he was in all matters of war and statecraft, even where he was mistaken. His French didactic prose is devoid of that mystery which gives such a vibrant quality to the language of Voltaire and Diderot, and in Germany to Lessing's didactic works. Frederick's French prose not only lacks all the qualities of warmth and intimacy but even—and this is difficult to prove but can be sensed—the tension between its German content and the foreign medium of expression. I am thinking of passages like the following:

> As I said before: The first step is to perfect the language. It must be planed and polished, must be shaped by skillful hands. Clarity is the first rule for all those who want to write or speak, since they must illustrate their thoughts and express their ideas in words.

This passage has neither Gallic charm nor Germanic force; it is neither witty small talk nor imperious bidding, but a limp juxtaposition of occasional thoughts and professional concern in which the author's power falters, even though he thinks correctly and writes clearly. This discordance becomes even more obvious if we read similar passages in the writings of Prince de Ligne. Ligne was not nearly as great a man as Frederick, but he was more gifted because he felt the awakening of his language while his spirit was still slumbering and because he had been awakened in it and by it, never completely leaving the depths from which it came to him. Frederick the Great tried in vain to escape from his all too Prussian youth by entering into the spirit of the French-European language. He faltered in his flight whenever he strayed too far from his German deeds and from his French diversions, and especially when he tried to legislate German acts of the spirit with French words and the earnestness of a Prussian king.

Just as Frederick the Great wrote treatises containing operational and tactical rules in order to instruct his generals and make his presence felt even in their planning, so his essay on German literature was first of all meant to convey a few orders to some of his more independent subjects whom he could not reach directly. In this case, he had to state the reasons for his orders more explicitly than in his own specialty, for in literature his will was not as binding as on the battlefield. Here, it was not a matter of citing a few specific cases to which the writer could promptly apply prescribed rules, but of creating a fixed frame of mind capable of accommodating the constantly evolving demands of history and of the future. He therefore prefaced the main body of the essay, concerning the teaching of the various kinds of writing, with a historical survey of the important European literatures, or rather with an exposé of the universally recognized ideals and models of literature. In his enumeration of the four Golden Ages—that of Pericles and Alexander, that of Cicero and Augustus, that of the Medici, and that of Louis XIV—he adopted the order given by Voltaire in the introduction to the *Siècle de Louis XIV*. This book had established the first progressive sequence in the history of civilizations other than divine scripture, and had gone beyond the annals, chronicles, memoirs, and collections of documents that had hitherto satisfied the historian. Frederick did not actually copy Voltaire, but he owed the very direction of his endeavors, his views of what is important and what is not, and his perspective of time to the man whose words had first taught him to see the mind as a historical phenomenon. It is true that he praised the Greeks for their harmonious language, which he considered an essential advantage and one of the reasons for the beauty of their literature. This observation did not come from Voltaire but from his own struggle with his unwieldy native language. Later too, in the prescriptive part of his essay, he placed special emphasis on enhancing the harmony of the German language and proposed summary remedies, such as vocalic endings. This is a child's rationalistic belief that anything that has been observed can be reproduced. In a similar vein Napoleon on St. Helena expressed regret that he had not promulgated an edict abolishing all exceptions to the rules of the French language. (Frederick's endeavors in this direction were later to elicit many angry and sarcastic comments from Klopstock, who felt prompted to exalt the German language above the Greek.) One of Frederick's Voltairean—i.e., antitheological and antimetaphysical—statements stressed the fact that Greek literature was created by poets; and poets, he said, are professional experts in *tours heureux* and *expressions pittoresques,* so that their followers learned to express themselves with *grâce, politesse,* and *décence.* The Romans, he continued, had long been occupied with war and had been more concerned with force than with style. Having come to *lettres* only after the fall of Carthage at the time of Scipio, they reached the maturity of their language and style only with Cicero and Augustus. Basing his judgment on Cicero's treatises and example books, *De claris oratoribus* and *De oratore* (probably in the translation of Bourgoin de Villefore) and on his rhetoric, *Ad Herennium,* Frederick accepted a few good orators between Scipio and Augustus—the Gracchi, Antonius, and Crassus. For Frederick, Greek and Latin were either naturally harmonious or refined by their poetic origins, and he contrasted them with the unharmonious sounds of northern Europe and its civilization.

Without prejudice but in favor of his nation and his region, he had to admit that the language of Germany was still half-barbaric, split into many dialects, disorganized, and rough. He pointed out that the languages of classical antiquity were unified since earliest times and very widely used, so that their expressions, sanctioned by great artists, could by tacit agreement become universal conventions and consequently binding, unquestioned, and appealing. Here is the concept of classicism in two aspects: positively, as a choice of rules and models that must be followed; negatively, as the despot's desire to eliminate any particularities of language, speech, or expression which might obstruct or confuse his long-range planning. It shows the same tyrannical mentality that was betrayed by Napoleon's misgivings about exceptions, or by Caesar's advice to writers to avoid obsolete or unusual expressions, as a ship's captain avoids shoals.

In Frederick's case, this attitude was expressed by the statement that in German the meaning of the sentence is drowned in irrelevant bombast. The lack of measure, of directness, of tautness—in short, of classical order, irritated him, and he sought to justify his irritation by a survey of German literature where he looked in vain for a German Homer, Virgil, Anacreon, Horace, Demosthenes, Cicero, Thucydides, or Livy. It may be significant that he did not include Aeschylus and Pindar, but it may also be that he would have thought it pedantic to enumerate the entire canon. He also mentioned Catullus, Tibullus, and Propertius, and placed them above Gessner's much-praised idylls. Phaedrus and Aesop he compared to Gellert, the only German to have done well in the minor genre of the fable. He considered Canitz a weak imitator of Horace —no doubt he knew him better as a councilor of his royal grandfather. But he did say that some of the German philosophers can be placed side by side with the famous ancients—perhaps even above them. He was thinking of Leibniz and Wolff, but as mathematicians rather than as stylists. In his opinion German historians hardly existed; such as they were, Mascov was probably the most thorough. He considered Quandt of Königsberg, the court preacher, as the only German to have shown his compatriots what harmonious language was; but since no one responded, he had abandoned his efforts. The praise was a personal gesture of the royal patron; it hardly constitutes the canonization of a German classic. Frederick also praised Christian Ewald von Kleist's anonymously published *Frühling* for achieving harmonious sound by using a mixture of dactylics and spondaics. Here, too, there is an element of royal patronage for an officer whose cultural endeavors did not escape the perceptive attention of this keen administrator. In a later section of the essay, where he made his literary survey, Frederick no longer remembered the name of Kleist. But he probably felt that the absence of rhyme made German poetry sound classical and that this form should be imitated. Klopstock, the restorer of the soaring verse of antiquity, was altogether rejected, because Frederick did not like his theological subject matter. He also condemned the entire German theater as stilted, vulgar, and contrary to the rules. The only exception was Ayrenhoff's *Postzug* (1769), which he considered a good exposition of mores.

After this interlude—sitting in judgment of contemporary German literature, and allowing for extenuating, that is, outside circumstances—Frederick returned to the development of harmonious sound and comprehension and looked to other countries that could furnish models and rules—France and Italy. His guiding idea was the "Re-naissance" of the arts and sciences after the dark Middle Ages. Here, too, he tried to find models and to establish their recognizable preconditions as well as their teachable rules. The House of Este, Lorenzo de' Medici, and Leo X, he said, had become patrons of the arts and sciences in Italy, while Germany was rent asunder as the theologians set man against man, and while France was kept from cultivating the arts by the Wars of the League, until Richelieu renewed the cultural plans of Francis I and Louis XIV brought them to fruition.

In content and style the next section of Frederick's essay is the most original. Here the author, out of the full measure of his own experiences and insights, evokes the suffering of Germany during the wars that were fought while France was recovering and flourishing. Here the elegant disquisitions of the *bel esprit* almost yield to a prophetic rumble, and the horrors he has seen in the Seven Years' War vibrate in his lament about the Thirty Years' War. The pupil of Voltaire cries out against the famous French cardinal and the glorious monarch who had been so highly exalted by his teacher, and, almost despite himself, the isolated German breaks out of the sociable European. Here is the same intense anger that had exploded at the triumph of Rossbach and Zorndorf, groaned at the defeats of Kunersdorf and Colin. Here the bitter wit of a man who suffers with the world and hates mankind comes through in passages that are reminiscent of Shakespeare's *Timon* rather than of Voltaire's *Candide*.

> While the Turks besieged Vienna and Melac laid waste to the Palatinate, while houses and towns burned to ashes, while undisciplined mercenaries desecrated even the preserve of death and tore dead emperors from their tombs to rob them of their miserable coverings, while desperate mothers fled with their starving children from the ruins of their country—were sonnets to be composed and epigrams wrought in Vienna or Mannheim?

In this act of accusation Frederick justified German barbarism not only as a king who yearns for a Golden Age of his own, but also as a German patriot whose heart is filled with the terrible fate of his people and as a victim of the foreign language which keeps him from expressing his deepest feelings. Beneath the glittering surface of such sentences with their vain figures of speech, there is a dark undertone reaching down to the ancient depths that have yielded Walter's warning calls, Hutten's curses, Grimmelshausen's apocalyptic sighs, Lessing's heart-sick wit, and even the resigned muttering of Goethe's old age—all the desperate or pleading responses of full hearts to the empty quarreling of the Germans, all the sorrow of these fertile minds in the face of the madness of our fellow men. The encompassing pity for the misery of the world, a feeling every deep person will at some time experience so sharply that he must weep at his own role in that foolish comedy, came to this great German when he looked at his state. He did not wish to serve it in blind submission and knew that he must remain a free and watchful individual; as a victorious ruler he wondered for whom he had gained his victories.

From this involuntary outburst Frederick returned to his arbitrary prescriptions or palliatives, not without propagandistic pride in his own achievements for the state and praise for his wise ancestors. They, he wrote, have cultivated the fields, rebuilt the devastated homes, replenished a new generation, cleared the wilderness.

> Population growth has stimulated manufacture, and the luxury trade—ruinous to a small state, but beneficial for the circulation of money in a large state—is growing apace. . . . Germany is rich in flourishing towns and cities, and the ancient Hyrcanian forest is covered with extraordinary edifices. . . . German manliness has not only repaired old damages, but is preparing for new growth. . . . No longer is the citizen languishing in misery. . . . Parents are able to educate their children without sinking into debt. . . . Generous competition is springing up everywhere. . . . Losses and missed opportunities are being compensated by hard work. . . . Indigenous style is aspiring to national glory.

In this paragraph, Frederick is more than a *bel esprit*. He is speaking as a political economist and theorist, as a progressive master of reality who, like blind old Faust, deadens his ever-present anxiety by unrelenting activity. And because of this activity, we must honor his anxiety, just as the dramatist shows Faust's end and his ultimate endeavors only as a parable, as an emblem for the flight of a driven mind from endless, futile brooding into useful work in the necessarily limited Here and Now.

After these digressions of a proud or despairing statesman, Frederick, the literary amateur, devoted his attention to the improvement of the German language. With good common sense, he advanced perfectly plausible rules—which were invalidated only by the fact that they were unnecessary. For Frederick knew German literature no better than the citizens of Schilda knew the nature and properties of the crab, of light, and of salt; and he gave advice without the slightest knowledge of the case. Here are some of his suggestions: the German language should be planed and polished, but its unwieldiness should not be replaced with shallowness. The great ancients, who sharpen the sense of language and promote clarity of thinking and knowledge, should be studied in the text, but in a critical fashion, without blind idolatry—especially since the highly praised neighboring nations were already beginning to rest on their laurels. Teachers should be made to give up their stiff, schoolmasterly attitude and their bombast (some samples are included) and brought to simple logic through mathematics. The German language should be tightened, clarified, and strengthened by translations of the best classics, such as Thucydides, Xenophon, the *Poetics* of Aristotle, Demosthenes, Epictetus, Marcus Aurelius, Caesar, Sallust, Tacitus, and the *Ars Poetica* of Horace; among the French, La Rochefoucauld's *Réflexions ou sentences et maximes morales,* Montesquieu's *Lettres persanes* and his *Esprit des lois.* The German language should take on vocalic endings, vulgar expressions should be expunged, clear logic should be taught to teachers and students from the works of Christian Wolff or from Bayle. Being a contemporary of Lessing and sharing his views on this point, Frederick denied the possibility of creating geniuses, but like Lessing, he wanted to train already existing talents and to rectify current abuses by models and rules. As models for the writing of history—its style, not its content—he once again recommended Livy, Sallust, Tacitus, as well as Bossuet, Vertot, and Robertson's *Charles V*. Thus he made a rapid survey of all areas of literature, pointing to this and that with his cane; but I shall pass over the details.

The truly remarkable thing in all of this is Frederick's imperious attitude. He found time to catalogue all the intellectual treasures of the world with a view to what he considered their proper use for civilization. Even when acting as a literary critic, he could not help treating autonomous intellectual creations as he would treat matters of high policy. This is reminiscent of Napoleon, who once ordered a French scholar to report to him, by the day after next, what Kant's teaching was all about. Frederick's straightforwardness was disturbed, more than Napoleon's, by the pretension of a *bel esprit* which he could not quite suppress, and by the smug attitude of a patron and connoisseur of the arts. Yet in the end the imperious ruler reappears beneath the rustling of paper, the resigned and pessimistic sage beneath the commanding tone. It is as the prophet of a German Golden Age which he was not to experience that Frederick sadly takes leave, a Moses who sees the Promised Land without entering it. And as we put aside this depressing essay we see him in the same awesome light that envelops his entire life, cold and clear, sallow as the evening—the German outsider who asks his tormented "why" and holds fast to his obstinate "nevertheless."

PART FOUR

Two Assessments

FRANZ MEHRING

An Enlightened Despot?

This polemic by a brilliant Marxist publicist, which appeared
in Germany shortly before the First World War, effectively attacks
the absurdities of nationalist exploitations of the Frederician legend. Mehring also provides useful social and economic correctives
to the standard interpretations of German political historians; but
his own exaggerations and his view of Frederick as a traitor to
the German national cause are basically unhistorical.—EDITOR.

IN 1840, the centennial of Frederick's ascension to the throne,
the Young Hegelian, Friedrich Köppen, published a pamphlet,
dedicated to his friend Karl Marx, in celebration of the event.
"According to a popular tradition," he wrote, "after a hundred

From "Ein aufgeklärter Despot?" by Franz Mehring, in *Neue Zeit,* XXX
(1912). Translation copyright © 1972 by Peter Paret.

years man is reborn. The time has come! May Frederick's resurrected spirit descend on us, and with flaming sword destroy all enemies that are blocking our entry into the Promised Land! Let us swear to live and die in his spirit!"

Nearly fifty years later, in 1886, the centennial of Frederick's death, old Emperor William, known in his youth as the "shrapnel prince," said: "Everything great and good that blesses our land today is based on the foundations that he laid." We don't need to explain in detail what it was that this limited drill-sergeant admired as "great and good" in the Second German Empire; suffice to recall the grandeur of our Prussian Junkers, our parasitic militarism, the profiteering in meat and bread, the anti-socialist laws, the state's subordination to Russia. Now who is right? The brash Young Hegelian, barely thirty years old when he wrote, or the dull Hohenzollern prince of nearly ninety?

It is worth considering this question for a moment because the patriotic drum is now being sounded in honor of the 200th anniversary of Frederick's birth on January 24th. A few days later, on the birthday of our present emperor, the two anniversaries will be celebrated with the usual commotion. Among other things, the Kaiser has commissioned Professor Koser, director-general of the Prussian State Archives, to write an essay about his ancestor, which will be distributed in 100,000 copies to the Prussian students as a present from their emperor. It is true that Professor Koser is the author of an adequate biography of Frederick; but his new piece is probably suitably characterized by Mephistopheles' statement: "The best that you know you can't tell the brats anyway." And so far as the anniversary articles already published in the bourgeois press are concerned, without exception they carry the stamp of the most submissive loyalty.

Not to keep my readers in suspense, it was old William rather than young Köppen who was right, and right three times over. At most we can object that Frederick did not lay the foundations of the Prussian state but simply strengthened them; the bases themselves antedated him, having been the outcome of the particular historical development of the Brandenburg-Prussian military colony since the Middle Ages. Frederick always refused to modernize these foundations, or even to repair them; all he did was to expand and reinforce them—and this is true all the way from the authority of the Prussian nobility to the state's subordination to Russia. In every area of his rule he clearly followed a regressive line—with the single exception of the judicial system, where he did attempt some reform, only to bog down again in the most capricious, absolutist manipulation of laws. To hear him celebrated as the model of an enlightened despot can only be considered biting mockery to anyone at all familiar with Frederick's history.

Nothing mattered more to him than to maintain the feudal-medieval social stratification of nobility, peasants, and burghers in his state. Elsewhere in Europe it was the task of enlightened despotism to assist the rising middle classes in order to win allies against the nobility; Frederick, by contrast, choked off the towns and pampered the nobles. He overwhelmed them with still more privileges than they already possessed in this blessed land. It is Frederick's true legacy that he placed the whole military and civil machinery of the state so firmly in the hands of the Junkers that we have never been able to tear it from them. If he didn't protect the towns against the nobility, he didn't protect the peasants either; at most he sought to restrict the dispossession of free farms so that he would not be deprived of recruits for his army and of tax-payers. These were the sole considerations that guided his attempts at "reforming" the medieval relationship between manorial lords and peasants. He found nothing objectionable in the Junkers' disgraceful exploitation and abuse of the country; but he insisted on his share of the blood and sweat that was squeezed from the peasants, who at that time formed the great majority of the population.

His financial administration, especially after the Seven Years' War, was a highly refined instrument of exploitation, but even for his day its policies were already old-fashioned. He raised taxes—particularly taxes on the peasantry—to unbearable and unheard-of levels. That the state possessed cultural obligations was a concept that was entirely foreign to this great spirit. He allowed the schools to decay completely. Intellectual slavery never celebrated such orgies as under the scepter of this wise ruler. His censorship was a fitting ancestor of our anti-socialist legislation.

He was no better in the area of foreign affairs. Nothing is as silly as to praise him for possessing "national loyalties." Had anyone appealed to Frederick's patriotism, Frederick would certainly not have sent him to prison, but he might have committed him to an insane asylum. He would have been delighted to yield his Rhenish possessions to France, and East Prussia to Russia, if in return for this sacrifice he could have gained Saxony. It is equally absurd to admire his struggle against Austria as an act in the national interest. His only wish was to win territory, to rob the Hapsburgs of a province. And in this enterprise he was supported not by the strength and will of the nation, but by foreign powers that sought to keep Germany completely impotent. Today even Prussian historians, if they still retain a spark of honest scholarship, don't deny that without French help Frederick could never have captured Silesia.

Frederick knew, of course, that the French did not help him without ulterior motives. By supporting him, the Bourbons contributed to the internal conflict and dissolution of Germany. But that did not prevent him from becoming a French vassal. To be sure, he found more than one model for his policy among his illustrious forebears; French gold had always enjoyed popularity at the Berlin court, even if it could only be earned by betraying Germany. Nevertheless, none of his ancestors had gone so far as Frederick in shamefully disregarding the honor of the nation.

He pocketed the profit of his betrayal, but the curse of treason dogged him for the rest of his life. When French domination became too onerous for him, his efforts to shake it off only led him into English vassalage. In the Seven Years' War England used Prussia to conquer America in Germany, but when the English no longer needed Frederick they tossed him away like a squeezed lemon, and he could save himself only by becoming Russia's lackey. The shame of Russian rule in Germany is still another of Frederick's legacies. He ended his reign lying humbly in the dust at Catherine's feet. Internally raging, but obedient, he helped drive the Poles and the Turks into her net. In the Turkish campaigns he supported Catherine with subsidies; in the first partition of

Poland he was forced to accept the greatest part of the shame while being content with the smallest bone of the victim.

The final, irrevocable judgment of Frederick and his achievements was rendered at the Battle of Jena. To salvage the hero it has been claimed that not he but his incompetent successors suffered the defeat. But incompetent though these successors undoubtedly were, it remains senseless to pretend that within two decades they ruined everything that Frederick had supposedly created in over forty years. On the whole they maintained his system pretty much as he had left it; in some respects they even improved on it. In 1806 Prussia's antiquated class-structure undoubtedly appeared even more decayed than it had in 1786; but it was the values of the new generation that had changed, not the essence of the state. The reformers of the first decade of the nineteenth century—such men as Stein and Arndt—were led by a true instinct when they damned this un-German king, whose greatness had ruined Germany and whose memory was Germany's shame.

In view of all this, how can we explain that the king's name has nevertheless retained a certain popular appeal—that his memory has stimulated a man such as Carlyle to write his biography and an artist such as Menzel to depict his life and deeds? How explain that the Young Hegelians gushed over his memory, and that as late as 1858 the progressive Lassalle could compare Frederick to Lessing as a liberator of the German spirit? We could answer this question with a trite commonplace by saying that among the blind the one-eyed man is king. Compared to the degenerate pack of princes of his times, Frederick was a real man; and in the same way he towers over his predecessors and successors in the Hohenzollern dynasty. At least he carried on his evil work with a degree of energy and seriousness that was alien to his peers. Good fortune did not make him smug, and the steadfastness with which he bore misfortune deserves respect: rather than allow insults to what he believed to be his royal dignity, he was prepared to take poison and depart this world. He had nothing in common with the moronic wastefulness of contemporary princely courts, nor with the hollow glitter of their megalomania, which took seriously the silly curiosity of the vulgar masses, interpreting demonstrative attention as sincere love of the monarchy or even as admiring loyalty to the person of the monarch. Frederick quite correctly regarded such patriotic rowdies as scum. During the king's visit to Breslau the philosopher Garve argued the point. "Yesterday when Your Majesty entered the city," he said, "and the population assembled to see its great king, it was hardly a rabble." Frederick replied much more philosophically than the licensed sage: "Put an old monkey on horseback, let him ride through the streets, and the mob will gather just as quickly." How far in advance of his time he was with such a statement—let alone how far ahead of our own age!

Frederick may be considered an enlightened despot, not in the historical sense but as an individual. He represented the most oppressive slavery of the spirit, but he refused to assume "the shabby mask of hypocrisy," and never sought to decorate his tyranny with pious turns of phrase. To laud him as a precursor of German classical literature and philosophy belongs among the absurd legends that nourish bourgeois literary history. But Frederick was certainly enlightened in the sense of his admired Voltaire: he belonged to that enlightenment of which ordinary people are supposed to know nothing. And in his writings and letters he never pretended otherwise. He exploited religion as a tool of despotism; he tolerated the Jesuits when Pope Ganganelli abolished the order; he protected Lutheran orthodoxy against all enlightenment attacks, so that even his lamblike admirer Gleim mocked: "he left us every freedom, even the freedom to be dumb." But personally Frederick was disgusted by every form of religion, and refused to pervert religion to beautify his policies: he never praised his successful theft from the Hapsburgs as the work of God's grace. A whole arsenal of mean and even witty gibes at religion and religious objects can be assembled from his writings.

That in no way excuses Frederick's despotism, as Lessing was only the first to recognize. The Prussian realm was and remains the most enslaved in Europe, Lessing said, despite all the antireligious stupidities that were current in Berlin. It was fortunate for Frederick's reputation that his successor returned to the demonstratively pious tradition of the dynasty—in spite of the wild immorality of his personal life. Frederick William II crowned his disgusting hypocrisy by claiming, or having his lackeys claim, that it was Frederick above all who had given rise to the free-thinking attitudes that were now being combated. Without in any way deserving it, Frederick thus gained the reputation of having been a bearer of enlightenment. After Jena his historical role was again accurately interpreted by the Prussian reformers. Another reversal occurred after the final defeat of Napoleon. When the Holy Alliance cloaked the most brazen despotism in pious garments, Frederick became a hero of the Enlightenment for the second time, the more so since Prussia pursued contemptible and shameful policies, and her leaders during the 1820's and 1830's did all in their power to darken the memory of the heretical monarch.

Familiar is Heine's angry outburst in 1832 "against Prussia, this tall, sanctimonious drillmaster with a big stomach, a big mouth, and a corporal's cane that he dunks in holy water before beating people with it. This Christian-philosophic militarist, made up of thin beer, lies, and North German sand. This stiff, hypo-critical, deceitful Prussia—a true Tartuffe among nations!" Heine could write such words only in a foreign country. In a sense it is the other side of the coin for Köppen, the radical Young Hegelian, writing seven years later under the constraints of censorship, to appeal to Frederick, who at least never tried to sanctify his corpo-ral's cane. Köppen held up the mirror of Frederick's thought to contemporary Prussia, so that the state would recognize its rotten-ness and choke on it—which, to be sure, it failed to do.

Today we know only too well that real battles with living op-ponents cannot be fought by appealing to ghosts—especially not ghosts of Frederick's stripe, the Philosopher of Sans Souci, who loved and served the Junkers no less well than do our present rulers. The nation continues to curse Frederick's despotism—and the more disastrous the after-effects of Frederick's reign, the more vehement the nation's curse. To celebrate the king's two hundredth anniversary as a national holiday would degrade all national feel-ing.

The date may be more suitable as a dynastic holiday. In the long
row of Hohenzollern who have preceded and followed him,
Frederick is distinguished by a few human qualities—in particular,
by the disdain of that "rabble," which in these days will celebrate
him most loudly.

HEINRICH RITTER VON SRBIK

Destroyer and Creator

FREDERICK BECAME THE GREAT DESTROYER of the
Holy Roman Empire of the German nation, and of its Austrian Hapsburg leadership. It has been justly observed that he completely discounted the imperial authority's claim of "sacred majesty." In his eyes it was nothing more than an "old fixture and a
tried device of Austrian policy." Once and for all he put an end
to the conflict between Prussian autonomy and loyalty to the
empire that had still paralyzed his father's political energies.

From *Deutsche Einheit,* Vol. I, by Heinrich Ritter von Srbik. Munich: F.
Bruckmann, 1940, pp. 98–107. Reprinted by permission of F. Bruckmann
Verlag. Translation copyright © 1972 by Peter Paret.

His youth was lonely.[1] His sensitivity alienated him from the barrack-square behavior of his brutal father; he was forced to dissimulate, became a dreamer without the wish to work, swayed by political fantasies but without genuine schooling in politics, familiar only with the history of international relations. Even as a young man, longing for freedom, not truly religious, full of enthusiasm for literature and philosophy, quite unsoldierly, compelled to work in the government bureaucracy, Frederick felt no genuine allegiance to emperor and empire. The crown prince showed no gratitude to Charles VI, who on the one hand protected him against his suspicious and cruelly vindictive father and assisted him with a yearly pension, but also maneuvered him into marriage with an unloved princess of a minor dynasty. But even the abortive idea of marrying the daughter of Emperor Charles himself had meant no more to Frederick than gaining "a few duchies" as dowry. As early as 1731 he was considering the expansion of Prussia by acquiring Swedish Pomerania, Mecklenburg, and the territories of Jülich and Berg; he viewed Austria simply as one major power among others. His alienation from the German Empire increased during his service with Prince Eugene in the Rhine campaign against France. In 1734 his ambition for glory and power, ambivalently linked with a philosophic demand for a policy of justice, brought him to favor an alliance with France. Then during his years in Rheinsberg—a period of study and reflection, when his desire for conquest waned and concepts of political morality seemed to dominate his thought—he was further embittered by Charles's failure to keep his promise to help Prussia acquire Berg. And as he observed his father's inability to act decisively in foreign affairs, his French sympathies triumphed fully. The defeats of the imperial armies in the Turkish Wars he regarded as a judgment of God. His early essay, *Considérations sur l'état présent du corps politique de l'Europe,* adopted the traditional arguments of German particularist liberties by con-

1. For the following, see A. Berney, *Friedrich der Grosse. Entwicklungsgeschichte eines Staatsmannes* (Tübingen, 1934), and the same author's "Über das geschichtliche Denken Friedrich des Grossen," *Historische Zeitschrift,* CL (1934).

trasting Austrian "despotism" with the independence of the member states of the German Empire. He was still far less a realist than a theorist, who drew inspiration from political idealism and his philosophic and literary ambitions. When the author of *Antimachiavel*—a work already suffused with an elemental drive for power—at last ascended the throne, his hatred of the emperor and his refusal to subordinate Prussia to the empire led him to call the imperial authority the "old phantom of an ideal that once had been powerful," but "at present is insignificant."

Frederick dismissed the death of Charles VI as "a trifle." But he changed course. Not the territory of Berg but Silesia became his goal. Whether his claims were valid or not mattered nothing to him. His new actions were guided by ambition, thirst for glory, and sober power politics. For the sake of specific Prussian interests he did not hesitate to turn against Austria and support the Bavarian claimant to the imperial crown, Charles VII, who served the purposes of French policy. The sole "concrete, juridical, supreme moral authority" to which he subjected himself was the Brandenburg-Prussian monarchy. In his view, the Holy Roman Emperor should no longer even formally be superior to the king of Prussia, but his equal; in the new imperial system sponsored by France, Prussia, and Bavaria true power was to rest with Prussia, the burden with Charles VII. In 1744 Frederick frustrated the return of Alsace from France to the Empire. By working through the imperial constitution he tried to unite the German states under Prussian leadership for the benefit of the Bavarian emperor and Prussian power. He failed; but despite his defeat the scheme of such a union remained a guiding theme of his reign. He attempted to give the Bavarian emperor an adequate financial base by secularizing the South German ecclesiastical principalities, just as the association of imperial circles was to provide the military basis. But the king of Prussia was to receive the title of "permanent lieutenant-general" of this imperial army, and its supreme command. For Frederick the new empire was simply a weapon in his conflict with the Hapsburgs, a means by which Prussian hegemony in Germany might be achieved. That too became a "Frederician" tradition. After Prussia's imperial policy had failed, he considered the authority of the new emperor, Maria Theresa's husband Francis of Lorraine, as nothing more than a "chimera." The position of the Austrian dynasty in Germany remained the enemy of his kingship. It is of highest symbolic significance that in 1750 the traditional public prayers for the emperor were prohibited throughout his realm as an "antiquated, badly contrived custom." To the king of Prussia a new province appeared more valuable than the "empty title" of emperor. It is difficult to imagine how the imperial prosecution for breaking the public peace, with which he was once threatened, could ever have been carried out; or how, at the coronation dinner of Joseph II in 1764, a man such as he could have performed his duty of chamberlain of the empire and borne a silver fingerbowl filled with water during the ceremony.[2]

Possibly the political ideas of the Askanian dynasty, his remote ancestors, influenced his thinking, without his being aware of it.[3] In any case, his political and territorial aims are clearly recognizable: the conquest of Bohemia, this outer fortress of the Hapsburg core; or, if that could not be accomplished, at least the separation of Bohemia from the Austrian sphere of influence. Frederick did conquer another advanced strongpoint, Silesia. A third, Saxony, together with Mecklenburg, he planned to take in 1758 and 1759, at the peak of his military success; but these intensely desired acquisitions remained beyond his grasp. His war against Joseph in 1778 and his creation of the League of German Princes in 1785 further weakened Austrian influence.

The destruction of Austria was not a permanent element of his political thought. But had French and Spanish plans to dismember the Hapsburg inheritance with the help of Prussia and Bavaria succeeded, the Belgian and Italian possessions of the Hapsburgs would have fallen into the hands of the Latin powers; Bohemia would have become the basis of a Bavarian empire, as Silesia did become the basis of Hohenzollern dominance, and a fragmented Germany would have become the toy of France.

2. A. Schulte, *Der deutsche Staat* (Stuttgart, 1933), p. 152 f.
3. Compare R. Schmidt, "Der preussische Einheitsstaat und der deutsche Bundesstaat," *Zeitschrift für Politik*, XVI (1927), 228.

Prussia's victory deprived the Holy Roman Empire of the German nation of Silesia, not legally but in fact. Frederick considered the conquered province as a territory detached from the empire, a duchy as sovereign as the Duchy of Prussia, which lay beyond the empire's borders. He reduced the territory of the empire in order to enlarge the European significance of his kingdom. . . . But to be sure, what did traditional imperial jurisdiction over Silesia signify to a monarch who held that the empire was nothing more than a republic of principalities, which eventually would separate into independent states! Cocceji's reforms of the Prussian legal system removed the last bonds between the monarchy and the imperial courts. The scheme Frederick pursued in the fall of 1759, that of partitioning northern Germany between Hanover and Prussia, "which should tear themselves away from the empire and form independent empires," demonstrates the harsh magnitude of his destructive and innovative policies.[4]

Frederick's conquest of Silesia meant more to Austria than the criminal plucking out of a brilliant jewel from the Hapsburg diadem of kingdoms and provinces. What mattered was not only the loss of a priceless factor in the economic life of the monarchy and a reduction of its population by 1,200,000 inhabitants.[5] The loss of Silesia severely damaged the German basis of the Central and East European power structure of the Hapsburgs, which had already been weakened by the renunciation of Lusatia to Saxony. With Silesia gone, Bohemia—the bridge between German civilization in the northeast and southeast—was delivered to a future of Slav predominance. Deprived of her former primacy in Germany, Austria was also relieved of her traditional and valuable obligation of acting as the empire's first protector against France. The Hapsburgs were robbed of the territory that had once extended their authority into northern Germany, and Austria's advantageous strategic position in relation to Poland and Hungary was ruined. Finally, the loss of Silesia drove Austria still further in the direc-

4. G. B. Volz, "Friedrichs des Grossen Plan einer Losreissung Preussens von Deutschland," *Historische Zeitschrift*, CXXII (1920), 267 ff.
5. A. Fournier, "Maria Theresia und die Anfänge ihrer Handelspolitik," *Historische Sudien und Skizzen* (Vienna, 1908), II, 41.

tion of becoming a purely Danubian state, and by reducing her German territories compromised her mission of extending and deepening German civilization in eastern Europe.

The new duality of political power in Germany (the remaining medium-sized and small states could not form a united third force) was accompanied by a spiritual division. Austria, the state that personified the old imperial idea, was now challenged by an individual whose authority derived not from the state over which he ruled but from his personal heroism. The thing that most impressed many segments of the German people was that for seven years a single man, possessed of incredible moral energy, fought a battle to the death against great powers, until he triumphed. They admired the German prince who defeated the French, who secured central Europe for Germany by acquiring West Prussia while Austria was still seeking to achieve the same goal in the southeast; they admired the prince who with growing self-denial, total dedication to the cause of the state, and with a profound though unreligious sense of responsibility, became the creator of a new political force.

And this prince was not the emperor. On the contrary, the emperor belonged to the dynasty of Lorraine, a foreign sprig grafted onto the old imperial family, an alien who owed the imperial crown to his Hapsburg spouse. The prince who came to personify German honor to many, and who became a German hero, was the great enemy of Austrian imperial power—the champion of a state that strove to outdo the Hapsburg, Wettin, and Guelph dynasties, the creator of a Prussian as well as of a "national" sentiment. Beyond Prussia's borders, the people's pride in the great Frederick had no specifically Prussian content. Men admired his will, energy, and leadership, his masculinity, courage, and readiness to sacrifice himself for the fatherland; they saw in him the creative preceptor of a new political force, even if it was only that of a particularistic German state. These were the magically seductive qualities that enabled so many to ignore the break with the age-old universalistic ideal that he represented, and the enormous damage that he dealt to German influence and power in southeastern Europe—it was these qualities that filled many non-Prussians with admiration for a hero who was so lacking in national feeling. There can be no doubt that Germans benefited greatly from their new self-assurance and from the new political energies that Frederick generated. But the cost of these gains was extremely high.

Just as the Reformation had not been the work of Luther alone, but possessed strong roots in the past, so the establishment of Prussian dominance was not due solely to Frederick's political genius. In the Middle Ages had not Henry the Lion rebelled against the universalism, the Italian policy, of Emperor Frederick Barbarossa? With the Hansa League had not a degree of political and economic separatism developed in North Germany? And who can deny that the emperor and empire had left the Hansa and the Teutonic Order to their own devices, that Hapsburg power had not been able to protect areas where vital forces of the German people were faced with highly significant cultural and political tasks in the interest of Central Europe and of European civilization in general? Over the centuries the rugged colonial territories of northeastern Europe nurtured a reserved, sober, severe culture, radically different from the open, old German and Austrian type. Later Lutheranism exerted a profound spiritual and psychological influence on the new culture.[6] This helps explain why in the minds of many contemporaries Frederick's wars against Austria could appear as the struggle of Protestantism against the Catholic Austrian emperors. However much Frederick originated and initiated, he also completed a centuries-long process of detachment and development in the north—a part of the country that had never been dominated by the imperial authority of the Catholic Hapsburgs to the same degree as central or southern Germany. If an inherent necessity had led to the creation of the Austrian state, a similar need could also be found, though not to the same extent, in the growth of the new North German power. By responding to this need, Frederick's personality and individuality acquired symbolic force affecting the course of German history down to the present, and presumably into the distant future as well. The

6. Compare H. Dankworth, *Das alte Grossdeutschtum* (Frankfurt a. M., 1925), p. 29 f.

king's character became a creative element in the entire German people, and has retained influence even though the type of political organization for which it was innately suited has long disappeared.

Frederick influenced and formed the attitudes of millions of Germans, and yet he possessed little consciousness of German culture.[7] His spiritual affinities lay with the French Enlightenment and rococo, to which he had been exposed since childhood, and whose values he made his own during the calm years at Rheinsberg. His philosophy was shaped most strongly by Fénelon's ideal of the moral ruler—the first servant of his people's happiness—and by the skepticism of Pierre Bayle, Hobbes,[8] Locke, Montesquieu, and Voltaire. Among German writers only Christian Wolff influenced him significantly. Frederick believed that in some distant future a universal German culture would blossom; he himself did not partake of it. But in his first war he matured as statesman.[9] As soon as the needs of the state dominated the day, the ruler's fiery energy and the philosopher's enlightened rationality were freed from the bonds of humanitarian principles. He renounced political systems based on ethics, acknowledged the relativism of political conditions and actions, and came to understand the reality of politics. The demon of passionate kingship triumphed, and the concept of *raison d'état* overwhelmed the ideologue. The ten years' "armistice" between the Silesian Wars and the Seven Years' War completed the development of the *roi philosophe,* who sought to understand politics and his own nature, to recognize universals, to relate specifics to the general, and to dispose over a "system of government that was as precisely structured as a system of philosophy." When the young Frederick first formed his views of royalty he did not yet despise man, his desire to be useful was still linked with love for the people; his drive to increase the power of the state was still coupled with his wish to create happiness through justice and to educate his subjects to serve state and

7. Compare W. Langer, *Friedrich der Grosse und die geistige Welt Frankreichs* (Hamburg, 1932).

8. G. Beyerhaus, *Friedrich der Grosse und das 18. Jahrh.* (Bonn, 1931), p. 11 ff.

9. For the following see Berney, *Friedrich der Grosse.*

community of their own free will. It seems that the conflicts of his youth—the tension between reflection and action, doctrine and practice, ethics and *realpolitik*—never completely disappeared in this human being, who despite everything cannot be denied greatness.[10] But in the dreadful experiences of the Seven Years' War he gave himself over completely to the idea of ruling in the interest of the state; the element of duty tamed his personal impulses, and in a sense he buried his own self under the ideal of the state. His political rationale, his manner of thinking exclusively in terms of *raison d'état,* which so sharply distinguished his views from the dynastic and patrimonial concepts of his ancestors, overpowered his passions, and the element of duty brought harmony to the discords of his personality.

The Seven Years' War marked a deep incision in his thought. Afterwards the freethinking opponent of every Christian dogma and of all religious culture, the Prince of the Enlightenment for whom even Protestantism was no longer an adequate intellectual basis, the skeptic, misanthrope, and lover of reason, restricted the reach of the Enlightenment to the realms of administration, the sciences, economy, and law—the firmness of his philosophic antagonism to Christianity notwithstanding. Now persuaded that the mass of the people was not fit for the truth, he renounced all ideas of creating a state on the basis of philosophic principles, and, a true stoic, for the sake of the state opposed the enlightenment of the people. He elevated practical life above philosophy, and overcame his former instincts and attitudes to achieve a new tolerance.[11]

Frederick's determination to infuse his subjects with the concepts of duty and service, to view men as the substance of the state without existence by and for themselves, to maintain the unfinished monarchy—which conquests alone had raised to the level of a great power—in a state of constant readiness, to achieve financial and military strength by the most rigorous methods of drill and administration—all these qualities of the bleak genius, who was tortured by so many demons, necessarily left profound marks on

10. The reference to F. Meinecke's work *Machiavellism* goes without saying.

11. See Beyerhaus.

his people. The so-called Prussian national sentiment is inseparably bound up with the life of this terrifying drillmaster, for
whom even his own brother felt a deadly hatred. The mechanistic
and authoritarian tendencies of the engineer who supervised the
state's machinery entered deeply into the character of his people.

The bureaucratic, coldly rational, enlightened despot failed to
encourage men's political and cultural autonomy; and in the consciousness of the subject the state grew into the all-powerful
authority. We have said that Frederick repressed his own longing
for glory; but could the Prussian and German people ever forget
his victories at Leuthen and Rossbach? Frederick's early expansive,
acquisitive policies gave way to defensive diplomacy; but the new
Prussian sense of honor remained inseparable from Prussian ag-
gressiveness and martial glory. In Mirabeau's words, Frederick's
death was greeted neither with regret, sorrow, nor praise; nevertheless, the sense of security that men enjoyed in his slave-state led
to their psychological attachment to this state. The former optimist
of the Enlightenment, with his faith in the power of education,
who had traveled the spectrum from humanitarian and moral
political theories to the elevation of power as such, finally to reach
the pure ideology of the state, created a specifically Prussian political attitude, whose fateful implications for Germany's future
could not possibly be sensed by his victimized contemporaries.

The Prussian people that he formed was the object, not the subject, of the state. It was divided by firm class-distinctions. Officer
corps and bureaucracy were the main pillars of the hard, anti-
humanistic concept of the state—its members on the average not
exactly characterized by initiative or readiness to assume respon-
sibilities, and tending to pedantry; but they were honest, with a
strong sense of duty, severely trained to economy and conscientious
effort. The nobility remained the favored source for officers and
bureaucrats, its social attitudes determined by state service and
ownership of the land—a vigorous class, loyal to the crown, but
its special interests interfering with the achievement of true social
unity. Through trade and commerce the middle classes provided
much of the state's revenues. The peasants formed the army's manpower pool, consequently their social position was protected, just

as similar considerations for the power of the state led to the retention of the nobility's social and economic privileges. Veterans, with all the qualities and drawbacks of the professional soldier, were the preferred candidates for subaltern posts in the administration.

This Prussian people, demonstrating constant, disciplined industry, incorporated an idea that cannot be denied a certain ethical value: the idea of service for the state. Above all it had been *one* proud and courageous man who had raised the state from a minor kingdom to a great power, from a principality of the Holy Roman Empire to the second political force in Germany. Training and will, logic and organization, a culture of reason—with Kant and the philosophy of idealism its supreme embodiment—practical realism and energy linked with a reflective sense of principle—these are the characteristics with which the Frederician state completed the development of the Lutheran, North German, Prussian type. It was a creation alien to the German national spirit of such eighteenth-century thinkers as Friedrich Karl von Moser, who, loyal to the empire, condemned the "abortion of a military-patriotic form of government" that had emerged in the "territories of upper and lower Saxony." [12]

The old king, burnt out, in a worn uniform, became the symbol of Prussian ambition, of Prussian expansion and aggression, but also of a Prussian sense of duty and self-sacrifice. Frederick had changed the hybrid electorate-monarchy, the "spider-legs without body," into a vigorous and vital power, a state that was forced to destroy the empire if it was to continue growing. When Frederick died, his army was reputed the best in Europe, the treasury was filled, the population of the monarchy had more than doubled since his accession, and the "King of the Border Zones" had become ruler of the fifth power in Europe and the second power in Germany.

12. F. Meinecke, *Cosmopolitanism and the National State* (Princeton, 1970), p. 31.

Bibliographical Note

THE SCHOLARLY LITERATURE on Frederick and on Prussian history in general is so voluminous that in a brief survey it is tempting to mention only works in English. Since many interpretations of continental scholars are not yet fully reflected in Anglo-American historiography, however, the reader may find it useful to have some German works listed as well. Titles marked with an asterisk contain important bibliographical information.

The best comprehensive account of Prussian history remains Otto Hintze's *Die Hohenzollern und ihr Werk* (1915). Hintze's remarkable essays on the development of Prussian institutions are included in the three volumes of his *Gesammelte Abhandlungen*

(1962–1967), a selection of which will appear in an English edition being prepared by Felix Gilbert. Prussia's constitutional and legal developments are reliably surveyed in Fritz Hartung, *Deutsche Verfassungsgeschichte* (1959).* The second volume of Hajo Holborn's *A History of Modern Germany* (1964) integrates recent interpretations of Prussia's rise to power in a thoughtful narrative. The Marxist view of Prussian history is incisively presented in Franz Mehring's essays, *Zur preussischen Geschichte*, 2 vols. (1930). A good brief summary is Sidney B. Fay, *The Rise of Brandenburg-Prussia to 1786*,* revised by Klaus Epstein (1964).

The most important sources for our understanding of Frederick are his own writings and instructions, collected in *Oeuvres de Frédéric le Grand,* 30 vols. (1846–1856), ed. J. D. E. Preuss; his official correspondence, *Politische Correspondenz,* 47 vols. (1879–1939) ed. R. Koser, G. B. Volz, et al.; and such documentary publications as Frederick's correspondence with Grumbkow and Maupertuis, and the memoirs and diaries of his reader, Henri de Catt, both edited by R. Koser in the series *Publicationen aus den K. Preussischen Staatsarchiven* (1898 and 1884). The basic biography is Reinhold Koser, *König Friedrich der Grosse,* 4 vols. (1912).* A concise study that combines the history of ideas with political and military analysis is Gerhard Ritter's *Frederick the Great* (1968), translated with an introduction by Peter Paret. George P. Gooch's *Frederick the Great* (1947) is a collection of essays on the king and his times. Thomas Carlyle's well-known *History of Frederick the Great,* selections of which have recently been republished with an interesting introduction by John Clive (1969), seems to me more enlightening about Victorian England than about its proper subject. Contemporary accounts and opinions of Frederick are collected in G. B. Volz, *Friedrich der Grosse im Spiegel seiner Zeit,* 3 vols. (1926).* In an important article, "Friedrich der Grosse und seine sittlichen Anklager," *Forschungen zur Brandenburgischen und Preussischen Geschichte,* XXXXI (1928), 1–37, Volz analyzes the contemporary rumors of Frederick's homosexuality and finds them to be baseless. The most careful study devoted to Frederick's physical appearance is A. Hildebrand, *Das Bildnis Friedrich des Grossen* (1940).

The outstanding work on Frederick's father is Carl Hinrichs, *Friedrich Wilhelm I. König in Preussen* (1941), which unfortunately does not go beyond 1713. In its subtle delineation of the interactions between Frederick William's character and his social, ethical, and political environment, Hinrichs' biographical sketch is far superior to anything written about Frederick himself. Simpler in design and execution is the comprehensive biography by R. R. Ergang, *The Potsdam Führer: Frederick William I, Father of Prussian Militarism* (1941). Hinrichs published the documents relating to the conflict between father and son and to Frederick's trial in *Der Kronprinzenprozess* (1936). Chester Easum has written a sound, conventional biography of Frederick's brother Henry, *Prince Henry of Prussia, Brother of Frederick the Great* (1942).

The most significant analyses of Frederick's political philosophy and attitudes are Wilhelm Dilthey's long essay "Friedrich der Grosse und die deutsche Aufklärung," in the third volume of his *Gesammelte Schriften* (1927), Friedrich Meinecke's discussion in *Die Idee der Staatsräson*—translated by Douglas Scott under the inappropriate title *Machiavellism* (1957), and A. Berney, *Friedrich der Grosse. Entwicklungsgeschichte eines Staatsmannes* (1934). A brief, brilliant contribution are the pages on Frederick's political testaments in Felix Gilbert's *To the Farewell Address* (1961).

Basic to our knowledge of Prussian administration in Frederick's day are the several series of documents and interpretation published under the general title *Acta Borussica* (1892–1933). Walter L. Dorn's three articles, "The Prussian Bureaucracy in the Eighteenth Century," *Political Science Quarterly* (September 1931–June 1932), constitute a useful distillation in English. An informative study on a special topic is Wilhelm Mertineit, *Die friederizianische Verwaltung in Ostpreussen* (1958). Hans Rosenberg, *Bureaucracy, Aristocracy, and Autocracy: The Prussian Experience, 1660–1815* (1958)* is a stimulating exploration of the interaction of social privilege and bureaucratic power, which does not always avoid the dangers inherent in imposing modern sociological and political concepts on eighteenth-century conditions. Two good related studies are Fritz Martiny's *Die Adelsfrage in Preussen vor 1806* (1938) and Otto Büsch's *Militärsystem und*

Sozialleben im alten Preussen (1962),* whose discussion of economic factors is usefully supplemented by William Henderson, *Studies in the Economic Policy of Frederick the Great* (1963). Frederick's legal policies are treated in Herman Weill, *Frederick the Great and Samuel von Cocceji* (1961).

Modern scholars have on the whole shown less interest in Prussia's foreign policy than in her administrative and military history. Among notable older works in the field are Max Lehmann, *Friedrich der Grosse und der Ursprung des Siebenjährigen Krieges* (1894), Leopold von Ranke, *Zwölf Bücher preussischer Geschichte* (1874), of which Books 7 to 12 treat the period from 1740 to the early 1750's, the same author's *Die deutschen Mächte und der Fürstenbund* (1875), and Harold Temperley, *Frederick the Great and Kaiser Joseph* (1915). Two good recent monographs are Wolfgang Stribrny, *Die Russlandpolitik Friedrich des Grossen, 1764–1786* (1966), and Herbert Kaplan, *The First Partition of Poland* (1962).

The basic work on Frederick's campaigns and military policy remains Curt Jany's far too uncritical *Geschichte der preussischen Armee*, Vols. II and III (1928), which incorporates the detailed studies of the Historical Section of the German General Staff. Frederick's strategy has received a classic analysis in the fourth volume of Hans Delbrück's *Geschichte der Kriegskunst* (1920). Two more recent studies of the links between political and social ideas, strategic thought, and military organization and administration are contained in the first volume of Gerhard Ritter's *Staatskunst und Kriegshandwerk* (1953)—translated by Heinz Norden under the title *Sword and Scepter* (1969)—and in Peter Paret's "The Frederician Age," from *Yorck and the Era of Prussian Reform* (1966).*

Contributors

ERNST FRIEDRICH RUDOLF VON BARSEWISCH, born in 1737, served as cadet and officer in a Berlin infantry regiment throughout the Seven Years' War. He kept extensive diaries, which formed the basis for subsequent memoirs that are among the most realistic accounts of military life in the eighteenth century. They were first published in Berlin under the title *Meine Kriegserlebnisse in den Jahren 1757–1763* (1863).

WILHELM DILTHEY (1833–1911) was one of the originators of the systematic study of the history of ideas. The principles that he developed in his seminal theoretical work, *Der Aufbau der geschichtlichen Welt in den Geisteswissenschaften,* were applied in his essays on the history of ideas in Germany from Leibniz to the end of the eighteenth century, from which the selection in this volume is taken.

WALTER L. DORN (1894–1961) taught at the universities of Chicago, Wisconsin, Ohio State, and Columbia. He was a knowledgeable scholar of eighteenth-century Europe, whose volume *Competition for Empire, 1740–1763* (1940), in William Langer's series *The Rise of Modern Europe,* continues to be widely used in American colleges.

CHESTER V. EASUM was born in 1894 and taught history at the University of Wisconsin for more than thirty years. Besides his biography of Prince Henry of Prussia, he has written on Carl Schurz and on topics of contemporary history.

CHIEF BAILIFF FROMME, landowner and Prussian official, was a nephew of the poet Johann Wilhelm Ludwig Gleim, to whom he sent his account of his meeting with Frederick. Gleim published it two years before the king's death, under the title *Reisegespräch des Königs im Jahre 1779.*

GEORGE PEABODY GOOCH (1873–1969), the prominent British historian and editor, was above all a specialist in the history of diplomacy. He also wrote on historiography, on cultural and political topics, and was the author of several collections of essays dealing with Frederick, Maria Theresa, and their times.

FRIEDRICH GUNDOLF (1880–1931), literary historian and translator, was a close associate of the poet Stefan George, with whom he shared the ideal of the artist as the supreme representative of spiritual values in the modern world. His literary studies—especially his influential books on Shakespeare and Goethe—uniquely combined precise textual analyses with psychological and historical interpretations of the poets and their environment.

CARL HINRICHS (1900–1962) spent the first half of his career in the German archival service. In 1944 he was appointed professor of history at the University of Halle, and later taught at the Free

University of Berlin. His study of Frederick's father, *Friedrich Wilhelm I* (1941) has become a standard work. After Hinrichs' death, his most significant papers on the institutional, intellectual, and political history of Prussia were published under the title *Preussen als historisches Problem* (1964).

FRANZ MEHRING (1846–1919) was a leading German radical publicist in the decades before the First World War. Among his most important longer works are a Marxist critique of bourgeois interpretations of Prussian history and German literature in the eighteenth century, *Die Lessing-Legende* (1893), and his fundamental history of German social democracy, which achieved twelve editions in the quarter century after its initial appearance in 1897–1898.

FRIEDRICH MEINECKE (1862–1953), the great German historian of ideas, analyzed Frederick and the Frederician state repeatedly in his long career. Two of his major works have been translated into English: *Die Idee der Staatsräson* (*Machiavellism*) and *Weltbürgertum und Nationalstaat* (*Cosmopolitanism and the National State*).

GERHARD RITTER (1888–1967) was professor of history at the University of Freiburg for most of his academic life. He wrote on late scholasticism, the Renaissance, the Reformation, and the interaction of political and military factors in German history from the eighteenth century to 1918, and was the author of biographies of Luther, Frederick, and Stein. His association with the conservative opposition to Hitler led to the publication after 1945 of a significant study of the German resistance—*Goerdeler und die deutsche Widerstandsbewegung*.

HEINRICH RITTER VON SRBIK (1878–1951) taught at the University of Vienna for many decades. In his major works—a biography of Metternich, four volumes on the "unity of Germany," and a two-volume study of German historiography from the Renaissance to the present—he developed a comprehensive rather than a narrowly Prussian or Austrian view of the German past.

PETER PARET studied at the University of California (Berkeley) and at the University of London. He is mainly interested in German intellectual and social history and the history of war. Before going to Stanford University, where he is now Professor of Modern European History, Mr. Paret was a research associate at the Center of International Studies at Princeton University and taught at the University of California (Davis). He has been a member of the Institute for Advanced Study at Princeton, a fellow of the Center for Advanced Study in the Behavioral Sciences at Stanford, and most recently a research fellow at the London School of Economics. With John Shy he wrote *Guerrillas in the Nineteen Sixties* (1962); since then he has written *French Revolutionary Warfare from Indochina to Algeria* (1964) and *Yorck and the Era of Prussian Reform* (1966). He has also translated and edited Gerhard Ritter's *Frederick the Great: A Historical Profile* (1968).

AÏDA DIPACE DONALD holds degrees from Barnard and Columbia and a Ph.D. from the University of Rochester. A former member of the History Department at Columbia, Mrs. Donald has been a Fulbright Fellow at Oxford and the recipient of an A.A.U.W. fellowship. She has published *John F. Kennedy and the New Frontier* and *Diary of Charles Francis Adams*.